DEATH AND THE MINES

Brit Hume

Rebellion and Murder

Death and the Mines

in the United Mine Workers

GROSSMAN PUBLISHERS · NEW YORK · 1971

For Clare

Copyright © 1971 by A. Britton Hume
All rights reserved
First published in 1971 by Grossman Publishers
44 West 56 Street, New York, N.Y. 10019
Published simultaneously in Canada by
Fitzhenry and Whiteside, Ltd.
SBN 670–26105–x
Library of Congress catalogue card number: 75–106294
Printed in U.S.A.
Second Printing

Acknowledgments

There are so many people without whom this book would not have been started, let alone finished, that it is impossible to name them all. I shall mention some: Ralph Nader, who gave me the idea and arranged the contract; Jeanne and Don Rasmussen, who showed me the ropes in West Virginia; my colleagues Ben Franklin and Ward Sinclair, whose work I have raided freely; my boss Jack Anderson, who gave me needed encouragement, plus time off with pay; Tom Stewart, my editor, who went over this book line by line, something I understand is rare these days.

CONTENTS

DEATH AND THE MINES

1

It had turned suddenly cold and a light snow was falling when Jerry Davis picked up the battered lunch pail he had inherited from his father and left home to work the midnight shift at the Number 9 mine for the last time. His wife, a plump, pretty woman, had packed an extra sandwich in case her husband had to be away from her and their five young children longer than usual. The extra food is a precaution taken by the wives of many coal miners, an effort to improve their husbands' odds in an industry where accidents which trap men in the earth are still a frequent occurrence. It was a twelve mile drive over rugged mountain backroads from the farm where Davis lived to the portal where he and the other men who worked in the west end of the huge mine went underground. When he arrived, the men in the bathhouse were discussing the things miners usually talk about in late November: the opening of hunting season, then only a week away; and the increased danger of a mine explosion created by the chill autumn weather, which tends to dry out the atmosphere underground. But the hazards of the "explosion season," as late fall is known among coal miners, could hardly have increased Davis's apprehension. An unusually intelligent and thoughtful miner, he had long been deeply troubled by the conditions in the mine. As he gathered with other members of his section crew to ride the cage-like elevator to the workings six hundred feet below ground, he was not comforted by the memory of the previous night, when excessive accumulations of flammable gas had halted work for several hours.

The Consolidation Coal Company's Number 9 mine is located at Farmington, West Virginia, a tiny mountain community which overlies the rich "Pittsburgh" seam of bituminous coal where it extends into northern West Virginia. Until Wednesday, November 20, 1968, Farmington was virtually unknown outside the state, except to a few sports fans who might have been aware that Sam Huff, the famous linebacker of the New York Giants and the Washington Redskins, was born and grew up there, the son of a coal miner. The town is six miles west of Fairmont, a city of twenty-seven thousand people, which is the unofficial capital of the mountain state's northern coal region. The northern field is one of the most productive in the nation. The coal lies far below the surface in most places, but the beds are as much as seven feet thick. The area has long been a stronghold of the Consolidation Coal Company, which operates eight large mines in the vicinity of Fairmont and maintains its regional headquarters in Monongah, just south of the city. Monongah is famous in coal annals as the site of the worst disaster in the industry's history, a 1907 explosion which killed 361 men.

Alva Gerald Davis was a short, wiry man of twenty-six, with lean features and an alert gaze. He had grown up in the tumbling hill country around Fairmont and he liked it there. An outdoorsman who loved to hunt and fish, he would have worked full time on his 175-acre farm if he could have made enough money at it. He had tried for several years to make the place go as a dairy farm, but with a growing family and no other income, he had finally been forced to give up his herd and go back to work in the mines. He had first worked as a miner when he was nineteen. He signed on at a small, low-paying, non-union mine where he learned to operate a roof bolting machine and run a coal shuttle car. These skills got him his job with Consolidation in 1967. The troubles that were to make his life as a miner almost unbearable began about a month after he started work at "Consol Number 9."

Davis was working on a section in the northwest end of the mine one day when a company foreman came by to check for gas in the atmosphere. In deep shaft mines like Number 9, methane gas is a major safety hazard. Its presence is detected by a device called a flame-safety lamp which was invented in 1815 and has not been significantly improved since. Its glass-encased flame will rise in the presence of methane without igniting the gas itself. On this occasion, the boss found that his lamp had gone out. As Davis watched, the foreman ignored a basic safety precaution: he relit his lamp in the working area, where the danger of gas accumulation is greatest. Davis was astonished. Even in the primitive non-union mines where he had worked, such a practice was rare. Had the gas, which is invisible and odorless, been present in any sizable quantity, the lamp, its flame exposed for relighting, could have touched off an explosion. Davis reported the incident to the union safety committee, which made a formal complaint to the company. When a hearing was held, the foreman denied the violation. Davis was called a liar and a troublemaker. Nothing came of the complaint, but Davis soon found that it was not forgotten. He was taken off his regular job and assigned to what miners call the "labor gang." This involves unskilled work and is usually reserved for inexperienced men. Davis's job was to stand alone in remote passageways to monitor conveyor belts carrying coal to central loading points. Most mines operate on the "buddy" system, where every man has a companion worker who looks out for him. But Davis worked alone watching the belt and this bothered him more than the drudgery of the job itself. Sometimes an entire shift would pass without his seeing another miner. He often worried that, if he were injured, he could lie hurt or unconscious for hours before help arrived.

Davis sought repeatedly to be reassigned to one of the working sections where the coal is actually mined and where he could do the skilled work for which he was qualified and would not have to work by himself. Every request was ignored by the company. His uneasiness increased to the point where he began seeing a doctor and was given pills to calm his nerves. After one brush with a foreman, he was fired. He filed a grievance through the union and was reinstated two weeks later, but without back pay. He became convinced that the company intended to keep him on his lonely job until he quit. But quitting was no solution. Miners who have difficulties with coal companies and end up leaving often find it extremely difficult to get work at another mine. Industry officials insist there is no such thing as a blacklist, but many miners suspect otherwise. So Jerry Davis stuck it out. Finally, after more than a year, he was given work as a roof bolter. He was sent to a section in the far southwest corner of the mine, miles from any other working area. The spot was extremely gassy and the roof leaked so much it was like working in the rain. Nevertheless, Davis thought the section foreman was a fair and safety-conscious man and he liked the other five miners who made up the crew. He was determined to make the best of the job.

Besides Davis and his mates, about eighty other men worked in the west end of Number 9 on the midnight or "cateye" shift. Most were assigned to eight sections located not far from the shaft at the Llewellyn Portal where they entered the mine. A few other miners worked in the eastern end of the mine, but most of this area was mined out. For Davis's crew it was a three-mile trip through pitch-black tunnels from the bottom of the shaft to their section. On this night, the crew was joined by two additional miners as they rode the underground train, or "mantrip," to their jobs. These two miners, whose job took them to every section of the workings, had the task of building cement stoppings to seal off the entrances to worked out passages. The purpose of this is to prevent fresh air, which is circulated with huge fans, from being drained off before it reaches the places where men are working. After the previous night's gas accumulations, Davis was glad to see the two men. One of them, Bud Hillsberry, was a friend with whom he sometimes went hunting. Until four-thirty that morning, the shift went routinely. One problem was encountered when the roof, or "top," as miners call it, weakened above the "face" where the coal is dug. To make certain it did not give way, Davis stayed at the face and installed extra roof bolts during the regular dinner break while the others were eating. Roof bolts are long steel pins which are driven into the layers of slate and other rock above the mine passages. When used properly, they bind the strata together to form a beam which will prevent a cave-in. Davis didn't mind the chore: unlike most of the safety matters which concerned him so seriously, a safe roof was something he could make sure of himself, and he was glad for the chance.

To officials of Consolidation, largest coal producer in the nation, the Number 9 mine was a source of pride, a part of the hope for the future in an industry that had looked for a time as though it had no future. With 375 employees and an annual yield of two million tons, it ranked among the company's eight largest mines. Its vast network of tunnels and galleries ranged over an area equal in size to Manhattan, much of it worked out but much of it still to be mined. Estimates were that the mine's vast store of virgin coal would last thirty to forty years. As far as the men in company headquarters in Pittsburgh were concerned, Number 9 was safe, too, although it was in one of the nation's gassiest seams of coal. Eight million cubic feet of methane seeped into Number 9's atmosphere every twenty-four hours. Four giant exhaust fans were counted on to draw fresh air through the working areas and out of the mine, carrying the explosive gas with it. Further, a kind of fail-safe system had been installed to shut off all power underground automatically if one of the fans broke down, thus curbing the possibility that accumulated methane would be ignited by faulty electrical equipment and warning the miners to leave the mine until the fans were working again. Fourteen years earlier, almost to the day, sixteen men had died when improper use of explosives underground touched off a pocket of gas and turned the mine into an inferno. That accident occurred just a month after the mine had been purchased by Consolidation. Veteran miners recalled that the 1954 disaster was followed by a period of unprecedented attention to safety precautions in Number 9. At one time during the late 1950s, each shift in Number 9 was kept on duty an extra hour every day to spread rock dust, a crucial explosion preventive, throughout the mine. A key ingredient of any major explosion is coal dust, which is deposited in large quantities throughout every mine where modern "continuous mining" machinery is used. These huge devices claw the coal loose from its bed with giant rotary bits, eliminating the old method of dislodging it with explosives. The machines stir up prodigious amounts of fine coal dust which settles along the floor and walls of a mine. This "bug dust," as miners call it, is highly combustible. Once churned up and ignited by a methane explosion, it can convert a minor blast into a major holocaust that spreads throughout a mine. The industry has yet to develop an effective means of preventing the dust from accumulating, so it still relies on an age-old process known as "rock dusting." If the coal dust which has accumulated is diluted with chemically inert rock dust to concentrations of less than sixty-five percent, it ceases to be flammable and the possibility of a mine-wide explosion is eliminated. In gassy mines such as Number 9, there is no more basic safety procedure than thorough rock dusting.

During the recessions of the late 1950s, when coal was in a deep slump, the Number 9 mine was closed. When it reopened in 1960, the old timers who had been around in the period after the 1954 explosion felt that the concern for safety that had marked those days seemed to be missing. Rock dusting was confined mostly to the main tunnels with the return airways—back corridors through which air is routed after it has circulated through the working sections—being given less attention. Complaints about safety matters were often ignored, and in some cases, such as Jerry Davis's, miners felt they were punished for raising the issue. The mine was visited several times a year by federal inspectors, but the men had long known they could not count on these occasional checks to assure that safety was given a high priority by the company. The foremen always seemed to know when an inspector was coming and his arrival was invariably preceded by a flurry of activity aimed at making the mine appear as sound as possible. The federal mine-safety laws then in effect had been passed in 1952 and had not been revised since. Their enactment was the last episode in a legislative history that had earned the coal industry lobby in Washington a reputation for working its will with Congress.

The first federal action on mine safety was the 1910 bill which created the Bureau of Mines in the Interior Department. The new agency was empowered to study mining methods with the object of recommending safety improvements. The law specifically ruled out "any right or authority in connection with the inspection or supervision of mines." Coal's safety record continued to be the worst in American industry and in 1941, Congress concluded that some action was needed to supplement the timid regulation afforded by state mine departments. "Investigation reveals no common standard of safety among the states, no common regulations and, in addition to this, a lack of uniform enforcement of such regulations as are in effect," read a report made by a House committee. The result was a law which empowered the Bureau of Mines to make "annual or necessary inspections" of mines. But the federal inspectors still could do no more than recommend safety improvements; compliance was optional. In 1947, a federal safety code was written as a guide for inspectors, but a Congressional survey showed that only about one-third of the code's recommendations were being observed. Then, four days before Christmas, 1951, 119 men were killed in a mine explosion at the Orient Number 2 mine at West Frankfort, Illinois. The holiday disaster stirred nationwide shock and indignation. President Truman sent Congress recommendations for strong legislation. And John L. Lewis, the redoubtable president of the United Mine

Workers of America, pleaded before Congress, in vivid rhetoric, for a strong law. By this time, more than 114,000 men had been killed in coal mines since the official death count was started in 1839. An average of 119 men—the number that perished at West Frankfort—had died every seventeen days since 1900. There had been twenty-five disasters in which more than a hundred miners were killed. Denouncing the states for "this abominable record of slaughter unequalled in the civilized world," Lewis said:

> It is something to go down the rows of a hundred burned and dismembered and blackened corpses lying on the floor of a gymnasium in a public building and look at them and know that a few hours before they were walking about in the form of men, even as you or I, and that there they lay, disfigured, changed from the form of human beings to something beyond imagination, and then be expected to emerge from that scene of horror with patience and with tolerance for the men who come before this committee and say, "Don't pass any legislation. Let me continue to do as I will. I hope some day to be able to operate my mine without killing so many men. But don't rush me! Don't rush me!"

But the law that emerged gave the Bureau of Mines the authority to correct only conditions which might lead to a "disaster." This was defined as an accident which kills five men or more. Such accidents, although widely publicized, accounted for only about ten percent of the deaths in coal mining, with the rest occurring in isolated mishaps, chiefly roof falls. Further, the law prescribed no penalties for violations except a provision allowing an inspector to order a particularly unsafe mine closed until its safety deficiencies were corrected. The law exempted all mines employing less than fifteen men from its provisions, although these smaller operations had notorious safety records. The bill also contained what President Truman called "complex procedural provisions . . . which I believe will make it exceedingly difficult, if not impossible, for those charged with the administration of the act to carry out an effective enforcement program." In signing the measure into law, the president called it "a sham." Nevertheless, the bill was clear on one point: a blanket of rock dust was to be maintained in all mines where coal dust accumulated in quantity. And in all sixteen inspections made in the five years leading up to November 20, 1968, the Bureau of Mines had cited Consol Number 9 for insufficient rock dusting. So serious had the problem become that one veteran miner, whose work took him throughout Number 9 each night, brought it up in the meeting of his United Mine Workers local on November 17. Although two of the union's top regional officials had been present, no action had been taken by the time the "cateye" shift began the following Wednesday.

A sudden rumble shook the windows and rattled the gas lines at Sam Stout's frame farmhouse up the mountain hollow just beyond the big mine fan. Stout, a retired coal miner, and his wife were awakened by the noise.

"It sounds like that pumphouse blew up," she said.

Earlier that night, as the weather grew cold, Stout had lighted a gas jet in the small block shed behind his house to keep the water pipes and pumping equipment housed there from freezing. At first he thought his wife was right. He got up and walked into the kitchen of the one-story house and peered out the back window. As he gazed down the shallow hillside where the pumphouse was, he could see no flame or smoke. "It's not the pumphouse," he said.

"What time is it?" his wife called back from the bedroom.

Stout glanced at the electric clock above the stove. The kitchen was dark but there was a light on in the adjoining hallway and Stout could see the hands of the clock. "It's four o'clock," he said. He went back into the bedroom and lay down again.

A few moments later, his wife sat up. "Something is smothering me," she said. "That fan must be down."

Stout hadn't noticed it before, but she was right. The massive mine fan, whose constant whirling din was a sound the Stout family had grown used to, was silent. It was one of two fans used to ventilate the busy west end of Consol Number 9. The other was located at the Llewellyn Portal where Jerry Davis and his crew had gone underground earlier that night. "Well," said Stout, "I guess the motor must have burned out and the blades must have been thrown off and that's what made the racket that shook the house." Having been a miner for thirty years, Stout was familiar with the way such equipment worked. He knew well the danger that could result from a ventilation interruption, but he felt certain the trouble with the fan could not have escaped notice in the mine. He soon began to notice the smoky odor that had bothered his wife, who was an asthmatic. Both found they could not get back to sleep. When what seemed like more than an hour had passed and the fan was still not running and Stout could see no one trying to repair it, he began to worry. His son-in-law, who was staying at the house, was awake and Stout asked him to telephone the lamp house at the Llewellyn Portal to find out what was wrong. By this time, though, it was too late. The calls got no answer.

Sam Stout was later to be summoned by the federal government and the state mining department to give his version of the events of November 20 at a hearing in Fairmont. His recollections would not square with those of several other witnesses. Lawyers for Consolidation and government investigators would call his testimony into question, suggesting that it was too dark in the kitchen for him to see his clock or that he had misread the hands. Despite their doubts, Sam Stout and the other members of his family who were present that morning would remain convinced that the mine fan behind their house was out of order at four A.M. Moreover, the hearing would make one fact clear: the fail-safe system, which was supposed to shut off all electricity in the mine if a fan broke down, did not work. Some miners even said privately that the company had deliberately wired the fan switches to by-pass the system so that production from the entire mine would not be discontinued by trouble in one area.

Jerry Davis had finished shoring up the roof when the rest of his crew came back from dinner at five A.M. He then made his way to the gallery called the "dinner hole" where the men usually spent their half-hour break. The dinner hole was just a crosscut between two tunnels. It contained no tables or chairs, nor any facilities for cleaning up. Its furnishings were a garbage can and a few empty rock dust sacks to sit on. Davis took his time eating, using practically all of his thirty minute break. When he finished, he got up and was preparing to go back to work when Bud Hillsberry passed by. Hillsberry was standing next to a cement stopping a few feet away when Davis saw him. "Say, Bud, where are you going to go hunting on Monday?" Davis asked. Hillsberry stepped into the crosscut to answer, but he never got a chance. The place shook slightly and the stopping next to which Hillsberry had been standing was ripped out and hurled down the tunnel near the two men in a furious rush of air and smoky dust.

At that moment the lights went dim, then flickered in the shed aboveground several miles away where the miners' helmet lights were stored. Russell Foster, the miner on duty in the building, then heard a deafening blast. It erupted from the Llewellyn shaft just outside with enormous force, blowing the headhouse off the portal and sending debris raining all over the surrounding area. Foster groped through the sudden darkness and found refuge beneath a staircase. The flood of debris continued for several minutes as thick grey smoke billowed from the wrecked mine shaft.

The explosion reached the other members of Davis's crew, who were at work at the face, as a sudden, overpowering surge of air. Their working area immediately filled with dense smoke and dust. Visibility was zero. Lewis Lake, a veteran miner who ran the huge continuous mining machine, thought at first that it was smoke from a burning electric cable. He dove onto the mine floor hoping to find clear air there, as it usually was when the atmosphere filled with the hot cable smoke. Nezer Vandergrift, who operated one of the shuttle cars that carried away the coal, knelt on the floor of the car and held on to the seat to avoid the force of the blast. Charles Crim, who had accompanied Hillsberry into the section that night to build stoppings, was pushing a wheelbarrow along a passageway some distance from the others when he felt the impact. He was thrown headlong about forty feet down the tunnel, wheelbarrow and all. Somehow, he was not hurt.

When the whistling rush of air began to die down, the members of Davis's crew began to call to each other through the darkness and smoke. Most of the men were still unsure of what had happened, but George Wilson, the section foreman, had no doubt. As the men at the face began to group together, Wilson said, "Boys, this is something we've never seen before. There's been an explosion." The men decided their only hope was to make their way toward the new air shaft that had been drilled at a place called Mahan Run, about a thousand feet from where they were working. The shaft was used only for air intake and had no elevator, but it was a possible source of fresh air in an atmosphere that soon would be filled with deadly carbon monoxide. In fact, it was probably the presence of this shaft between the spot of the explosion, several miles away, and the place where the men were working that saved their lives by releasing some of the enormous pressure of the blast. So, continually shouting to each other so that no one would be lost in the darkness and smoke, the five miners, unhurt but still in great peril, headed for the Mahan shaft.

Jerry Davis had known immediately what had happened. Moments after the blast, Crim had crawled into the dinner hole on his hands and knees. Davis told him and Hillsberry to wait while he looked for the rescue equipment which was stored on every section. Once they had it, they would look for the other five and then try to make it to the bottom of the Mahan shaft. As Davis groped toward the place where the equipment was kept, he could hear the rest of the crew coming toward him. He called to them and, when they reached him, he told them he knew where to find the rescue gear, which included two gas masks and nine "self-rescuers"—breathing devices which filter out carbon monoxide for up to two hours in the aftermath of a mine fire or explosion. After the equipment was located and distributed, the men grouped together at the dinner hole and started out for the shaft, carrying their lunch buckets and coats with them for what would be a cold and possibly very long wait. It was then that someone remembered Paul Henderson, although by this time it was too late to help him. A young miner and the son of a man who worked on another shift, Henderson had only been underground about four months. He had a job similar to the one Davis had been given during his year of difficulty with the company. He stood at a loading point to monitor the movement of coal on a belt. His job kept him far from the rest of the crew and he worked alone. Davis and Ralph Starkey, one of the other miners, set out to look for Henderson while the others waited for them at a spot where they found the air to be fairly clear. When the two men reached the place where Henderson worked, there was no sign of him. All Davis could find was his lunch pail. He opened it. It was full of coal dust, an indication that Henderson had survived the force of the blast, perhaps while eating, and had put the lid back on his lunch pail before seeking safety. He had apparently gone the wrong way toward the ruined Llewellyn Portal— the apparent area of the explosion—instead of toward Mahan Run. Davis and Starkey shouted for him, but got no answer. So Davis wrote a message to him in chalk on the side of a coal car directing him to come to the Mahan shaft. Later, Gary Martin, one of the members of the crew who donned a gas mask, returned to look for Henderson, but in vain.

When Davis and Starkey rejoined the others, they made their way to the base of the shaft. Cold, fresh air was still coming in when they arrived, so the men decided to save their self-rescuers until they were absolutely needed, as they were certain to be before long. Although no one spoke about it, all the men knew that another explosion might come at any time—once a major blast occurs, disrupting ventilation and igniting coal dust, the chance of another one occurring soon is considerably heightened. The miners were safe for the moment, but they had to make contact with someone aboveground who might be able to help them. There was a steel pipe, four inches in diameter, which had been lowered down the shaft from the surface, 513 feet above them. It seemed to offer the only means of communication with the surface. The men took turns whistling and shouting into it and banging on it with a stick of wood. For more than an hour and a half, they received no reply. Then about eight A.M., there was another explosion. For a while, the force of it reversed the course of natural ventilation which had been drawing fresh air down the shaft to where the men huddled below. The atmosphere began to grow murky again and Davis could smell the odor of burned coal dust which had been so strong just after the first blast. Davis began to feel weak and nauseated, and the headache he had had for some time grew worse. Both Vandergrift and Starkey passed out and repeatedly had to be revived so they could keep their self-rescuers in place. At one point, Lewis Lake, who had seemed to be doing well, lost consciousness. Gary Martin, wearing one of the gas masks, slapped his face to awaken him. "Lewis, if you don't wake up and help me, we're going to lose two or three of these men," Martin said. When Lake came around, he got up and tried to help the slightly built Vandergrift who seemed to be fading. He and Martin held him up and rubbed his wrists and slapped his face to revive him and keep his circulation moving. It was bitter cold now and snow was falling down the shaft. Vandergrift rallied a little and Lake took off his coat, and gave it to him, and gave his gloves to Starkey, who was also having a bad time.

They had been waiting huddled at the bottom of the shaft for more than two hours, and their hope of rescue was ebbing, when someone finally responded to their calls for help. A man shouted down to them from the surface to find out how many survivors were gathered there. He then went away, promising to bring help. At least another hour went by, however, and all the men were growing weaker and increasingly woozy from the carbon monoxide that periodically wafted into the atmosphere around them. Finally, rescue workers arrived at the top of the shaft and dropped down supplies and gas masks on a rope. Then a telephone receiver was lowered and the miners were told that efforts were being made to get a crane that could hoist them to safety in a bucket. It was not until about ten o'clock that the big bucket finally came down. Vandergrift and Starkey were the first to be lifted out, then Davis, Wilson and Lake, followed by the other three. All were rushed to a nearby hospital. They recovered, but they were the last to come out of the mine that day. Thirteen men who were at work in the east end of the mine far from the explosion escaped unhurt shortly after the original blast, but seventy-eight others were still in the mine when the official count was made known after nightfall. By then, a horde of newsmen had arrived to cover what appeared to be the worst mine disaster since 1951. And at ten P.M., as the reporters, the officials, and the relatives of the miners crowded into a Consolidation company store near the mine to await developments, a third explosion sent flames hundreds of feet into the night sky above the Llewellyn Portal. Although no official would say it, the blast ended what little chance there had been of reaching the trapped men. Raging underground fires and the danger of another explosion at any time would prevent rescue teams from reaching the sections of the mine where the men had been working.

The events of November 20, and the nine days of helpless waiting that followed before the mine was sealed to extinguish the underground fires, were an experience the reporters and television crews at the scene would never forget. The newsmen found themselves thrown together with the families of the missing men. All waited together amid the Christmas decorations in the cinder-block company store for news of the rescue efforts. Many of those with relatives underground went more than two days without sleep. As the days passed and the information given at each briefing held out less and less hope of a miraculous rescue, shouts of anger and cries of grief greeted the statements by company officials. Thanksgiving day came and went, adding a note of irony to the pathetic vigil. On the afternoon of the blast, West Virginia Governor Hulett Smith made the first in a series of appearances by top government, industry and union officials. "We must remember," he told the crowd assembled at the rear of the store, "that this is a hazardous

business and what has occurred here is one of the hazards of mining."
The next day, W. A. (Tony) Boyle, the president of the United Mine
Workers, arrived on the scene. Those who recalled the outrage of John
L. Lewis in the aftermath of mine disasters were surprised when Boyle
said, "As long as we mine coal, there is always this inherent danger." He
added that Consolidation was "one of the best companies to work with
as far as cooperation and safety are concerned." J. Cordell Moore, an
assistant secretary of the Department of the Interior, echoed Boyle's
praise of Consolidation. "The company here has done all in its power to
make this a safe mine," he said. "We don't understand why these things
happen, but they do happen."

The truth was that, compared with the rest of the industry, Consolidation had a good reputation in safety matters. During the year before,
eighty-two percent of the nation's 5,400 underground mines had been
cited for safety deficiencies. The industry had the highest injury rate in
the country—more than four times the national average. In 1967, 220
miners had been killed and more than six thousand had suffered disabling injuries. The repeated violations of anti-explosion procedures
that had been found in Number 9 were not unusual, as vital as the
precautions are. (In fact, the explosion created such a rush to clean up
other mines that many equipment suppliers ran out of rock dust in the
weeks following the disaster.)

The tense and emotional days after November 20 were marked by a
number of heated exchanges between reporters and company officials.
Many of the newsmen who came from out of state had been surprised
to find that such a thing as the company store they were using as a press
room still existed. And they were equally surprised at the reaction of
Boyle, Smith and others to the tragedy. Thus, when William Poundstone, a Consolidation executive vice-president, asserted during one
briefing that the mine had been "safe" prior to the explosion, he found
himself fending off an hour-long barrage of questions. One reporter
later remarked that he could think of no better example of an unsafe
mine than one in which seventy-eight men are killed. At the height of
the discussion, Poundstone said, "I think I have more important things
to do than argue this point." Another Consol spokesman explained that
the safety violations recorded by the Bureau of Mines were analogous
to deficiencies found in annual automobile inspections. He said they
were of little importance. But the newsmen were getting a different

story from relatives of the missing miners. One reporter was told by a veteran miner whose brother-in-law was among those trapped that the conditions in the mine were "lousy." He said it was "filled with gas" and "something was bound to happen." Poundstone said, however, that the mine was only "technically gassy," a contention that was contradicted by W. R. Park, a senior Bureau of Mines official, who called it "extremely gassy" and another Consol official who said it was "excessively gassy."

In the week after November 20, at least fifteen other major blasts ripped through the mine and there were countless lesser "popoffs" of ignited methane gas. Finally, on November 29, the mine was ordered sealed, a step the company had known was inevitable for days but which had been postponed at the request of relatives of the entombed miners, who remained hopeful to the last. By this time, tests of the underground atmosphere made by boring holes into the mine indicated that there was too much carbon monoxide and too little oxygen for anyone to have survived, even if they had somehow succeeded in avoiding the force of the explosions. The prevailing mood as this final action was taken was one of fatalistic acceptance, the same resignation which characterized the early attitudes of Boyle and the other officials at the scene. It was an attitude shared by many miners who had lived for years with the daily prospect of sudden death. Most of the men who worked in Number 9 said they would go underground again as soon as work was available. Among a few, the feeling was different, however. Jerry Davis had made up his mind long before the bucket was lowered into the mine to lift him to safety that he would never set foot in another coal mine. As soon as he was healthy, he took his family to a town near Akron, Ohio where he took a job with a trucking company. Nezer Vandergrift went to work in a steel plant not far from Farmington. Both men took pay cuts to accept their new jobs.

2

Three weeks before Tony Boyle confronted the stricken relatives of seventy-eight of his union's members and praised the company in whose mine the men were trapped, a federal jury in Lexington, Kentucky reached a verdict which helps to make Boyle's behavior understandable. The jury found that the United Mine Workers had, since 1950, conspired with the Consolidation Coal Company and other major producers to create a monopoly in the coal industry. It awarded more than $7 million to a small company it found had been almost driven out of business by union contracts tailored to the needs of the big companies. It was the second time in three years the UMW had been found guilty of antitrust conspiracy with the major coal operators. As surprising as these unprecedented verdicts might seem, they could have come as no shock to thousands of coal miners who had been wondering for years what the leaders of their union were up to. For in the aftermath of the bitter strikes of the years that followed World War II, an era of labor peace had come to the coal industry. Gone were the inevitable strikes, the tumultuous public bargaining sessions, and the constant threats of national coal shortages during the walkouts. In their place were closed-door negotiations between UMW chieftains and a delegation representing nearly the entire coal industry. Invariably, these resulted in new contracts without a strike. So complete was the change in the relationship of these traditional antagonists that when John L. Lewis retired in 1960, his testimonial dinner was attended by a number of coal operators. He was a "labor statesman," the coal men said, who had long since forsaken his unreasonable ways to bring about smooth union-management relations for the benefit of all.

The beginning of the process that ultimately brought Tony Boyle to the scene of a mine disaster to praise the company is rooted in the dire economic problems which confronted the coal industry in the years after World War II. The fuel demands of the war economy had kept the industry going, but when the conflict was over, technology appeared to have caught up with King Coal. The home heating market began to vanish. Oil and gas pipelines made these fuels available to home owners everywhere and no one wanted to keep a pile of coal in his cellar when his furnace could be stoked automatically from a tank or pipe. This development was especially devastating to the anthracite industry. The hard, glassy coal burned slowly and cleanly and was good for heating, but it had few other uses. Its production, which had been fading for some time, went into a steep decline from which it could not recover. The once-teeming mining communities of northeast Pennsylvania rapidly became depressed areas whose young people departed in droves for regions and industries whose boom days lay in the future, not the past.

The much larger bituminous industry seemed destined for a similar fate. In addition to losing its home heating market, soft coal also lost the railroads, which turned to diesel power. The steel companies, which used bituminous coal to make coke, remained a dependable market but one which was much too small to sustain the industry. Nevertheless, coal had captured a share of the thermo-electric market and in this there was hope, although the competitive problems were serious. The big steam generating plants could convert quickly from one fuel to another, depending on which was cheapest. Soft coal's competitors seemed likely to remain fairly stable in price, while growing transportation and labor costs made rises in the cost of coal seem inevitable. There was only one way they could be averted—by large scale mechanization of the mines. This would cost hundreds of thousands of men their jobs but, in the end, might save the industry.

The likelihood that the industry could undertake the kind of automation program needed to stabilize the price of coal and make it competitive seemed slim indeed in the postwar days. For one thing, the coal industry had always been hidebound and slow to take advantage of technology. What technological advances there were in the industry were usually made by supply companies or government agencies, rarely by the coal companies themselves. While there was a new attitude, born of necessity, among the executives of the largest producers, the fragmented industry included hundreds of small companies. The big operators stood a chance of raising the capital needed to overhaul their operations, but the smaller companies, many of them marginal, which accounted for much of the nation's coal production, simply didn't have the resources. In addition, there were natural problems which made extensive automation impossible in some areas, such as eastern Kentucky where the coal beds were extremely narrow. The huge continuous mining and automatic-loading machinery that had been introduced in some of the thick-seam mines in the northern coal fields would never fit in the narrow beds to the south. Then, of course, there was the labor problem. The United Mine Workers was the biggest, richest, and most powerful labor union in the land, and mechanization meant elimination of jobs on a vast scale. Few realistic observers expected the salvation of the coal industry to grow out of this unpromising combination of circumstances.

In these difficult days, the triumph of John L. Lewis and the UMW over the coal barons became complete. With the companies clinging desperately to the markets they still had and fighting to overcome the image of instability that their history of strikes and labor strife had produced, the operators were at Lewis's mercy. And, for a time, it seemed he would take full advantage of their vulnerability. He escalated the union's contract demands and brought the miners out on strike again and again.

In 1946, Lewis demanded that the operators pay a royalty on every ton of coal produced in union mines to establish and maintain a welfare and retirement fund for the miners and their families. It was an unprecedented proposal and the operators rejected it out of hand. When the contract deadline arrived on April 1, the miners struck. On April 10, with negotiations deadlocked, Lewis walked out of the talks. "To cavil further is futile," he told the industry representatives. "We trust that time, as it shrinks your purse, may modify your niggardly and antisocial propensities." By mid-May, the strike was still on, although the miners had gone underground during one two-week interval to avert a national fuel shortage. The government seized the mines on May 22. A week later, Lewis and Interior Secretary J. A. Krug agreed on a contract—including provision for a welfare fund financed by a five-cent per ton royalty—under which the government would operate the coal industry. The mines reopened, but within months were closed again after Lewis accused the government of violating its contract. The strike was called in defiance of a federal injunction and it led to Lewis's now-famous confrontation with the courts in which he and the UMW were fined $3.5 million for contempt. The fine was later cut to $700,000 by the Supreme Court and the mines reopened. But by June of 1947, the industry was still in government hands.

The mines were due to revert to control of their owners on June 30, but there was still no agreement between the companies and the UMW. As the deadline approached, Lewis made it plain he would accept no contract that did not provide for continuation of the new welfare fund. "If we must grind up human flesh and bones in an industrial machine—in the industrial machine that we call modern America—then, before God, I assert that those who consume coal, and you and I who benefit from that service—because we live in comfort—owe protection to those men first, and we owe security to their families after, if they die. I say it! I voice it! I proclaim it! And I care not who in heaven or hell opposes it!" By July 8, 1947, sixteen months after the original demand was made, Lewis had won his greatest bargaining concession ever—a new contract was signed ratifying the welfare fund and raising the royalty to ten cents a ton.

That year, bituminous coal production hit an all-time high of 630 million tons. But by the next year, the competitive progress of oil and gas limited production to less than six hundred million tons. By the end of 1948, it had slumped to 437 million tons, and there could no longer be any doubt that coal was in serious trouble.

In 1949, the union and the industry were again locked in bitter struggle. In June, Lewis ordered his men out on strike for a week after contract talks that had begun in late May became deadlocked. Then Lewis sent the miners back to work on a three-day week for the rest of the summer. The operators, infuriated, responded by cutting of payments to the welfare fund. The move forced the fund to cease all benefits except emergency medical care. The miners responded by going out on strike again in September for seven weeks. Christmas passed with no agreement, nor any really serious bargaining. In January, miners in Illinois struck and the walkout spread until it had paralyzed the industry. In February, the Truman administration got a Taft-Hartley injunction ordering the UMW to send miners back to work. It appeared the operators might, for once, be gaining the upper hand. But the miners refused to go back despite instructions from union headquarters to do so. The government sought to have the union fined for contempt, but the Federal Court in Washington found that a legitimate effort had been made to get the men back on the job and the motion was dismissed. The operators, who had hoped that the Taft-Hartley law might reverse the odds against them, had again been foiled and they knew they were beaten. Within days, a new contract was signed which, among other things, reorganized the welfare fund and raised the royalty to 30 cents a ton.

Although the operators could not have known it during this dark hour, when coal's survival as a major fuel seemed so much in doubt, 1950 was to mark the beginning of a new relationship between Lewis and the men he had so long tormented with his militance and scathing rhetoric. Late that year, he negotiated a new contract, in private for the first time, with a newly organized, industry-wide bargaining unit. It was signed without a strike on January 18, 1951. From that day forth, Lewis allowed the big companies a free hand in a process of mechanization and consolidation that would see more than 300,000 men lose their jobs. Thousands of small mines closed down, unable to meet the twin imperatives of automation and industry-wide labor contracts. Besides allowing the larger coal companies a free hand in mechanizing their operations, Lewis encouraged them to borrow from the National Bank of Washington, which the UMW controlled. During the 1950s, the union bank loaned millions to coal companies to assist them in their modernization.

It seems clear that Lewis thought the modernization and consolidation of the coal industry could be accomplished with a minimum of impact on the mining regions. The layoffs would be painful, but the expanding postwar economy would absorb many ex-miners. The young men who might otherwise have gone underground could seek opportunity in other areas. The welfare fund would provide pensions for the older men. It was to be a relatively orderly process and, for a while, it was.

But the recessions of the late 1950s derailed the program, cutting back coal demand, accelerating layoffs and making other jobs extremely scarce. The effect was catastrophic in Appalachia, an area already seriously affected by the lean years in the coal industry. Thousands of miners, too young to retire but too old to pack up and start over elsewhere, were cast adrift in the hills. The result was that hundreds of small coal pits that had been forced to close by the terms of the union contract reopened, manned by miners laid off from the larger mines. The union contract was no longer an obstacle. Men were desperate for work and these non-union "dog-holes," as they were called, offered jobs. Soon these primitive operations took over a sizable share of the nation's coal market by undercutting prices charged by the larger union companies. So great was their growth in the mountains of eastern Kentucky that the union's hold on the region was effectively broken.

To avoid being driven from regions where the terms of the union contract and the availability of unemployed miners made the idea of going non-union appealing to coal operators, the UMW resorted to "sweetheart" contracts. Under these clandestine arrangements, both sides agree to ignore portions of the national contract. In some cases, the welfare royalty, which was raised to forty cents per ton of coal in 1952, would be reduced. In others, wages were cut. In hundreds of mines, both were below contract levels. The "sweethearts" soon became an established fact of industrial life in southern Appalachia. They did not stop the growth of non-union mining, but they contributed mightily to the disillusionment and bitterness that were later to spread through the union's entire membership.

Yet "sweetheart" contracts were not the most extreme measure taken by Lewis under the selective labor-management partnership he had created to save the coal industry and the UMW. He had also secretly engaged the UMW in a bizarre financial deal with Cyrus Eaton, the famed railroad tycoon, through which the UMW purchased control of a major coal company. The company, the West Kentucky Coal Co., had been one of the nation's only major non-union producers. Before Eaton came along, its owners showed no signs of giving up their anti-union attitude. Using capital put up by the UMW—without the consent (or even knowledge) of the membership—Eaton gradually bought a controlling interest in the company. When he became board chairman in 1952, West Kentucky finally signed a contract with the UMW. Over the next decade, the UMW funneled $25 million in loans into the company.

After the facts of the deal became known to the membership, the company was abruptly sold at a loss of $8 million. The union chieftains explained to the members that the loss had been worthwhile because the company was organized at last.

When Lewis stepped down after four decades as the union's president in 1960, the outline of his legacy was already clearly visible in the Appalachian coal fields. For Lewis, as much as any man, had shaped the scene that confronted Senator John F. Kennedy as he made his famous campaign swing through the region on his way to the White House.

The coal industry, given up for dead a decade earlier, was alive and looking ahead to better days. But the men whose money had been freely loaned to promote the mechanization of the mines had been put out of work by the hundreds of thousands. "Sweetheart" contracts abounded in the hills. Non-union mines, operated under the crudest conditions, were flourishing. The accidents for which mining was notorious continued unchecked. No new federal mine-safety laws had been passed—or even sought—since 1952. Miners' lung disease was a serious and growing problem, but one that was altogether ignored.

Thousands of impoverished ex-miners, used up and cast aside by the coal companies, could be found in scores of dismal Appalachian towns that lay along the railroad tracks and polluted streams running through the flatlands and hollows around the big mines. Out of work and out of luck, there was little they could do, for mining remained the region's only industry. Some tried to return to the subsistence farming that had supported the region in the days before the coal barons came, but the soil was black with coal dust and the crop yield was meager. So most just sat on their front porches and gazed at the steep highland slopes that had once been scenic but now were scarred by strip mining or obscured by huge smoking slag heaps—the trademark of an industry that, for all its new machinery, remained remarkably primitive.

Thus it is not surprising that the handsome, rich, young Senator from Massachusetts was deeply affected by what he saw in the mountains. The Kennedy administration took office in 1961 with a commitment to major reform of the policies that governed life in Appalachia. But this sense of the need for change was not shared by the men who inherited control of the United Mine Workers from John L. Lewis at the start of the decade.

The presidency of the union fell to Thomas Kennedy, who by then was seventy-three years old and in poor health. To replace Kennedy as vice-president—and heir apparent to the top job—Lewis chose William Anthony Boyle, a volatile, if shy, Irishman who had been Lewis's administrative assistant since 1947. In contrast to John L., whose bushy eyebrows and bulldog jowls were familiar to every miner in the country, Boyle was an obscure figure who had worked in his boss's shadow. He was a diminutive man with sandy hair that had receded exactly halfway back on his head, and a penchant for nattiness that ran to bright shirts and ties and a fresh rose in his lapel each morning.

Boyle hailed from Montana where he had been born in a mining camp, the son of an immigrant coal worker. His father had gone to work in the mines of Scotland when he was nine and, as the UMW's publicity releases noted with pride, Boyle's grandfathers and great-grandfathers on both sides of the family had worked in the mines of Great Britain. The full story of "Tony" Boyle's rise to power in the UMW is hard to trace, but it is known that he became president of the union's district in Montana in 1940, seven years before Lewis called him to Washington to be his chief aide and the union's main contract troubleshooter. As Tony moved up in the world, so did his two brothers, Jack and Dick—but not without Tony's help.

When Tony Boyle went to Washington to become Lewis's right-hand man, Dick Boyle was appointed to succeed him as the president of UMW District 27 in Montana. The appointment was made despite the fact that the younger Boyle had never been a coal miner and the union constitution requires an officer to have five years' experience in the mines. After Dick Boyle took over, the union used its influence to bring about the shutdown by federal mine inspectors of several major mines in the vicinity of Roundup, Montana. Although the closures were ostensibly for safety reasons, both state and federal mining officials later called them "unwarranted" and "selective." The one company that was not affected by the actions was the Mountain State Coal Co., whose president was Jack Boyle. The closings, which occurred at various times during the 1950s, affected all of Jack Boyle's major competitors and eventually forced them out of business. At one point, both the U. S. Bureau of Mines and the FBI had considered investigating the matter, but it was dropped after Marling J. Ankeny, director of the mines bureau, declined to press for the probes.

In 1957, Tony Boyle journeyed to Montana to testify before a legislative hearing into possible revisions of the state's mine safety laws. Boyle opposed the bill, which would, among other things, have required roof bolting in all mines in the state. Although roof bolts are the most modern method of support, and collapsed roofs have long been the leading cause of death in coal mines, Boyle claimed the bill would "legalize the killing of men in coal mines." He told the committee that his brother would close his mines if the roof-bolt requirement were enacted. Less than a year later, four men died in a roof fall at Jack Boyle's "Montana Queen" mine. A state coal mine inspector who investigated reported that the roof was "not properly supported."

Boyle figured prominently in one other public controversy, outside of his family dealings, during his years as Lewis's right-hand man. This grew out of the UMW's all-out organizing drive begun in 1950 in the coal fields of southwestern Virginia. Production was expanding in this corner of the state, which adjoins West Virginia, Kentucky, and Tennessee. There never had been a strong union tradition in the area, however, and most of the new mines that opened were small, non-union operations. This was painful to the UMW, which had hoped that any increases in coal production would mean additional royalties for the new welfare fund. Non-union mines, of course, paid no royalties. They were also an embarrassment to John L. Lewis. So the union hired field workers to carry its message to the unorganized. Uncooperative coal operators were subject to demonstrations by hired pickets. After two years, however, the drive had made little progress and it was increasingly marred by violence. Equipment and buildings owned by recalcitrant operators were destroyed, frequently by dynamite blasts that resounded across the mountainsides and valley bottoms in the night. Non-union workers were threatened and harassed. In the midst of this, on February 28, 1952, a suit was filed in the county court at Wise, Virginia, asking $350,000 in damages from the UMW. The plaintiff was Charles Minton, a former UMW worker who claimed he had been fired and blacklisted by the UMW because he refused to carry out the union's order that he murder two coal operators. The suit said Minton was given the order by Tony Boyle.

In his suit, Minton told the story as follows: When John L. Lewis became dissatisfied with the progress of the organizing effort in Virginia, he summoned the Virginia field staff to a meeting in Washington. He re-emphasized his determination to bring the Virginia mines under the union banner. "Organize these small mines and damn the law suits," he said. "We'll take care of them." Later, Lewis sent an aide to District 28 headquarters in Norton, Virginia, with instructions that the operators be given "a good taste of rough stuff." Until then, the field workers had successfully discouraged the idea of violence. But after the aide's visit, Minton and another organizer were called aside by George Griffiths, secretary-treasurer of District 28, at union headquarters in Norton. Griffiths ordered them to blow up an electrical substation owned by the Gladeville Coal Company in the nearby town of Glamorgan. Minton and the other field worker obeyed, blasting the installation to bits with three cases of dynamite. For their work, the two saboteurs were paid "a handsome reward." The Gladeville incident was only the first in a series of dynamite blasts at non-union mines ordered by district officers.

Later, Minton was summoned to meet with Tony Boyle, "agent extraordinary of the United Mine Workers and personal agent of John L. Lewis," in Knoxville, Tennessee. Boyle told Minton he had been chosen to murder C. P. Fugate and Harry L. Turner, co-owners of the Gladeville Coal Company, who apparently had not been made more cooperative by the destruction of their electrical substation. Minton "was given to understand that if he would commit this crime, he would be supplied the finest counsel which could be obtained and that should he go to prison his family would be well supplied with funds during his absence and that he himself would receive a substantial reward." Minton refused. He was abruptly transferred to another job. Not long thereafter, he was fired. He then found he was unable to get work as a miner because the union "conspired to impoverish plaintiff and to prevent him, by indirect means, from obtaining employment in any of the coal mines located in District 28 of the United Mine Workers of America, or elsewhere." In its reply to Minton's suit, the UMW made a blanket denial of his charges. Nevertheless, Minton's action opened the way for nine other suits, totaling about $1 million, by coal operators whose property had been damaged but who previously had no evidence on which to sue. None of the cases, including Minton's, ever came to trial. They were settled out of court in a matter of months.

Reports circulated at the time that the companies received about $200,-000, but this was denied by union officials. There was no word on the terms of the union's settlement with Minton.

The incident would later return to haunt Tony Boyle. Asked about it publicly, he would claim he did not recall it. Several reporters who tried to look up the suit in the courthouse at Wise would find that there was record of it, but that the papers themselves were missing.

Thomas Kennedy became seriously ill in 1962 and Boyle took over as acting president of the union. When Kennedy died early the following year, authority passed quietly into Boyle's hands. Little had changed since Lewis had departed as president, and the succession of Boyle, the hand-picked heir, seemed to assure that nothing new was in the offing. Business went on as usual in the baronial old building in downtown Washington that had been the union's headquarters for more than twenty-five years. The building had once been an exclusive downtown men's club, and its paneled walls, high ceilings, and brass chandeliers made it seem a quaint place for a major labor union to be conducting its affairs in an age of glass-walled skyscrapers. But the union's headquarters, like its policies, had been good enough for John L. Lewis, and they would be good enough for Tony Boyle.

In the gritty coal hamlets of the Appalachian back country of 1948, no institution filled a greater need than the United Mine Workers Welfare and Retirement Fund. Medical facilities in the coal regions were terribly inadequate and health and sanitary conditions in the area perhaps the worst in the nation. In the labor contract made between Lewis and the government during the federal control of the mines in 1946, the U. S. Navy Bureau of Medicine was assigned to make a study of health conditions in the mining communities. When the study was made public in March, 1947, its findings shocked the nation.

"Ninety-five percent of the houses are built of wood, finished outside with weather board, usually nailed direct to the frame with no sheathing. Roofs are of composition paper. Wood sheathing forms the inside finish. The houses usually rest on posts with no cellars. . . . The state of disrepair at times runs beyond the power of verbal description or even of photographic illustration since neither words nor pictures can portray the atmosphere of abandoned dejection or reproduce the smells. Old, unpainted board-and-batten houses, batten gone or going and boards fast following, roofs broken, porches staggering, steps sagging, a riot of rubbish and a medley of odors.

"There is the ever present back-yard privy, with its foul stench—the most common sewage disposal plant in the coal fields. Many of these ill-smelling backhouses, perched beside roads, along alleys, and over streams leave their human waste exposed, permeate the air with nause-ating odors, and spread disease and death. . . .

"The evidence is convincing that three-quarters of the hospitals are inadequate. The distances involved in transporting an injured miner from the mine to the hospital is recorded for 188 mines. The average distance is seventeen miles. The distances range from one to 160 miles.

"Theoretically, the miners' wages allow for the extra hazardous na-ture of their occupations. Yet evidence clearly indicates that their earn-ings do not permit sufficient reserves in savings bonds or personal insur-ance to compensate them in case of permanent disability resulting from accidents and serious illnesses."

The new welfare fund provided retirement pensions of $100-a-month for men who had never before had such benefits. In addition there was a rehabilitation program for sick and injured miners, free medical care for miners and their families, including those on pensions, cash aid for the disabled, death benefits and maintenance assistance for widows and orphans. When a white-haired, hollow-cheeked, sixty-two-year-old coal miner named Horace Ainscough received the first UMW pension check in September, 1948, he is said to have remarked, "God bless the day John L. Lewis was born." It was a comment that could hardly have seemed too effusive to anyone familiar with the conditions the welfare fund was established to combat.

By the early 1950s, it became evident that despite the infusion of cash for miners' medical care from the fund, the facilities in the coal regions were simply not adequate to meet the great need. In 1952, the tonnage royalty was raised to forty cents, and the fund's trustees, led by Lewis, announced its most ambitious project: ten modern hospitals would be built in the mining regions of Virginia, Kentucky and West Virginia. Four years later, the hospitals were finished and dedicated. They cost the fund $30 million, but they brought high quality medical facilities to the region for the first time. Now the fund's regional offices could recruit their own doctors from the top young specialists in the nation to practice in the mountain regions at outstanding new facilities.

Even as these hospitals were dedicated, however, many miners and their families had begun to feel that the fund was not doing all that they had come to expect of it. The terms of the agreement establishing the fund placed absolute authority over its administration in the hands of the three trustees. By 1956, this authority had been exercised twice in ways that dealt stunning blows to many miners and their families. In 1953, the trustees decreed that the twenty years of service in the coal industry required for eligibility must have occurred within the thirty years prior to application for a pension. The result of this change was that many men who had as much as forty years underground and who had stood by Lewis and the UMW through some of their bitterest battles found themselves excluded from the pension for which they had worked so long. Many such men had become ill or otherwise disabled during the 1940s or early 1950s and were out of the mines during the years immediately preceding their sixtieth birthdays, at which time they were eligible to apply for a pension. If they filed their applications after 1953 and had not been working during the previous decade because of disability, they could not receive a pension.

In 1954, the trustees suddenly terminated the fund's cash aid for the disabled and income for widows. The announcement of the change said only that these programs had been "temporary," but no one in the coal fields had any idea that these were other than permanent benefits. These two programs had helped more than eighty thousand miners and thirty thousand widows and their children. About fifty-five thousand persons were still dependent upon this assistance for their livelihood when it was abruptly cut off.

Despite these setbacks, complaints about the fund were seldom heard in the mining regions during the 1950s. Many thousands of men received their pensions and medical benefits on schedule and without difficulty, and the coming of the hospitals to the mountains made criticism seem like quibbling, especially when John L. Lewis was still in charge of the UMW and was a trustee of the fund. But more setbacks were in the making. The arrival of the recessions of the late 1950s had a harsh impact on the coal industry, and production declined sharply. By 1956, it had climbed to five hundred million tons from its 1949 total of 437 million. But in 1959, production tumbled to 412 million tons, and the welfare fund was caught short. The fund ran a $12 million deficit in 1959 and a $21 million deficit in 1960, as its income slumped with the decline in coal production.

When the fund's annual report came out in 1961, it showed a balance of $99 million, the lowest in seven years. A painful series of benefit retrenchments was in progress. The fund announced that a miner's hospital and medical benefits would be cut off after one year of unemployment, regardless of the reason. Six months later, the monthly miners' pensions were reduced from $100—which they had been since the fund's inception—to $75. In October, 1962, the fund, again without a full explanation, announced that the ten coal field hospitals it had dedicated only six years before would have to be closed or sold. The hospitals were finally disposed of, eight by sale to an agency of the Presbyterian Church. The other two were closed. The fund has never made public what it lost on the transaction, but the sum is generally considered to have been around $16 million.

Of all the cutbacks in the welfare fund's benefits there was none that caused greater disillusionment than the announcement, in October 1962, that medical benefits would be cut off for union men who worked in mines whose owners had not been meeting their royalty payments. The decision was announced by Miss Josephine Roche, a seventy-seven-year-old confidante of Lewis, who was both the fund's director and one of its trustees. "The flagrant failure of the operators" to pay their royalties, she said, "left the fund no recourse but to terminate all benefits granted to the employes." It struck many as unorthodox to cut off benefits to miners because their employers didn't pay their debts, and the situation was made worse by the fact that many of the mines had been operating under verbal "sweetheart" agreements—their owners thought they could withhold the royalty payments with impunity.

In the steep mountain coal country of eastern Kentucky, the impact of this decision was particularly serious. Many miners, unaware of the "sweetheart" deals that led to the action, blamed their employers for their lost benefits. Mines were dynamited, coal cleaning plants were vandalized, and roving militants fanned out through the region, closing down mines by merely setting up picket lines and letting the deep pro-union convictions of the miners do the rest. Even in the poor, strife-ridden Kentucky coal industry, no UMW member would cross a picket line.

If the men who moved to retaliate against the Kentucky mines could have had a fuller understanding of the forces at work in the coal fields in the early 1960s, they might have directed their bitterness elsewhere. The small coal mines, unable to mechanize and faced with national labor contracts agreed upon between the UMW officers and the big coal companies, were operating on the slimmest of profit margins. The union had tolerated non-payment of welfare fund royalties to keep many of these mines from going non-union and thereby contributing to the UMW's decline in Kentucky, Virginia, and parts of West Virginia. But the crunch of the recession had made things tougher all around, and the fund's crackdown—a doublecross in the eyes of many small coal operators—was accompanied by lawsuits demanding back payment of royalties. It was in a counter-move to such a suit that a small Tennessee coal company first won an antitrust case against the UMW and the big coal companies. The decision in the celebrated "Pennington" case was later overturned by the Supreme Court, but the high court affirmed that a labor union's exemption from antitrust laws could be forfeited if it entered into an economic conspiracy with management. (It was under this ruling that the federal jury in Lexington, Kentucky later made its decision against the UMW shortly before the Farmington disaster.)

Anyone who believes in the coal conspiracy theory—which has now been accepted by the courts—cannot escape the conclusion that the actions against the miners employed by companies not meeting the welfare royalties were part of the scheme. For the results were precisely what the UMW and the big companies appeared to want: labor strife and violence at the small mines, which were an increasing competitive nuisance to the big companies with which the UMW had cast its lot. And the termination of hospital benefits was not the only step taken by the fund that seemed aimed mainly at hurting the small mine operators.

In 1965, the fund trustees made several more decisions that look highly suspicious in light of the courts' findings of conspiracy between union and big management. The monthly pension was raised, but not all the way to $100. The fund was again running a healthy surplus as coal, helped out by the end of the recessions and a booming demand for electricity, had gotten squarely on its feet again. There was enough money to raise the pensions to $100, but the trustees decided something else had to come first. They lowered the retirement age from sixty to fifty-five, while pensions were raised only to $85. Reporters who asked about this action were told that the union hoped the lower retirement age would encourage older miners, if they were laid off at larger, union mines, to retire instead of going to work in the expanding non-union segment of the industry. Further, the twenty-year service requirement for a pension was modified to require that a miner spend his final working year in a union mine. Thus a man who had labored forty years in a union mine and who was forced by economic circumstance to work his final year in a non-union mine would not be entitled to a pension, whereas another man who had spent nineteen years in non-union mines and then went to work for a union mine in his last year would be eligible. The intent seemed clear: the small mines, nearly all of them non-union, were getting labor from the layoffs at the larger union mines, and the fund was adjusting its eligibility requirements to choke off this labor supply. Later the same year, the pension was raised again to $100, but by that time the miners had already seen how the fund was setting its priorities.

There were other aspects of the fund's management which, while not so quickly grasped by the miners, were later to become major objects of controversy within the union. In 1957, the fund began publishing annually a brief audit report which explained in general terms what was being done with its accumulated assets. At the time, the fund had an unexpended balance of $145 million. More than $27 million of this was listed as on deposit in a so-called "general" checking account, which union officials later acknowledged was at the National Bank of Washington—the bank in which the union had acquired a controlling interest. This account was separate from, and much larger than, those used to pay the pension checks and administrative costs of the fund. From 1957 until 1968, the balance in the account, which drew no interest, fluctuated from a low of $12 million in 1961 to a high, in 1967, of $72 million. Even when the fund was running heavy deficits at the turn of the decade, millions were still on deposit in this account. While thousands of miners were being refused pensions or having their benefits reduced or cut off, money that could have provided badly needed income for a great many of them was lost because of this curious policy of allowing huge sums to earn nothing in a checking account of unknown purpose.

Although the coal miners had no way of knowing it at the time, the swollen checking accounts at the National Bank of Washington were part of a concerted scheme to enrich the union-owned bank. It all started late in 1949 when Lewis had a series of secret meetings with Barney Colton, a soft-spoken, courtly Washington banker who was to become President of the UMW's bank. At their second meeting, the two men discussed plans to transfer both the union's and the fund's accounts to the National Bank of Washington. By early the next year, just after the new contract raising the welfare royalty was signed, the fund had deposited more than $36 million in checking accounts at the bank. The arrangement drew strong objections from the coal industry's representative on the welfare fund's board of trustees, Charles A. Owen, president of the Imperial Coal Company. At a meeting in August, 1950, Owen told Lewis and Josephine Roche, the close Lewis ally who was the fund's "neutral" trustee as well as its director, "It is undoubtedly the law that a trustee should not deposit funds in a bank which he controls or in which he has a substantial participation. Amongst other criticism, he may cause the dividends upon his stock to be enhanced by the Bank's use of a large deposit of his trust's funds for loan purposes. Also conflicting interests may arise; or losses may occur." Owen's complaints fell on deaf ears. Lewis had no intention of changing the fund's investment policies and Roche was completely in accord with his wishes, whatever they were. Although Owen made other attempts to have the policy changed, they all failed. And Owen's industry colleagues apparently were unwilling to risk upsetting the newly tamed lion of labor by making a major issue of the matter.

The fund made other curious investment decisions. Between 1962 and 1966, it sold about $46 million of government securities prior to their maturity date. These transactions, made in a period of spiralling interest rates, resulted in a loss of about $4 million. The fund claimed that this was only a "paper loss," designed to free the money for investment in higher-yield securities. But this explanation is puzzling, for during the same period, the fund was increasing the size of its "general" checking account from $23 million to $48 million—an odd course for an organization willing to take a $4 million loss in order to acquire higher-yield securities.

As the fund grew to be a source of deep disappointment among many miners, the union leadership itself had also begun to stir resentment, particularly in the coal regions of northern West Virginia, eastern Ohio, and southwestern Pennsylvania. Here, the local economy was more diversified and the dependency upon coal not as great as in the southern mining fields. The schools were generally better, the standard of living higher, and the miners not the benighted, isolated group that manned the pits to the south. Miners lived alongside men who worked in other industries, chiefly steel, and they were acutely aware of the huge gains that other labor unions were making with each new contract. Allegiance to Lewis and the UMW tradition of absolute solidarity was strong, but it was eroding rapidly by the time Tony Boyle became president.

The contracts negotiated by Lewis during the previous decade had been "open-ended"—they remained in effect until either side decided to terminate them. The purpose of this arrangement was obvious. Coal was in a recovery period, but continued progress, as the recession proved, was by no means certain. Lewis did not want to be bound by the usual two-year contract, which would force him to squeeze bargaining gains out of a shaky industry that he was trying to nurse back to health. Thus from 1958 to 1963 the UMW had no new contract. The only changes the miners got were the cutbacks in welfare fund benefits.

The passage of the Landrum-Griffin Act in 1959 gave the UMW hierarchy another headache. The miners' union had long been considered one of the wealthiest of all labor organizations but no one—least of all the membership—knew for sure how much the union had. The new law, which was aimed at assuring the democratic operation of labor organizations, required unions to file annual public statements of income, expenditures, and assets. When the UMW's first was filed in 1960, its contents made front-page news. It showed that the union had a staggering $110 million in assets, including a controlling interest in the National Bank of Washington and a sizable interest in the West Kentucky Coal Company and in American Coal Shipping, Inc. The 1960 report and the two that followed it also revealed that the union had shelled out nearly $7 million between 1959 and 1961 to pay off defaulted loans, which the UMW had guaranteed, made to coal companies by the National Bank of Washington. These facts were slow to penetrate the southern Appalachian coal fields, but the news spread like wildfire among union men to the north and added to their growing restiveness.

In the anthracite region of northeast Pennsylvania, 1960 brought another piece of the jigsaw puzzle into place and helped to assure that the anthracite miners would be ready joiners of any insurgent movement within the UMW. The anthracite region had been the first organized by the mine workers, and for years it was the nation's prime coal producing region. At the turn of the century, a young man named John Mitchell, fifth president of the UMW, had organized miners of differing nationalities and languages for an industry-wide strike that brought the eight-hour day to the coal miners. It was a legendary event in labor annals, and it established a proud union tradition among the hardy immigrant stock that lived in the crowded, grey cities of the region extending from Pottsville north to Scranton. From this solid base in the anthracite country, the UMW moved into the unorganized bituminous territories in its famous organizing drives of the 1920s and 1930s.

The fading of the glasslike anthracite coal as a major fuel had dramatically reduced the size of the Pennsylvania industry, and had apparently caused Lewis and his associates to give the region up for dead. A special pension fund established for the anthracite industry had deteriorated, because of low coal production and rampant non-payment of royalties, to the point where pension checks were reduced from $100 to $30 a month. Little effort was made by the UMW to collect the unpaid royalties and the men of the region told bitter stories of the coziness between their district officers and the coal company bosses. Thus it came as no surprise to the miners of the region when August J. Lippi, president of the union's District One, the heart of the area where the UMW was born, was convicted in June, 1960, of accepting a $10,000 bribe from a coal company to assure labor peace in 1956–57.

The recovery of the coal industry was complete by the time Tony Boyle became the eleventh president of the mine workers' union on January 20, 1963. Coal consumption was up to 422 million tons, and the feeling among industry experts was that the battle with oil and gas for the electricity generating market had been won. The average price per ton of coal was $4.48—more than fifty cents *below* what it had been in 1948. The average miner was producing nearly fifteen tons per day, thanks to new machinery, compared to about six tons per day in 1948. The only real threat to coal in the electricity market was atomic energy. Experts were predicting that the atom would take over a larger and larger share of the electricity market and would one day control it all. But for the forseeable future, coal production was expected to rise dramatically because the electricity market was growing so fast that even an increasingly small share of the market would mean huge gains in coal consumption. As Tony Boyle stepped from the shadow of his mentor, Lewis, to take command of the organization, he seemed at first to be aware that the UMW's massive assistance to the coal industry had finally paid off and had made a return to the old adversary relationship possible. "This automation and mechanization has gone far beyond what Mr. Lewis was talking about when he urged the mines to mechanize," Boyle said in a widely quoted speech. This remark was taken as a sign that the free hand granted the industry in laying off men to make way for machines would no longer be extended, that Boyle had heard the rising chorus of demands for job security, paid holidays, and the other fringe benefits so long deferred while the industry battled to avoid extinction.

But by August of 1963, Boyle had still not reopened the contract with the industry. The voices of discontent were beginning to grow loud. The ferment was especially strong in the northern bituminous region, where a group of local union leaders was trying to organize a strike to force the union to reopen the contract. Unofficial estimates were that such a strike might keep twenty thousand men off their jobs. In Washington, Boyle said nothing about the dissident movement. The hierarchy's position was voiced by Raymond Lewis, brother of John L., who had been installed to replace Boyle as the vice-president. There was no intention of reopening the contract, Lewis said. "I don't think the contract can be reopened on the say-so of a few men," he added. Replied one Pennsylvania union president, "They practically come out and tell us to mind our own business." Added another local officer, "They keep telling us the industry is sick. Nonsense, we're the ones that are sick." The dissidents wanted a new contract for a variety of reasons, but they made it plain that the main one was a drastically improved seniority clause. Many coal companies were laying off older men and keeping younger ones so that they could avoid the uneconomical process of retraining veterans who might only have a few years of work remaining in their careers. Instead, they were investing the training in new men with whole careers ahead of them. This practice was sound economically, but it did not go over well with miners who had been members of the union for many years and felt that protection of their jobs should take priority over corporate economizing.

Simultaneously, another rebel movement was shaping up in Kentucky where about three thousand miners threatened to go to Washington to urge a new, separate contract for the small mines so that they could remain open under the union banner.

A strike in the Pennsylvania fields was headed off at the last minute when Joseph Yablonski, the rugged-looking, gravel-voiced president of the union's District 5 at Pittsburgh, made a personal appeal at a weekend meeting of the rebels. The fiery Yablonski, who was liked and trusted by most of the miners, said that Boyle would "give serious consideration to your suggestions." Although Yablonski made no promises, his comments succeeded in convincing the men that Washington was listening. And on December 18, Boyle indeed opened negotiations with the Bituminous Coal Operators Association, the big mine owners' bargaining unit. The move was welcomed by the dissidents, but they took a wait-and-see attitude toward Boyle's negotiating abilities. As Harry Knight, secretary of a huge Pennsylvania local, put it, "Unemployment comes first and then safety. The last thing we want is money and that's probably the first thing they'll offer us."

In January, Boyle submitted a list of fifteen bargaining goals to Edward Fox, chief negotiator for the BCOA. Newspapers were filled with reports that Boyle had broken with Lewis's policy of seeking all contract gains in the form of higher wages, a policy that had prevailed through the three previous contracts. Broader seniority rights and higher overtime pay—aimed at encouraging more hiring—were said to be highest on Boyle's list.

But when Boyle called the union's International Policy Committee, which ratifies contracts, to Washington on March 20, the word leaked out that the contract agreed upon embodied another $2-per-day wage boost—the same increment negotiated by Lewis in the last three agreements. When the contract was signed (no UMW wage policy committee ever voted one down) Boyle announced it with a grand flourish. It was, he said, "the best contract ever negotiated by the United Mine Workers." He claimed that the agreement provided for "mine-wide seniority." Boyle's comments satisfied the rebels for exactly one week—the time it took them to read and analyze the contract. They found that there were still no paid holidays and that the vaunted "mine-wide seniority" clause contained loopholes allowing the companies to continue doing virtually what they had been doing. Added to this, they discovered a provision, worth nothing to them in benefits, that required the major companies to pay eighty cents a ton into the welfare fund on coal purchased from non-union mines. Most small mines did not have cleaning and processing plants, and it was common for them to sell their coal to larger mining companies, who would process it in their own plants, called tipples, and then sell it as their own. Boyle and Fox pretended at a news conference after the contract was signed that this clause was a major bone of contention, but in view of the large mine owners' dislike of their smaller competitors, it seems unlikely that this provision met with much resistance.

Leaders of the northern dissident movement were furious. At a protest meeting in Bellaire, Ohio, a small industrial town just across the Ohio River from Wheeling, West Virginia, a series of speakers denounced the new contract. "It's a step sideways," said one miner. "Fox outfoxed Boyle," added another. Carl Bailey, an officer of local 688 at the Republic Steel Company's nearby Clyde mine, said the UMW's officers were "love birds with the coal operators." The dissidents demanded that Boyle come to the coal fields to explain the contract. He refused. A wave of wildcat strikes then swept across the northern coal fields. With roving pickets bringing out mines that did not shut down on their own, scores of mines were closed and about ten thousand men were idled for about a week before they gradually began to return to their jobs. The long era of "labor peace" in the coal fields was over, ended not by a union-backed strike aimed at the industry but by an unauthorized walkout directed at the union leadership.

The end of the 1964 protest strike marked only the beginning of the dissident movement in the United Mine Workers. The militant miners of Ohio, Pennsylvania, and northern West Virginia vowed to take their case to the union's quadrennial International Convention, scheduled for early September. And if they failed to get what they wanted there, there were always the union-wide elections in December, in which Tony Boyle would have to face a membership referendum on his performance for the first time.

In Washington, Boyle was also under pressure from the government to make changes. The UMW was composed of twenty-seven districts, all but two in the United States, and in only six of these were the members allowed to elect all their regional officers. The other twenty-one districts had most of their officers appointed from Washington. It was a practice that went back many years and had been legal until the passage of the Landrum-Griffin Act, which required the election of officers in all regional union divisions. The law permitted an international union president to take temporary charge of a district in case of financial mismanagement or contract compliance problems, but he was required to restore democratic procedures after eighteen months or face action by the Department of Labor. The law had now been in effect for five years and the UMW had made no effort to change its practice of appointing most of the district officers.

To the average coal miner, the men in the Washington headquarters were distant figures not directly related to their day-to-day existence. But the district officers were different. It was they who had the responsibility for enforcing the contract with the companies, and it was they who were responsible for prosecuting grievances filed under the contract. To a coal miner involved in a dispute with his foreman, the test of how well his union stood behind him was the performance of the district office in settling the issue with the company. During the decade and a half in which the UMW's primary concern was the rehabilitation of the coal industry, thousands of miners had come to feel that the men in their district offices saw their duty as enforcing the contract against the men, not against the companies. It was in response to complaints from miners that the Labor Department began to put pressure on Boyle to remove the so-called "trusteeships" in which the districts were held and to allow the election of officers. By August, however, there was no sign from Boyle that he would follow the department's wishes. The union argued that the districts were not subordinate divisions at all, but "administrative arms" of the international union. This argument, of course, left unanswered the question of why the election of officers was permitted in five districts. The desire for district democracy, or "autonomy," as the miners called it, had been an issue in the UMW before, but Lewis's influence had always been sufficient to keep any insurgent activity to a minimum. Now, however, times were changing. Lewis had retired and Boyle's first contract had stirred up strong resentment among the miners. Sentiment for autonomy increased, and the government's contention that the appointment of the UMW district officers was illegal added to it.

The last time a serious effort had been made to oppose the wishes of the UMW hierarchy at a convention was in 1944, and that was before Tony Boyle's time. During the twelve years that he was Lewis's administrative aide and protégé, the president's office heard virtually nothing but adulation from the men in the mines. Lewis had operated the UMW as a virtual monarchy since 1920, and the man he had trained to take his place had no intention of breaking that tradition, regardless of what the government and dissident members wanted.

Besides, things looked different from Tony Boyle's perspective. More than forty years of one-man rule in the UMW had created an atmosphere inside the grey, six-story headquarters overlooking McPherson Square in Washington in which criticism of the man at the top was considered treason. Lewis had suppressed dissent in the membership and had refused to tolerate it from his associates. When Lewis and UMW Vice-President Philip Murray, who succeeded Lewis as president of the CIO, quarreled in 1942, Lewis called a meeting of the UMW International Executive Board and had Murray cashiered from the union. Lewis's other lieutenants got the message, and thereafter he had no problems with dissent in his inner circle. It was natural that Boyle should expect to be treated in the same manner as his mentor and, inside union headquarters, he was. Raymond Lewis dared to oppose Boyle, but he only did it once. When Boyle had abruptly transferred John Mayo, International Executive Board member from District 4 in Pennsylvania, to head a temporary UMW office in Iowa, Lewis objected, claiming that Boyle had violated the union constitution. He got back a letter from George Titler, a Boyle ally who was president of the union's district in southern West Virginia. "What would John L. Lewis have done with a maverick of your ilk?" the letter asked. "The answer is simple: a kick in the pants with a hard-toe shoe.

"After John L. Lewis spent twelve years teaching Tony Boyle to be a master executive, why should a man who never worked in the mines, devoid of any executive ability, be picked up by the nape of the neck and the seat of the pants and thrown into a responsible, $40,000-a-year job, one heartbeat away from the presidency of this great union, and be allowed to throw roadblocks in the way of a fine executive working long hours, doing your work as well as his own. . . .

"For years I have considered you as a small end of nothing shaved down to a point. Your abominable letter has not changed my opinion. I recommend psychiatric treatment for both you and Mayo. Sane men do not drill a hole in the bottom of a boat while at sea."

Although theoretically a subordinate of Lewis, Titler ran no risk in writing his scathing letter. Once Lewis had challenged Boyle, he was a marked man. Within a year, Lewis had resigned and was replaced—by Titler, a disheveled character in his late sixties, with narrow eyes and a vast abdomen that made it nearly impossible for him to keep his shirts tucked in.

Aside from such unpleasant incidents as the squabble with Raymond Lewis, it was a comfortable life that Boyle and his intimates led in Washington. Boyle collected $50,000 a year in salary, plus an unlimited expense account. His fellow international officers each got $40,000 plus expenses. Further, the hierarchy had removed $850,000 from the union treasury and placed it in a special account in the National Bank of Washington to enable all international officers with ten years of service to retire at full salary. This action, taken without notifying the membership, was done in time to benefit John L. Lewis upon his retirement. Boyle and company also participated freely in another long standing UMW tradition—nepotism. Boyle's brother was the $27,000 a year president of District 27 in Montana in 1964, and his daughter, Antoinette, a lawyer, had been added to the district payroll at $23,000 a year, although there was some question as to what she was supposed to do. Secretary-treasurer John Owens had his son Willard on the union legal staff at $35,000 a year, and his other son Ronald was a member of the International Executive Board from District 6 at $16,000 a year. Harrison Combs, assistant general counsel of the union, had three other members of his family on the payroll, and International Executive Board Member John T. Kmetz had two of his sons on the staff. At least five other families were represented by at least two members on the UMW payroll.

As the September convention drew near, the hierarchy made elaborate plans to deal with any insurgent activity that might occur. The first move had been to break a long-standing practice of holding the convention in a city central to the coal fields. Recent conventions had been held in Cincinnati, but this year's was scheduled for Miami. The change was of considerable consequence to the large, militant locals in the northern mining regions, which had hoped to send a full complement of delegates to press for reforms. The union constitution required the International to pay for the transportation of one delegate from each local, but locals that were entitled to more than one had to meet the transportation costs of nearly all their additional representatives. Moreover, all locals were required to pay the lost wages and incidental expenses of their delegates. Thus the further from home the site of the convention, and the longer the convention lasted, the more it cost the locals to send representatives.

The hierarchy also took full advantage of the fact that there were still in existence approximately six hundred locals composed entirely of retired or inactive miners. Under the union constitution, when a mine closed down the local organized at that mine should close at the same time; during the past fifteen years of the industry's consolidation, hundreds of mines had shut down, but the International had simply ignored the constitution and allowed these locals to remain in existence. There were at least as many of these so-called "bogey" locals as there were active locals. Their members were usually either dependent financially on the welfare fund for pensions or old-timers who felt a strong allegiance to the union leadership that carried over from the glory days under John L. Lewis. Many of these locals had only a handful of members and some had only a single member. Nevertheless, the hierarchy issued convention credentials for each and urged them to send delegates. With the International paying the travel expenses and seldom any lost wages to make up, it was convenient for these locals to send a representative, and he was usually a man who could be counted on to be friendly to the union hierarchy.

In cases where potentially friendly delegates could not afford to make the trip, the administration had a way to make it easier for them. Jobs were available on any of the seven committees which reviewed resolutions before they went to the floor. These committees had as many as seventy members, and they were paid $60 a day for their services. In addition, 168 messengers, ushers, and sergeants-at-arms received the same pay. In all there were about five hundred jobs that Boyle could assign to whomever he pleased. When a local union could not afford to send all the delegates to which it was entitled, the district office would often insist that its extra credentials be turned in for distribution to someone chosen by the administration, frequently the district officer himself or a member of his staff. Always, these credentials were distributed to persons friendly to the administration. Locals that could not afford any delegates and that refused to turn their credentials back to the district office faced a fine for failing to be represented at the convention.

Virtually everything about this system of delegate apportionment violated the union constitution, which provided that all delegates "shall be elected directly from the local unions they represent." It further provided that the credentials committee "shall not transfer votes to any delegate unless authorized by the local union to do so." Often, locals were represented by persons they had never heard of, let alone authorized to vote for them. The constitution also said that "no appointed employee of the organization shall be a delegate from any local union other than his own." This provision was among the most widely and obviously flouted of all. For instance, Sam Nicholls, the appointed head of the union's virtually defunct district in Washington state, arrived at the Miami gathering with the credentials of five different locals.

As a result of these procedures the large locals were often represented by only a few delegates who carried as many as five votes. To diminish the influence of these representatives, the convention was run on a voice-vote basis. Thus a delegate representing five hundred miners at an active local had no more weight in the convention than a man sent by a defunct local with three members. This imbalance was partially offset by the fact that many of the "bogey" locals were represented by district officials who also carried several votes. To many miners, however, these subtleties of delegate apportionment meant little because of the manner in which the issues were brought to a vote.

Theoretically, the conventions were held for the purpose of voting on the hundreds of resolutions sent in by local unions, dealing with subjects ranging from constitutional amendments to bargaining objectives. Both Boyle and Lewis before him were fond of bragging that the UMW was unequalled in the democracy of its proceedings. The conventions were "more Democratic than the U.S. Congress," Boyle would often say. This is certainly open to question. All resolutions were screened through the committees appointed by the administration and headed by members of the hierarchy. Similar resolutions were lumped together and reported simultaneously. When the convention chairman, invariably an administration man, turned the floor over to the various committee chairmen so that their resolutions could be put to a vote, the resolutions themselves were never voted on directly. The committee chairman would offer his committee's report on a measure, and it was this report that was voted on—not the measure itself. The report, favorable or unfavorable, was without exception what the officers wanted. Thus those favoring any action not wanted by the hierarchy found themselves in a position of having first to line up enough votes to defeat the committee report, then somehow getting the floor to bring up the original resolution. Since the hierarchy controlled the chair, the ayes invariably prevailed and anyone who disagreed was gaveled down.

As the 1,173 UMW delegates assembled on September 1 in the ballroom of the Americana Hotel in Bal Harbour, Florida, it was clear that what little chance the insurgents had to effect some changes through the convention depended upon the outcome of the first day. It was then that the rules of the convention would be established, and any challenges to the credentials of delegates decided. By this time, the rebels had an additional rallying point in the candidacy of Steve Kochis, a tough-talking, tobacco-chewing miner from Bobtown, Pennsylvania, for the presidency of the union.

Boyle was ready for them. As the miners took their seats in the ballroom of the hotel, they noticed a group of men carrying white miners' hard hats, on the convention floor. On one side of their helmets was stenciled, "Tony Boyle." On the other it said "District 19," and no one who knew the union well could fail to recognize the significance of their presence. District 19 encompassed southeastern Kentucky and eastern Tennessee, an area that had long been marked by violent labor strife. Many mines had closed down and others had gone non-union in the midst of prolonged strikes. The UMW had lost its grip on the area, but nonetheless it kept the strike going and the district office in operation. During the last half of 1964, the International pumped $661,000 into the region, nearly five times as much as it gave to any other district, and about one third of all the money it paid to all the districts. Not surprisingly, the miners from District 19 felt a strong allegiance to the officers whose largesse with the organization's treasury kept their strike benefits flowing. Their presence as unofficial marshals did not bode well for anyone wishing to take issue with Tony Boyle. In addition, the convention floor was flooded with a variety of guests, including the wives of officers and delegates, and even a few coal operators. They were seated among the delegates, with no attempt made to segregate them.

As the proceedings got underway, John Kmetz took the podium to introduce Boyle to the delegates. He gave a long, adulatory speech: "Somewhere along the line, as I saw President Lewis watching him so closely, bringing him along, I knew that possibly the day might come, and I prayed that I would live and see that day, when he would be in the position that he is holding today. . . . My friends, a great leader, a true servant of all the workers, with a high sense of duty, with statesmanship, with courage, with patience and fortitude, an inspiration to all of the officers who have been working with him, I present to you now as the permanent chairman of this convention—President Boyle."

With that, hundreds of delegates, many of them waving placards emblazoned with Boyle's name and picture, stood to whoop it up for the beaming little man on the platform. The hoopla was intensified by five bands, which Boyle had ordered brought in from the coal fields on a special train. The delegates continued to chant and cheer and stamp their feet and wave their signs for about twenty minutes. Then they sat down, but Boyle hadn't had enough. The bands played on for another half-hour before the word came down for them to stop. The miners later learned that Boyle had paid $390,000 from the union's treasury to import the musicians.

After the music died down, a delegate from Boyle's home district in Montana presented him with a state flag. Then a representative from a defunct local in District 19 gave Boyle one of the white hard hats identical to those being worn by the marshals on the floor. Finally, Boyle began his speech.

"I am reminded at this time," he said, "of some irresponsible people who have been making irresponsible statements to the press. . . . I have read that there are some people who would return this union to its membership. Well, I have only been your president a little over a year and nine months, and I didn't know that I had taken it away from you. . . . Take it away from you? What would I do with it? . . . This is in line with the enemies of organized labor in this country. The enemies of labor, as you know, in 1947 spent money and time lobbying for that slave labor law known as the Taft-Hartley Act and they had it passed. Twelve years later, they weren't satisfied. Labor hadn't been shackled enough. So the enemies of the organized labor movement in this country decided it was time to give them another shot in the arm, and what did they do? They came to Washington and they found an unknown by the name of Landrum. Then they found another unknown by the name of Griffin. They must have impressed upon these unknowns that they would get their names in bold print if they would start out on a tirade to destroy the labor movement.

"So the slogan was 'let's give the unions back to the membership.' And Congress passed the Landrum-Griffin Act. . . . Who is giving aid and comfort to it today? A handful of a minority in these different labor groups. Your officers are too busy trying to repeal these obnoxious laws to be concerned with irresponsible people. The most criticism I can recall at the moment having received, and that which has bothered me the most since I have been your president, is the hundreds and hundreds of letters, telegrams, and telephone calls to the national office criticizing the president of this union because he won't invoke the 'basic law' against these irresponsible people. Sure, I had a reputation when I was in a local union of being a firebrand. I think I had somewhat of a reputation of that nature when I came to Washington. But you do mature, and you do become patient, and you do become tolerant with people for whom you feel sorry."

If Boyle's hour-long speech convinced any of his critics in the audience that he regarded them as merely irresponsibles for whom he felt nothing but compassion, their minds were quickly changed. The rugged crew from District 19 donned their helmets and took positions alongside each of the microphones on the convention floor. When the chairman of the Committee on Rules and Order of Business took the floor to introduce the hierarchy's program for running the proceedings, a number of dissidents rose to speak on the motion.

"Mr. Chairman, I haven't heard anything about the seating arrangement of the convention," said John Belch of the big local at Ronco, Pennsylvania. "Delegates and spectators are all together. When it comes time to vote, the spectators' voices could outnumber the delegates' voices. I think there should be a rule on seating arrangements at this convention."

"Let me assure you, Delegate Belch," replied Boyle, "that I don't think we have to worry too much, from the demonstration you saw here this morning, as to the closeness of the votes that might occur. . . ."

As Boyle spoke, a number of other miners tried to reach the microphones to protest the convention rules. Scuffles broke out, with the hard-hatted delegates punching, kicking, or simply grabbing those who wanted to speak. John Stofea, a twenty-three-year veteran of the UMW from New Eagle, Pennsylvania, turned around in his seat and saw the foreman from the U.S. Steel Company mine where he worked seated behind him. Incensed, he got up and strode toward a mike at the front of the room. Three of the white hats grabbed him and beat him into submission. One clubbed him with the edge of his helmet. He was led bleeding from the floor as the brawl continued. Those who reached microphones to speak found that they had been turned off. As the free-for-all calmed down, the Boyle rules for running the convention were gaveled through. The procedure for voice votes on committee reports, the mixing of delegates and guests, and the credentials of all delegates were approved, by voice vote, without another word spoken against them. By then, it was past lunch time and Boyle, without saying a word about the uproar that had just occurred, declared a recess until the following morning.

Although the dissidents strove manfully to win a few points, their struggle was utterly futile after the first day. As the proceedings opened the next morning, Joseph Yablonski, the president of District 5, in Pennsylvania, approached Boyle and threatened to take his delegation home in protest if there were any repetition of the first day's incidents. Boyle promised to allow anyone to speak who wanted to. But the hard hats were still stationed at the mikes, although they were sitting instead of standing. There was no further violence, but whenever it appeared there might be some debate, the chair resorted to unusual parliamentary procedure to get things back on course. One such move occurred when the administration brought up a special resolution to elect members of the international executive board. The constitution provided that the board should be elected, but Lewis for years had been appointing its members. The passage of the Landrum-Griffin Act had made this illegal, so the Boyle administration hit upon the idea of putting their hand-picked board members through at the convention with a single resolution to give the appearance of an election.

When the resolution had been read, Dallas Heltsley, a rebel from the union's District 23 in west Kentucky, rose to speak. John Owens, the seventy-two-year-old secretary-treasurer was acting chairman. He quickly gaveled the motion through before Heltsley, or anyone else, could say anything. Then Owens recognized Heltsley, who wanted to complain about the performance of Neil Beam, his district's international board member. "You were a little hasty, sir," he said. "I didn't have time to get to the mike before you got through reading [the resolution]. I would like something to say on this. Could I have the mike, please?"

"For what purpose do you rise?" demanded Owens.

"I rise to report on this executive board here, but you closed this thing out before I could get from my seat to the mike to say anything. I am Delegate Heltsley from local 1092, District 23. I wanted to speak here to the delegates to tell them that we have unrest in 23 and under the man whose name you have read there, Mr. Neil Beam. . . ."

"Just a minute, Delegate. That subject matter is not before the convention. If there is any matter in District 23's internal affairs that needs airing, I think you ought to present that to the proper authorities of the organization so they can make an investigation and ascertain the facts and correct them. You can't do that in this convention. You are out of order, sir. Please be seated."

Steve Kochis, the insurgent presidential candidate, also tried to address the convention while Owens was in the chair.

"For what purpose do you arise?" the secretary-treasurer demanded.

"I rise for a special privilege now, Mr. Chairman."

"Are there any objections on the part of the delegates?"

There were none and Kochis began to speak. "Mr. Chairman and International Officers, members of the United Mine Workers of America, ladies and gentlemen. I want to thank everyone here for giving me the right to speak. My name is Steve Kochis, Jr., from Bobtown, Pennsylvania, Local Union 6159.

"Mr. Chairman, I respectfully request special dispensation from the floor for the express purpose of summarizing the activities of the forty-fifth consecutive constitutional convention. There is no question in my mind or in the minds of all the delegates, regardless of geographical location—north, south, east, or west—that a premeditated and predetermined plan was put into effect to try to squelch the free voice of this convention. . . ."

"The Delegate will take his seat. He is out of order," interrupted Owens, who then launched into a fifteen-minute defense of the convention—despite the rule specifying that speeches last no more than five minutes.

The only issue on which there was any semblance of full debate was the question of district "autonomy." With the officers under pressure from the Labor Department to allow the election of district officials, Boyle apparently wanted it to appear that the established system had the full support of the membership. A Boyle loyalist, George Titler, brought to the floor the long committee report on the more than forty resolutions submitted favoring district autonomy. When the meeting was opened for comments from the floor, more than thirty miners spoke, all but a few opposing autonomy. More than half, however, were from the ranks of the $60-a-day committee members and convention functionaries. Those who opposed the committee report got the usual treatment. One delegate rose to say, "My local union, in the best interests of all members of the United Mine Workers of America, wishes this convention to have this resolution withdrawn." Replied Chairman Owens: "It is not a subject matter before the convention. Let's proceed with the matter before the convention."

When the convention ended September 11, it was a clean sweep for the Boyle administration. The convention voted to lengthen the president's term from four years to five and to raise the number of local union endorsements needed to challenge an international officer from five to fifty. Unfortunately for Boyle, the latter action came too late to rule out Kochis, whose nomination was already official. The autonomy movement was staved off, and all 279 resolutions dealing with the welfare and retirement fund were referred to the trustees of the fund and hence, to oblivion. All resolutions complaining about the manner in which the convention was scheduled, its location, and the fact that it was held during the Labor Day weekend, were "non-concurred" in by the committees that reviewed them and voted them down. In short, the union's hierarchy overwhelmed the dissenters on all issues.

Boyle's efforts to wrest a strong display of personal support from the convention delegates were not inexpensive. Aside from nearly $400,000 spent on music, the international shelled out more than $77,000 on souvenirs, including expensive portable radios that were given each delegate. The salaries and expenses for the convention committee members came to nearly $640,000 and some of these hirelings went home as much as $2,000 richer. Another $24,000 was spent on photographs. The expenses for guests came to more than $16,000. In all, the convention cost more than $1.4 million—approximately $900,000 more than the previous one, held in Cincinnati.

The convention produced only one development in which the dissidents could take hope. The Labor Department had given the union a last chance to grant autonomy to the districts at the convention. When the old system was again ratified, the department, spurred by complaints from miners, filed suit December 16 in U.S. District Court in Washington to force the Boyle administration to allow election of officers in six of the non-autonomous districts. As long as the suit had been in coming—the Landrum-Griffin Act had been in effect for five years—

it was of great importance, for if the absolute control Boyle exercised over the district officials were ever broken, his machine would be vulnerable. The court battle promised to be a protracted one, however, with the union attorneys using every means to keep the case from coming to trial for as long as possible.

If the convention had been a hopeless avenue of reform for the dissident elements in the United Mine Workers, the international election proved to be just as futile. Steve "Cadillac" Kochis was unknown to most miners and he had no money to conduct a serious campaign. Adding to his problems was the fact that no UMW president had failed to achieve re-election in more than forty years. It would take more than a tobacco-chewing rank-and-filer with no administrative experience to convince most miners to turn out an incumbent, even an unpopular one. So, in the December election, Boyle was returned to office by ninety-six thousand to nineteen thousand votes.

4

If Boyle had succeeded in outmuscling the growing number of working miners in his organization who were bitterly dissatisfied with his performance, he was soon to discover that their grievances would not go away, and that they had ways of expressing them that could be troublesome. In late August of 1965, two thousand men walked off their jobs temporarily in a dispute over the firing of a miner at the Freeman Coal Company in Farmersville, Illinois. They set up a picket line at two nearby mines owned by the Old Ben Coal Company and brought out another seven hundred men. The union district officers tried to get them back on the job, but the men refused to go until the miner was rehired. The company would not discuss rehiring him until the mines reopened. The stalemate continued for several days, until the miners began trickling back to work. It was a pattern that would continue to plague the industry.

Early that September, contract disputes at the U. S. Steel Company's vast Robena mining complex near Waynesburg, Pennsylvania, and at the Hannah Coal Company's Ireland Mine near Moundsville in the northern West Virginia panhandle touched off separate wildcat strikes that kept about ten thousand miners off their jobs for several weeks. The controversy at the Ireland Mine was particularly heated. It was caused by the firing of six men who took part in a brief protest walkout stirred by a safety dispute. Five of the six men were officers of the UMW local at the mine, and one was Karl Kafton, a huge, good-looking man who was one of the most articulate leaders of the rebel movement. The angry strikers used roving pickets to close down other mines across the coal fields of Ohio, northern West Virginia, and south-western Pennsylvania. The vast wildcat strike, which shut off about fifteen percent of the nation's coal production for nearly a month, finally ended when Boyle met with about a hundred of the strikers in Washington and pledged "every help" in having the six men reinstated. They never were, however, and the miners in the region never forgot it.

Early the following year, Boyle again found himself under pressure to reopen the contract. Coal output was rising steadily and other unions were making sizable gains in contracts. Although miners were generally considered well paid, they still lacked many of the benefits other workers had had for years. There was still no pay for sick or injured miners although coal continued to have the worst industrial safety record in American industry. Accidents killed 247 miners in 1964, thirty-one more than the year before. Miners' lung diseases were a growing problem. Miners took eight official holidays during a year, but they received no pay for them. There were still no sanitary facilities in the mines, and many mines were still without bathhouses. Those that had them did not even furnish soap. Although production was rising, employment in the mines continued to drop. Only about 116,000 miners were still on the job as the year began, a three percent decrease from the year before. Seniority and job security were still big issues. As Karl Kafton told one reporter, "Boyle is on the spot. If he doesn't reopen the contract, you'll be able to stuff his following into a phone booth."

This time Boyle did not resist the pressure for a new contract. He began negotiations in March with the big eastern coal producers with whom the union usually reached the agreement that set the pattern for the entire industry. Again there were reports that Boyle was playing down wages in favor of "fringe" benefits. A central demand was said to be for "helpers" on large mining machines, which would help to curb the downturn in employment by adding new jobs. But by the first week in April there was no new contract, and reports from the negotiations were that Boyle had now decided to soft-pedal his demand for the helpers and other work-spreading schemes. Then, unexpectedly, Boyle reached agreement with the huge Peabody Coal Company of St. Louis, and two other midwestern producers. The contract called for a $2.25

wage increase over two years and holiday pay for the first time, as well as increased vacation pay. Although most of the gains sought by the most rebellious miners seemed to be missing, the agreement expanded mine-wide seniority to include first claim on jobs at other nearby mines owned by the same company. The contract was treated by the big eastern producers as extravagant. The huge Bituminous Coal Operators Association flatly labeled the pact "too costly." Their seeming recalcitrance was all the miners needed—they had not been on a pre-contract strike in years. A huge wave of unauthorized walkouts immediately gripped the eastern segment of the industry—at its peak, more than fifty thousand workers were off the job. Although UMW headquarters put pressure on the men to return to work, the strike apparently succeeded anyway. Within two weeks the big eastern producers signed a contract similar to the one negotiated earlier. The men went immediately back to work. It was a sharp contrast to the turmoil that followed the signing of the contract in 1964 and it apparently convinced Boyle of his success in mending his fences with the miners.

Things went relatively smoothly for Boyle and his associates for the rest of 1966, and for most of the next two years. The UMW president concentrated on his duties as a leader in the National Coal Policy Conference, a joint union-industry lobbying organization that Lewis had formed a decade earlier to promote the interests of the coal industry. He went frequently to Capitol Hill to lobby against federal appropriations for atomic energy, always an object of official UMW scorn as a threat to coal's economic future. The only mine-safety measure anyone on Capitol Hill could ever remember hearing about from Boyle was a bill to bring mines with fewer than fifteen employees under the jurisdiction of the 1952 safety act from which Congress had exempted them. This amendment had several times passed the Senate, but the arguments of the small mine operators that the UMW and the big coal men were ganging up on them always found enough credence in the House to block it until it finally went through in 1965. After that, Boyle was silent on mine safety.

Adding to the general euphoria that enveloped UMW headquarters in the two years preceding the Farmington disaster was the fact that the Labor Department's suit to force election of district officers was adroitly entangled in red tape by Boyle's lawyers. The government, apparently in no hurry itself, also asked the court for repeated delays and offered little or no resistance when the union sought them. Four years after the original complaint was filed, the case was still nowhere near trial.

As the union officers went about their business, they were little noticed by the press or by most of official Washington. Boyle was joined in his fulminations against federal support of the atomic energy industry by a small coterie of coal-state congressmen and senators who stood ready to do his bidding whenever called upon. But since the UMW was not a member of the AFL-CIO and did not distinguish itself by participation in the social issues of the day, it managed to stay out of the papers. There were a few exceptions. The *Wall Street Journal*, the only paper that had followed the development of the rebel movement in 1964, always carried full reports on the frequent wildcat strikes that occurred thereafter. In 1965, Jerry Landauer, the *Journal's* crack investigative reporter, did a long article on the "sweetheart" contracts that had become a fact of life in the southern mining regions. The existence of these clandestine agreements, while always denied by union officials, was a paradoxical exception to the pattern of economic collusion with the larger coal companies that was soon to be officially confirmed by two federal courts. The "sweetheart" situation and the general strife that prevailed in the Kentucky coal country was also thoroughly covered by the *Louisville Times* and *Courier-Journal*. After Boyle's reelection in 1964, *The New York Times* published a story about him based on a long interview in which Boyle pledged a major effort to organize the non-union mines, which by then accounted for about 25 percent of the nation's coal production. *The Times* also carried a detailed story about the Supreme Court's landmark decision later that same year, which, while overturning the UMW's antitrust conviction in the so-called Pennington case, affirmed the concept of illegal union-management collusion in restraint of trade. In January, 1967, when a Federal Court at Chattanooga, Tennessee, awarded $3 million to two small Tennessee coal companies after finding that they had been put out of business by a UMW collusion with a large coal company, *The Times* ran the story on page one. But the newspaper did not follow up with any more thorough reporting of what had become of the union that had once terrorized management and made the nation jittery with its militance.

In retrospect, it seems hard to believe that the situation at UMW headquarters could have gone virtually unnoticed for so long. The cast of characters alone would seem to have been enough to catch some imaginative reporter's eye. Boyle's efforts to emulate the demigod Lewis had made him quite a colorful figure. His face was generally wreathed with a pugnacious frown that quickly became a scowl when he mounted a speaker's platform or took his seat to testify before a Congressional committee. While he could not match Lewis's brilliant rhetoric, he tried hard, making up for what he lacked in vocabulary and articulation by volume and fury. His public utterances were often incoherent, bombastic, and threatening, and accompanied by a full range of gestures—table-pounding, fist-shaking, and hand-waving. Although short and possessed of only half a head of hair, Boyle, who was sixty-three years old in 1967, flaunted a wardrobe that made him seem younger and more prepossessing. He had suits in a rainbow variety of colors, some with shoes to match, and a wide selection of brightly colored shirts and ties. His rose boutonniere was a trademark. But if his clothes did not reflect his age, his face had begun to show it. Although still freckled, his complexion had a pallid, almost ghastly cast that at times made him appear to be in ill health. His elderly wife, Ethel, also dressed in eye-catching garb that included miniskirts, when they became the vogue, and a dazzling array of jewelry. She had a crop of exceptionally bright, carrot-colored hair, and wore heavy makeup, including crimson lipstick.

Big George Titler was quite a contrast to the trim and natty Boyle. Although not tall, he weighed well over 250 pounds, most of them centered in his stomach, which was so vast that it seemed remarkable he could support himself on his short legs. While Boyle strove for a look of urbanity, Titler seemed to seek the opposite image. His dark brown hair, which showed very little grey for a man in his seventies, was always a bit unruly and his eyes often appeared nearly closed behind his glasses, giving him a sleepy look. His dangling shirttails heightened the country-boy appearance. His jackets were rumpled and seldom buttoned, and his pants were over-long and baggy.

Perhaps the most fascinating character at UMW headquarters was John Owens, the secretary-treasurer of the organization since 1947. When he turned seventy-seven in 1968, he was virtually bald and he apparently decided to do something to project a more youthful image. He purchased a none too realistic, light grey wig which he wore every

day, and he shaved off the moustache he had worn for years. The result-
ant change in his appearance was dramatic enough to make him unrec-
ognizable from his earlier photographs. This seemed not to faze Owens,
who was a remarkably spry fellow for his age. He had lost a leg in a
mine accident and got around on an artificial limb. Those not aware of
his impairment would not have noticed, for his walk showed only a
trace of stiffness that would seem normal to anyone his age. He was a
neat dresser and easily the most loquacious of all the union's officers.
At any time, whether during a convention, a trial or a Congressional
hearing, when Boyle needed a lengthy extemporaneous address to
filibuster him through a tight spot, Owens was called upon, usually under the pretext that he would "clarify" the issue. His perform-
ances were extraordinary. He could launch into interminable disserta-
tions that usually succeeded in so thoroughly confusing everyone that
the entire proceeding was thrown off course. One of his rhetorical masterpieces came at the 1964 convention when Steve Kochis demanded an
explanation of the $8 million loss the union had taken in buying and
selling the West Kentucky Coal Company. Owens began his reply by
reminding the delegates that the union was seventy-five years old and
ticking off a list of its achievements. He then launched an attack on
Republican presidential candidate Barry Goldwater, and indignantly
charged that "our two major political parties have demonstrated how
controlled conventions select the men for whom we vote for the highest
office in the land." Next, he took a swipe at the courts. Then he said the
union had had eleven presidents, and he proceeded to name them.
After that, he dished up some praise for Boyle and then went back to
the 1940's and the federal seizure of the mines and Lewis's being fined
$750,000. Next came a review of the achievements of the welfare and
retirement fund. When this had gone on for several minutes, Owens said
candidly: "But this isn't what I rose to talk to you about." But he talked
on about the fund for another fifteen minutes before he finally got to
his point. He reasoned that the $8 million loss was worthwhile in view of
the money paid in salaries to UMW members and the millions pumped
into the welfare fund in royalties—all of which were made possible
because the UMW had organized the company by the unorthodox procedure of buying it. When his case was completed, Owens kept going
for another twenty minutes, even managing to work Patrick Henry's

name into his discourse, which lasted at least an hour. The delegates gave him a standing ovation.

Owens, a friendly and personable old fellow, was well compensated for this unique service. In addition to the $40,000 a year he received in salaries and the two sons he had on the payroll, he was given quarters in a lavish suite at the Sheraton-Carlton Hotel, just two blocks from union headquarters. Between 1963 and 1968, the bill for it came to more than $68,000.

Although Titler and Owens were both international officers and theoretically exercised some authority, the UMW was a one-man show, and the only persons beside Boyle with any real power were those on whom he relied for advice. His most influential advisor was Suzanne V. Richards, an able, nondescript spinster in her forties who had been at Boyle's side since he first came to Washington. In the early days, she had been his secretary, but he came to hold her judgment in increasingly high esteem and eventually put her though law school and elevated her to the post of "executive assistant." She was paid $40,000 a year and was widely regarded as the "power behind the throne," particularly as Boyle became more and more caught up in controversies which were both unexpected and difficult for him to understand. Another whose power grew apace as the administration became embroiled in growing controversy was Edward L. Carey, the union's general counsel. An able lawyer, Carey had a reputation for aggressiveness acquired while he was an assistant federal prosecutor. His appearance and personality fit the image. He was a big-chested man with curly grey hair and a florid complexion. His mouth had a tendency to curl sullenly, even sneeringly, and the impression of toughness was heightened by his stentorian voice, which made it necessary for anyone talking to him by telephone to hold the receiver away from his head. Although he was less influential than Miss Richards, Carey's power in the organization ultimately reached a point where he was talked about as Boyle's heir apparent.

Although Boyle seldom made trips to the coal fields and was a rather obscure figure in Washington, a great deal of effort and money was spent trying to make him and the other officers appear to the members as ubiquitous and influential champions of labor. The chief instrument of this image-making was the *United Mine Workers Journal,* a tabloid bi-weekly whose format had not changed since the Depression. Its principal editorial content was usually the text of any statement or speech by Boyle, frequently published in full whether it dealt with a subject of interest to coal miners or not. Extensive coverage was also usually given to other members of the union hierarchy when they gave speeches. The publication was put out by Justin McCarthy, once a highly regarded labor reporter for the *Chicago Daily News* who had won a prestigious Nieman Fellowship at Harvard in 1948. McCarthy had gone to work for the UMW during Lewis's day, when the union had been caught up in the major labor issues of the time. His salary had risen to about $20,000, a lot for a newspaperman, and he was not inclined to rock the boat when asked to publish material that his news judgment told him had little interest for his readers. His assistant was Rex Lauck, son of a union functionary of earlier days, who did most of what little live reporting was needed for the publication. Most issues of the *Journal* were a mix of Boyle's speeches, canned features, obituaries, and crude cartoons promoting the theme that things are much better for union members than non-union workers. The back page of the publication was invariably given over to recipes and the inside back cover was devoted to cornball jokes and aphorisms culled from other publications. An example: "Is your wife a club woman?" asked a friend. "No," was the reply. "She's strictly a dish thrower." The inside front cover was always filled by what was called the "official roster" of the organization, which was simply a list of all the international and district officers. There was little mention of such issues as mine safety, except for an article three times a year, based on a Bureau of Mines press release, summarizing the number of deaths in the mines. The summary was printed without comment. The *Journal* never mentioned the dissident movement in the northern coal fields, carried no account of the 1964 convention brawl, and published no letters to the editor or other dissent from the official position of the organization.

When someone prominent in the organization died, the *Journal* went all out on the obituary, putting a black border around the headline and eulogizing the deceased in the most effusive terms. When Mart Brennan, president of District 7 in the anthracite region, died in 1968, for example, the obituary took up a full page and included a list of all the members of an "international commission" appointed by Boyle to attend the funeral. It also printed a list of all the other prominent union officials who turned out for the burial. All names were in bold-face type. Even the telegram sent to the widow by Boyle, Titler, and Owens was reproduced, in capital letters.

While an official like Brennan could get the full treatment by dying, most of the heavy coverage was reserved for Boyle, especially when he made one of his rare forays into the coal fields. The same issue that carried Brennan's obituary was dominated by stories about weekend trips Boyle, Titler, and Owens had made to the union's districts in Alabama and west Kentucky. Titler and Owens got generous coverage, but Boyle's was in a class by itself. His picture was on the cover and appeared in fourteen other places in the issue. Stories about the trips appeared side by side on the first news page of the publication and Boyle's name was in the lead paragraph of each, in bold face type. The next three pages were given over to the field visits—primarily to quotations from Boyle's speeches there. The following page was splashed with a reprint of an interview with Boyle by a small Kentucky newspaper in which he voiced his usual complaints about atomic energy. Just in case the reader had failed to get the flavor of Boyle's activities, two facing pages near the back of the *Journal* were devoted to a picture spread from the trips. Boyle was in the middle of all six pictures on one page and appeared in three of the five on the other. The lead editorial, written by McCarthy, said that Boyle's advice to the membership during his trip (his name once more made paragraph one in bold-face type) was "profound." The editorial then quoted, again in bold type, a slice of one of Boyle's speeches calling on the members to organize the non-union mines. This was a frequent Boyle theme, urging men who worked full time at arduous labor to do the enormously time-consuming and complicated job of organizing other mines for a union that had a $100 million treasury.

Though Boyle might have seemed miserly in seeking volunteer help from his membership to do the union's organizing, he could be magnanimous with the UMW treasury in other ways. Between 1963 and 1968, $25,000 was spent for portraits of the officers which were then mass-produced so that a set could hang in every UMW office and local meeting hall. This expense was enlarged by the fact that a new portrait of John Owens was needed after he completed his remarkable transfiguration by toupee. The union's records also show that more than $93,000 was spent for other photographs, mostly of the officers, during the same period. This figure did not include the cost of photographs taken for the *Journal*.

The organization's records also show that loyal employees were sometimes rewarded beyond their salaries. Willard Owens, son of the secretary-treasurer, for example, received a $10,000 "grant" for an unstated purpose in 1967. The same year, the union's assistant general counsel, Harrison Combs, got a "grant" of $5,000. Other officers received $21,000 in "contingent fund advances" during Boyle's reign and in 1963 alone received $10,000 in unspecified "incidental expenses."

There were other unusual disbursements, including a 1965 loan of $39,862 to John E. Kusik, a leading lieutenant of Cyrus Eaton and a top executive of the Chesapeake and Ohio Railroad. Asked by a reporter about the loan, John Owens refused to disclose a reason for it but said it had been paid back. When Boyle took over, an outstanding $375,000 loan to a coal investment firm, the Freeport Coal Company, was renewed. The loan had been made years earlier to help the company acquire a twenty thousand acre tract of coal land in Preston County, West Virginia, where all UMW organizing drives had failed. It was an apparent attempt to gain influence with whatever mining company subsequently leased the mineral rights to the tract. No company was interested, however, and the loan had not been paid back by 1968 when the union permitted Freeport to lease the property to a non-union operator.

During Boyle's tenure, the UMW also made contributions amounting to $542,000 to the support of the National Coal Policy Conference. The NCPC, in the interests of its combined union-management membership, had begun to extend its lobbying far beyond general promotion of coal in the interests of its combined union-management membership. It had reached into such areas as opposition to antipollution legislation and other measures that might have been of general benefit to coal miners and their families, if not to the economic short-term betterment of the companies.

As the 1968 convention approached, Tony Boyle expected no repetition of what had occurred four years earlier. The coal industry was in its best shape since the 1940's and its surge had made life easier for Boyle. The 1966 contract had not brought the coal miners abreast of many other industrial workers but it had been a great success compared to the one negotiated two years earlier. The welfare fund had been able to raise pensions to $115 per month in 1967, and even the pattern of increasing unemployment at the mines seemed to have been reversed. Indeed, industry officials were now talking about a manpower shortage brought on by rising coal demand and by the exodus of many young people from the mining regions to seek opportunity elsewhere. Although the industry's safety record was not getting better, and was responsible in part for the developing labor shortage, safety hadn't been a major issue in the union for years and the administration didn't expect it to become one at the convention. Nevertheless, Boyle hadn't enough confidence to return the gathering to the heart of the coal fields —it was to be held in Denver. Most of the other familiar precautions were in effect, and a few new twists had been added.

This time, there were only three bands to put on a demonstration for Boyle, and this economy cut the music expenses for the nine-day gathering in half, to only about $200,000. Transportation costs were up, though—$338,000 compared to $140,000 for the Miami convention. Instead of radios, the delegates were given cigarette lighters and electric clocks stamped with Boyle's name and picture, as well as gavels and souvenir pens. The cost of these trinkets was nearly $110,000. The Boyle-appointed committees were not as large as they had been in 1964 and their cost was reduced from nearly $640,000 to less than $400,000. It would have been still less had not the administration insisted on having a thirty-nine-member Committee on Appeals and Grievances, whose salaries and expenses came to $40,800, although there were no appeals nor grievances to be resolved by the convention.

Aside from the music, the souvenirs, and the thirty-minute demonstration on the first day, Boyle was also honored by a number of resolutions supposedly submitted by various local unions. Strangely, officers of some of the locals had never seen them before the convention. The measures, written in prose far too high-flown for most coal miners, called for Boyle's election to a lifetime term (this would have been illegal) and the doubling of his salary to $100,000 a year. Boyle received these tributes warmly, but turned them down with an "aw-shucks" display of modesty.

Among other high points of the convention for Boyle and his fellow officers was a song composed and sung to them by the Saint Ann's Band

of Freeland, Pennsylvania, which had also been present at the 1964
gathering. To the tune of "Hello, Dolly," the song went:

>   Hello, Tony, and hello, Johnny,
>   And hello to big George Titler, too.
>   You're looking great, fellas,
>   We're feeling great fellas,
>   To be led by men the likes of all of you.
>
>   Well, hello, Ethel, and hello, Phyllis,
>   And hello to Bernice in Ohio, too.
>   You're looking great ladies,
>   Really, really great ladies.
>   Your men-folks are lucky to have you.

Although the song had two more verses, it was surpassed for sheer dog-
gerel by another ditty, sung to the delegates by Joe Glazer, a hack
folksinger who usually appeared at UMW conventions billed as "labor's
troubador." Glazer, with help from *Journal* editor Justin McCarthy, put
together "The Ballad of Tony Boyle," which was not only sung at the
convention but reprinted by the thousands for distribution at UMW
headquarters. Sung to the tune of "The Foggy, Foggy Dew," the song
went this way:

>   When Tony was a young man, he went underground;
>   He worked at the miner's trade.
>   And many, many times the bosses passed the word,
>   "He's a dangerous renegade."

So it went for six more verses, finally concluding with this stanza of
general comment about the coal miner:

>   He digs coal in the wintertime,
>   And in the summer, too.
>   And when he gets his pension from the Welfare Fund
>   He says: "God bless the Union and Tony too!"

For all the ballyhoo, the convention did have a few serious moments.
One of these followed the introduction of the report of the union's one-
man safety division. Although discussion did not center on the report
itself, the document was filled with revealing information. Since the

previous convention, the report said, 953 men had been killed in coal mines and nearly forty-three thousand had been injured. Bureau of Mines inspectors had discovered nearly twenty-four thousand violations of the mine-safety law during the four year period. Of more sigificance, however, was the report's summary of violations federal inspectors found of the more stringent Federal Mine Safety Code. The code, which the government had no power to enforce, was part of the UMW's contract with the industry, and the job of seeing that it was observed was assigned to the union district officials. As the report put it: "Each district representative shall know the Federal Mine Safety Code and be made fully responsible for compliance with its various provisions. He will consider code compliance equal in magnitude with his other assignments, and will diligently strive to influence the responsible officials at the mine property to eliminate all code violations, particularly those which have existed during consecutive federal inspections and have been designated as repeat violations." The safety division report showed that there had been 128,300 violations of the code of which 75,469 were repeat violations. Yet even this discouraging report on the industry's attitude toward safety precautions and on the union officials' efforts to improve it appears to have been grossly understated. A Senate Committee later reported that between 1960 and 1968, there were more than 1.3 million violations of the code found by federal inspectors of which only 231,000 were corrected.

The report was put to the convention by Michael Budzanoski, a close ally of Boyle's who had succeeded Joseph Yablonski as President of District 5 in Pennsylvania. Budzanoski was secretary of the committee which reviewed the report. He spoke in glowing terms of the work of the safety division, never mentioning that it consisted of just one man. When he had finished, the usual motion to approve the report was made. Several miners rose to speak.

Ernest Porter of Boonville, Indiana was first to be recognized. He complained that unsafe use of explosives was a familiar practice at the mine where he worked although similar practices had recently caused several fatalities at a Kentucky mine. "Furthermore," he said, "the Bureau of Mines sends a schedule to the company informing them when their inspectors will be there, and a day or so before their arrival, we undergo a clean-up campaign. Even coal dust is wiped off the hand rails. When that inspector comes on the job, you will invariably find an assistant superintendent or the superintendent accompanying him, showing him the things they want [him] to see."

Although Porter's remarks contained no criticism of the Boyle administration, acting Chairman Louis Austin, the aging appointed President of District 23 in west Kentucky, apparently felt that even this mild protest should be smoothed over by some rosy comments from a Boyle loyalist. "The chair understands that Delegate Darcus from District 31 (northern West Virginia) desires to speak on this subject," Austin announced. John Darcus, a paid member of the convention Scale Committee, took the floor for a ten-minute speech praising Boyle's efforts on safety and a host of other issues. "You have heard about President Boyle being a nut on safety," he said at one point. Several other miners with safety complaints got the floor but their comments did not provoke any expressions of interest or concern from the platform. Charles Shawkey, a smart and militant young miner from West Virginia, reported that when the mine operators greeted the state safety inspectors at his mine, "they act like old friends, like they are having a reunion." Darrell Baker, from a Union Carbide mine not far from where Shawkey worked, told the convention that one state mine inspector "came to our mine and when he got out of the car and got his knee pads out of the trunk, he was so drunk that he dropped them. I feel that this is a disgrace. . . ." If Chairman Austin also thought it was disgraceful for mine inspectors to be drunk on the job, he gave no sign of it. Throughout the discussion, every complaint about safety matters was matched by a speech by one of the administration's friends designed to overcome any inference that the safety problems were the fault of the union leadership.

Although this discussion of mine-safety grievances was a failure in influencing the convention or the membership as a whole, there was one presentation that succeeded mightily in doing both. The convention occurred at a time of dawning awareness that miners faced a health problem equally as serious as accidents—"black lung" disease. Ralph Nader, the increasingly influential public safety advocate, had begun to beat the drums for action to combat the disease months earlier and had included strong criticism of the union in his public statements on the subject. Part of the Boyle administration's response was to trot out Dr. Lorin E. Kerr, an assistant to the Medical Director of the Welfare and Retirement Fund, to make a speech about black lung to the delegates. Instead of the usual convention combination of platitudes and self-congratulation, the delegates got an extraordinarily incisive and vivid exposition. Kerr, a gentle and nervous little man, was an authority on miners' lung diseases.

"Coal mine accidents take their daily toll but equally important are the hidden losses due to dust disease," Kerr said. "At work you are covered with dust. It's in your hair, your clothes and your skin. The rims of your eyes are coated with it. It gets between your teeth and you swallow it. You suck so much of it into your lungs that until you die you never stop spitting up coal dust. Some of you cough so hard that you wonder if you have a lung left. Slowly you notice you are getting short of breath when you walk up a hill. On the job, you stop more often to catch your breath. Finally, just walking across the room at home is an effort because it makes you so short of breath. This is what I am here to talk about. Call it miners' asthma, silicosis, coal workers' pneumoconiosis—they are all dust diseases with the same symptoms."

Kerr went on to explain in simple language the difference between the traditionally recognized miners' lung disease—miners' asthma or silicosis, caused by inhalation of silica particles in rock dust—and black lung or pneumoconiosis, caused by inhaling coal dust itself. "This clarification is important," he said, "because today many people still think that silica is the only dangerous dust and silicosis is the only disabling dust disease. They also maintain that coal dust containing little or no silica is harmless. Thus, according to them, there is no need to prevent coal dust or provide workmen's compensation for coal workers' pneumoconiosis.

"Contrary to these statements, beliefs, and attitudes, coal workers' pneumoconiosis is the most important occupational dust disease occurring in the United States today." Kerr then traced the history of medical knowledge of the disease. "By 1813," he said, "physicians were reporting the occurrence of black lungs in autopsied coal miners and twenty years later British doctors were claiming this was a disease associated with coal mining. From then until the end of the nineteenth century coal dust was generally acknowledged in Europe to be the cause of the black lungs and the shortness of breath occurring among coal miners.

"Unfortunately, in the early years of the twentieth century, efforts to suppress coal dust subsided. It was claimed that improved ventilation in the coal mines had practically eliminated the dangerous development of black lungs. There was also opposition to the idea that coal dust was a hazard. In fact, some medical leaders claimed that it was not only harmless but possibly beneficial. This medical denial of the existence or danger of coal dust has continued to be the position throughout the years of some company-oriented physicians motivated by enlightened self-interest and a desire to save money for industry."

However, Kerr noted, since 1942 black lung disease has been recognized as a compensable occupational disease in Britain, where it has since been the object of intensive research, resulting in dramatic strides toward elimination of the disease. But no such progress was being made in the United States. "The United Mine Workers Welfare and Retirement Fund found from its own records that in 1965 the death rate for coal miners from chronic lung diseases was four times greater than for all American males in the same age-group. . . . In addition, fund records indicate that the percentage of coal miners dying from pneumoconiosis, emphysema and other non-acute lung diseases has more than doubled during the last twenty years. . . . These and other American statistics are a grisly repetition of those reported by British investigators for the last twenty-five years. . . . It is safe to conclude from all available information that in the United States at least 125,000 miners have coal workers' pneumoconiosis. These are frightening figures. To those who question them I would say that in the last twenty years, at least one million miners have been exposed to a daily dose of coal dust.

"I can vividly remember, twenty years ago when I came with the fund, the constant stream of wheezing, breathless coal miners coming to the area office in Morgantown seeking relief from their struggle to breathe. I can also remember how overwhelmed I felt. Never in my earlier professional experience had I observed or heard of a single industry with so many men who seemed to be disabled by their jobs. I say 'seemed to be disabled by their jobs' because doctors said these men rarely had silicosis and it was unusual to find a physician who suspected that coal dust might be dangerous. The disability was called miners' asthma and it was accepted by miners and doctors as part of the job.

"We in the fund also became acutely aware of the unusual medical care these breathless miners required. They had more colds and other respiratory infections than other miners and these infections lasted longer. Some of these men would get so bad with a cold they had to be hospitalized, where they frequently would stay for two and three weeks, several times every year. Oxygen in the hospital or at home seemed to bring more relief than anything else. If all the tanks of oxygen these men have used were laid end to end, I would venture that a long green line would run at least six thousand miles—twice across the nation coast to coast.

"In searching for the cause of this shortness of breath we could not agree with those doctors who claimed it was due to 'compensationitis' or nervousness. I can assure you that were I as breathless as some of the miners I have seen I would be nervous too. But to claim it was due to nervousness and had nothing to do with dust was nonsense. I know of one doctor who even maintained that breathlessness was due simply to fear of coal mining.

"The failure to take earlier action," Kerr concluded, "constitutes what may be labeled in the future as the greatest disgrace in the history of American medicine."

After his discussion of the disease, Kerr outlined a program for combating it that included a major effort to suppress the dust underground, recognition of the disease as compensable, and limitation of miners' periods of exposure to dust. He pointed out that research on the disease in the United States had, even in its retarded state, been allowed to come to a virtual halt. In the main research project, which was being done by the U. S. Public Health Service at Morgantown, West Virginia, only thirty-five miners had been examined in an eighteen-month period. The program was supposed to involve examination of four hundred miners.

When Kerr was finished, a resolution calling for a massive lobbying effort in every coal state to have black lung included under workmen's compensation was introduced. It called for drafting of a model law and for full cooperation from each district office in trying to have the laws enacted. Like all other convention resolutions, the black lung measure sailed through, but unlike the others it was taken most seriously by hundreds of delegates who had grown increasingly concerned about mine dust and lung disease. Many of these men were officers in their local unions who were in a position to influence others to take up the cry for black lung compensation legislation.

Aside from Dr. Kerr's speech and the resolution that followed it, the convention was a routine affair, with none of the outbursts that had occurred at the Miami gathering. The delegates voted to endorse the presidential candidacy of Vice-President Hubert Humphrey, the first such endorsement given by the union since John L. Lewis put the UMW behind Wendell Willkie in 1940. Humphrey, who had shown several weeks earlier in Chicago that he was quite at home in a tightly managed convention, appeared in person to accept the UMW support. He and Boyle stood on the platform first with their arms around each other, then with their hands joined in the air, to acknowledge the cheers of the standing delegates. It was a rousing reception, but not as rousing, of course, as the one accorded Boyle when the convention opened. As it died down, Humphrey said, "Mr. President—Tony—the one and only Tony Boyle—it is good to be with you. . . . I am mighty glad to rub shoulders with this fellow Tony Boyle. He has been giving me advice and counsel for a long time. . . ."

How much advice and counsel Tony Boyle ever gave Hubert Humphrey is certainly open to question, but the UMW did give Humphrey something he needed much more than Boyle's advice—money for his campaign. The Democrats' campaign finance reports later revealed that a 1968 "Salute to Humphrey Dinner Committee" received a total of $30,000 from Robert Howe, director of Labor's Non-Partisan League, the UMW political arm, and from James Kmetz, the league's assistant director. The donations were made in the name of Howe and Kmetz and members of their families. It was unclear whether the money came from the union treasury, which would make the contributions illegal, or whether it came from a political fund raised by voluntary membership donations. The latter is a legitimate device for union campaign contributions.

Before the convention ended, Boyle admonished the delegates against giving their local unions any impression that the convention was rigged. "When you go back home with your little recording machines, play the full record. Don't just play the excerpts that you want to play to your local union. I would like for those to rise who will say, when they go home, that Tony Boyle gagged them and they didn't have an opportunity to express themselves at this convention. Were you gagged? Stand up. Let me take a look at you. Tell me now. Don't tell your local union. Where are you? I don't see any of you.

"I hope the security arrangements made by the sergeants-at-arms haven't inconvenienced you too much. You were required to have the proper credentials to attend these meetings. We had to do that, not because you wouldn't throw the hippies out if they came in, but for other reasons.

"Did you know that some hippies tried to come in during our deliberations? I suppose they wanted me to endorse long hair, or something, or no soap. When I was very young I hated soap—if my mother had caught me like that. . . ."

So, the 1968 convention ended with Boyle and his mates as secure as ever. The appointed convention committees had "non-concurred" in all resolutions not favored by the officers and the committee reports were voted through without exception. The distribution of convention credentials might have seemed more flagrantly unconstitutional than usual to some of the delegates (for example, two West Virginia locals were represented by Paul K. Reed, a retired union functionary who lived in Venice, Florida, and was virtually unknown to the membership) but this year, no one even bothered to object when the credentials committee report was brought up. Two changes in the union constitution were pushed through, one giving Boyle the power to fill vacancies occurring in all international offices except the International Executive Board. The other constitutional change gave the International Board—a majority of whose members were elected by resolution at the convention and thus, in effect, chosen by Boyle—the power to postpone the next convention. There was the usual debate on the question of autonomy, but, as was always the case, the administration's friends dominated the discussion and passed a committee report opposing any change. Boyle closed the convention with a lengthy speech, for which he received a standing ovation while the band played "Montana."

The convention had come in the midst of negotiations with the major coal producers for a new contract, and Boyle returned to the bargaining table immediately after leaving Denver. The talks found the operators in a relatively generous mood. Profits were up and coal demand was rising sharply. The industry's main problem seemed to be getting enough men to fill the rapidly developing job openings and curtailing the wildcat strikes that had plagued it throughout Boyle's administration. However, the contract deadline arrived before an agreement had been reached and, for the first time in seventeen years, there was an authorized strike by the United Mine Workers. It lasted less than a week, however, before Boyle and George Judy, president of the Bituminous Coal Operators Association, came to terms. The three-year con-

tract gave the miners an immediate $3 raise to $30.25 a day and provided two subsequent $2 raises to $34.25 a day by late 1970. Although
the big raise was the key provision in the contract—and the one most
likely to keep a young man in the coal fields from leaving to work elsewhere—there were several other important provisions. One was a
highly unusual $120 Christmas bonus for miners who had not taken part
in any wildcat strikes during the previous year. The seniority clause
was expanded to make length of service the basis for shift preference.
Vacations were lengthened for miners with more than ten years of service. And, Boyle announced proudly, the operators would now have to
furnish the soap at mine bathhouses. The big raise got the new contract
considerable publicity, but news stories generally neglected to point out
those benefits that were missing. There was still no pay for men idled
by sickness or injury, regardless of their length of service. The need for
a program to combat black lung was glossed over. In announcing the
agreement, Boyle said that this had been discussed but that it was decided to do nothing because legislation dealing with the problem was
before Congress—an explanation that seemed weak to many of those
concerned about the disease. Perhaps most important, in view of the
deluge of resolutions at the convention dealing with the welfare fund,
the royalty, which had been forty cents for sixteen years, was not
raised.

The *Journal* gave Boyle the full treatment in the issue reporting the
new contract. The cover had a picture of him shaking hands with Judy.
The back cover was filled by a picture spread, showing Boyle in six
different poses, titled "President Boyle at Work and At Ease." The
headline on the main story about the contract read, "The 'Boyle' Wage
Contract." Down one side of the page was the contract story, which
began as follows: " 'The President Boyle National Bituminous Coal
Wage Agreement of 1968'—as it was dubbed by International Secretary-
Treasurer John Owens—was signed in the International Executive
Board Room of the UMWA in Washington, D.C. on the afternoon of
October 14.

"It is the best contract in the history of the UMWA, according to
UMWA President W. A. Boyle's Associate Officers, Owens and Vice-
President George J. Titler. . . ."

As well as getting Boyle's name into the headline and the first two
paragraphs and managing to work in Owens and Titler, the *Journal's*

editor, Justin McCarthy, also found room for five more pictures of Boyle in the twenty-four-page issue, in addition to those on the front and back covers. On the opposite side of the page from the story on the "Boyle" contract was the text of a press release about Boyle's announcement of the agreement, immediately followed by the text of Boyle's statement about the contract.

Although it might seem that this kind of puffery would simply bore the membership into ignoring the publication, it is worth remembering that the *Journal* was virtually the only communication between the top union officers and the miners. While it was read thoroughly by only a few, most UMW members at least thumbed through, scanning the headlines, lead paragraphs and pictures. Many had been reading it for years and its format had not changed; it was still a 1930s-style newsprint tabloid. To the men who remembered it when it was the trumpet of John L. Lewis, it still had credibility, particularly since so little was written about Boyle and the UMW in other publications. Thus, until events began to change their minds, many miners thought of Tony Boyle as he was depicted in the *Journal*—a rip-roaring, two-fisted labor leader carrying on in the grand tradition of John L. himself. And it seems likely that any man who could allow this sort of hero-worship to be published about him must have come to believe it himself. A storm of controversy was brewing for Tony Boyle, but no one could have been less prepared. In his world, the issues facing the UMW were wage gains and the fight to retard atomic energy's progress. When questions were raised about job safety and health, about the unusual ways the miners' money had been spent, and about the curious management of the pension fund, Boyle would have no answers.

The explosion that dark and frozen morning in the West Virginia hills brought reactions of resignation and fatalistic acceptance from most officials—but not from all. Among the exceptions was a slim, white-haired, somewhat disheveled former college professor named Ken Hechler, who had represented the southwestern district of West Virginia in Congress for ten years. Hechler had introduced the belated Johnson administration mine-safety bill in the House two months before the disaster, and the relatives and friends of the trapped miners apparently remembered. Although his district did not include the Farmington area, pleas for help poured into his office for days after the explosion. Never in his decade in Congress had anything so affected Hechler. Normally a calm intellectual whose eager-beaver political style seemed awkward and forced, Hechler found himself outraged by the disaster. He was further infuriated by the admonition of one Bureau of Mines official whom he telephoned for a progress report on the rescue effort. "Now let's not go blaming anyone for this, Ken," the official cautioned. Several days later, when it was apparent that the seventy-eight men were lost, Hechler went into his office and sat down at his desk—known on Capitol Hill for the chaotic, foot-high stack of paper that covered its entire surface—and went to work at the old brown Royal typewriter with the green keys and pounded out a three-paragraph statement that signaled a dramatic change in his previously secure but prosaic political career.

"Coal miners don't have to die," Hechler wrote. "In a civilized society, it is nothing short of criminal to allow the present conditions to continue in the coal mines. Federal and state mine-safety laws are weak, most coal companies seem to know when the inspectors will appear, enforcement of safety standards is weak and entangled in red tape, the union leaders seem more interested in high wages than in health and safety, there is no aggressive attack on the health hazards of coal dust which cause black lung, the coal miners and their families have been steeled to take a fatalistic attitude toward death and injury and both Congress and the general public have been complacent and apathetic.

"From Monongah to Mannington, the same script is grimly familiar. The national searchlight is focused on a disaster. The company officials promise that everything possible is being done. The families wait stoically. The union leaders say that everything possible is being done. The surviving coal miners and their sons say that, of course, they will go back into the mines. Soon everybody goes back to the status quo until the next disaster strikes in the coal mines.

"Coal miners have a right to live, to breathe, and to be protected by twentieth-century safety standards. The nation must rise up and demand that strong and effective mine-safety legislation be passed by Congress."

Hechler's strong words, which were widely publicized, came as an unpleasant surprise to the many coal executives who lived in Huntington, West Virginia, and who had regarded him as a loyal ally. And, although his comments about the UMW officials questioned only their judgment, not their motives, the union hierarchy regarded Hechler's action as an unpardonable double-cross. But to Hechler's close associates, his aggressive plunge was no surprise, for they had long known this rather homely man, who looked older than his fifty-four years, as the most unorthodox of politicians.

A native of Long Island, Hechler had earned a Ph.D. in American history from Columbia and had taught there and at Princeton. Although his parents had been civic-minded Republicans, Hechler had a background in liberal Democratic politics that went back as far as his 1935 master's thesis entitled, "Will Roosevelt be Re-Elected?" Although the thesis was 350 pages long, it is best remembered for its final chapter, which contained only one word: "yes." Hechler was later research director at the White House during the Truman Administration and held the same job during the Stevenson-Kefauver campaign in 1956. In 1957, he joined the faculty of Marshall University, a small state-supported school in Huntington, West Virginia, where he taught political science.

Hechler's courses were conducted informally and with a showman's flair that made him enormously popular with his students. One of his favorite gimmicks was to telephone a major public official and interview him during a class with the conversation broadcast to his students by loudspeaker. His political connections enabled him to bring such prominent figures as Adlai Stevenson, the Speaker of the House, Sam Rayburn, and Jim Farley, Roosevelt's Postmaster-General and top political adviser, into his classes. Hechler never used his baptismal name, Kenneth, but insisted always on being called Ken, even by his students. In his lectures, he constantly stressed the theme that public participation in politics was the key to responsive government. "You are in politics whether you like it or not," he would often say. "If you sit it out on the sidelines, you are throwing your influence on the side of corruption, mismanagement and the forces of evil."

When asked why he left the more sophisticated worlds of Washington and the Ivy League for West Virginia, Hechler usually said he came seeking a taste of the small-town life. But there was always the suspicion that he had something else up his sleeve, and he did.

During the war Hechler had enlisted and reached the rank of major as a combat historian assigned to the European theater. His experiences provided the material for a narrative account of the famed American crossing of the Lundendorf Bridge over the Rhine at Remagen, Germany, in March of 1945. The book, entitled *The Bridge at Remagen,* was published in 1957 and was an instant success, providing Hechler with a lump sum of cash from royalties and the sale of movie rights. In addition, the professor's face and deep, pleasant voice were becoming familiar in the Huntington area through political commentaries he had been broadcasting for a local television station. The money and the recognition were all Hechler needed to convince him to make the race for Congress from Huntington, although many of his friends and the local political figures told him the idea was crazy. In late March, 1958, four months before the primary and seven months from the election, the war historian and professor crossed the bridge into public life.

His campaign was a shoestring, grass roots affair that relied mainly on his own energy and the volunteer help provided by a small legion of students who were attracted by his political philosophy. His knack for gimmickry and showmanship came in handy, too. Rising at dawn each day, he toured virtually every corner of the vast, ten-county area his district encompassed. Using an eye-catching red and white convertible with his name and his candidacy emblazoned on the side, he was on the road until nearly midnight each night. He passed out free copies of *The Bridge at Remagen,* and used his limited campaign kitty to buy newspaper advertisements reproducing letters written to him by President Truman and his former colleagues in the White House. Although anxious to build up his own credentials, Hechler refused to criticize his opponents, instead calling them "good, fine Democrats." For all his energetic campaigning, Hechler was still the underdog. Politics are played by the old rules in West Virginia, and a bachelor college professor from New York who had only been around a year and who was opposed by the party organization could hardly be considered a likely winner. But Hechler played the underdog role to the hilt, referring to his campaign as "the lonely battle," and this pitch, along with his tireless electioneering, paid off. As Robert Burford, the local Democratic county chairman, later put it, "Like everyone else, I hadn't given Ken a chance for the nomination. Then one day in Charleston I dropped in to chat with one of our candidates for state office. 'Who in hell is this *Hechler?*' he asked me. He went on to say that Ken had been dropping into creeks and hollows of his home county that no candidate for anything had bothered to visit in years. For the first time it dawned on me that he might win." Hechler won, all right, carrying seven of ten counties in the District.

But the general election was a more formidable obstacle. For one thing, it was a traditionally Republican district and Hechler's opponent was a popular two-term GOP Congressman named Will Neal who was also a well-known obstetrician in the area. "I delivered the voters," Neal would tell his supporters, "It is up to you to deliver the votes." Again, Hechler avoided personal attacks, calling Neal "an honest man of conviction. I respect him for his principles even if I may not always agree with what he stands for." He hit hard on the theme that the nation was in a "Republican recession" and passed out cheap campaign cards on which was written, "The recession makes it tough to print a better card." As his campaign treasury ran low, he could not match Neal's five-minute television broadcasts, so he put on ten-second spots that said, "We can't afford more television time, but I hope you'll vote for me anyhow."

As election day drew near, the Republicans knew Hechler was making a strong race and they tried for a last-minute sensation to give Neal an edge. Four days before the campaign ended, the Republican governor, Cecil Underwood, called a press conference to announce indignantly that Hechler had had copies of his book and campaign flyers stuffed into surplus food packages distributed by the state to the poor. "This is the most despicable display of political chicanery I've ever seen," Underwood said. The charge created an uproar, but Hechler responded calmly. He said he was not responsible for the package-stuffing but refused to attack Underwood. Instead, he had high praise for the governor and produced an autographed picture Underwood had given him before the race. The inscription read, "To Dr. Hechler, with appreciation for the intellectual leadership you are giving to West Virginia." Hechler's low-key reply to the last-ditch charge apparently worked. It was close on election day, but as late returns came in after midnight, Hechler moved into a slim lead which he held to win by about 3,500 votes.

Later, Hechler's rules for campaigners were published in the Congressional Record at the request of Senator Hubert Humphrey. The code, which was also praised in a floor speech by Senator John F. Kennedy, is as follows:

(1)   Pay attention to the average person.
(2)   Be true to your own personality.
(3)   Be constructive and campaign cleanly.
(4)   Turn every attack on you into an asset. Couple an immediate answer with your own constructive approach to the problem.
(5)   Remember—your most effective workers are under twenty (they're enthusistic) and over sixty (their word is respected).
(6)   Avoid "strategy meetings" that cause dissension, waste time.
(7)   Venture forth around the district every day. Don't be "desk-bound."
(8)   Don't tie your hands with job promises.

(9)   Don't promise the moon to pressure groups.
(10) Be able to laugh at yourself and enjoy it.

In his ensuing campaigns, Hechler stuck to his credo. The red convertible of his first campaign gave way to a jeep, also red, with his name on the side, and his constituents got used to seeing him riding around whenever he was home, usually wearing an old army parka that became a trademark. What he lacked in back-slapping politician's charm, he made up in energy and aggressive friendliness. His popularity increased steadily. Two weeks before the Farmington disaster, he had been re-elected by forty-thousand votes.

But somehow, the enormous promise that this resourceful professor-politician showed in his campaigns never seemed to carry over into significant action on any major issues in Washington. He was a ranking member of the House Science and Astronautics Committee, which was responsible for the space program, and was chairman of its subcommittee on Advanced Research and Technology. These assignments, though important, did not put Hechler into the midst of the kind of controversial national issues that enable a politician to make a name for himself. In addition, he belonged to a joint House-Senate Committee on Congressional reforms, but since the men with most of the power in Congress opposed reforms, the committee rarely met. Outside of his committee work, Hechler hardly distinguished himself. He inveighed against junk mail. He spoke up for the coal industry. He was chummy with the UMW hierarchy, particularly with George Titler, who came from West Virginia and had campaigned with him. He also got into an unfortunate squabble with John Slack, a fellow Democratic Congressman from a neighboring district, over the location of a new West Virginia airport. Although Hechler was unquestionably right on the airport issue and spent large sums of his own money to promote the cause, his efforts failed and left him with some bitter political enemies. In sum, while Hechler's liberal voting record was certified, his overall performance was not impressive and he remained an obscure figure in Washington. This nondescript image might have been partially the result of the extraordinary informality which prevailed in his office. He never made appointments, usually telling those who wanted to see him to call him shortly before they were coming. He went around in rumpled, ill-fitting suits with spotted neckties, and battered, scuffed shoes. The impression of disorder created by the promiscuous mountain of paper on his desk was heightened by the other piles of papers and the cardboard boxes, filled with miscellaneous documents, that were strewn about his office.

Although Hechler's sudden militance on mine safety was most infuriating to coal industry officials and the UMW hierarchy, he was not alone in refusing to take a "just-one-of-those-things" attitude toward the Farmington tragedy. Senator Gaylord Nelson, the Wisconsin Democrat, issued a statement calling the explosion "foreseeable and preventable." He accused the Bureau of Mines of "whitewashing" the safety deficiencies found in Number 9. Even some Bureau of Mines officials admitted to reporters that the closure of an unsafe mine was a rare occurrence. "It isn't intentional," one bureau official said, "but we may have slid into complacency like any bureaucracy."

Some of the most candid comments came from Stewart Udall, the lame-duck Secretary of the Interior who had presided over Federal mine-safety enforcement for eight years. In what one reporter called a "Soviet-style mood of confession," Udall declared at a mine-safety conference convened in Washington several weeks after the disaster, "We have accepted, even condoned, an attitude of fatalism that belongs to an age darker than the deepest recesses of any coal mine. At every level of responsibility, from the individual miner to the highest councils of government, we have looked with horror on the specters of death and disease that haunt our mines. Then we have shrugged our shoulders and said to ourselves, 'Well, coal mining is an inherently hazardous business' or 'It's too bad, of course, but as long as coal is mined, men will inevitably die underground.' These easy rationalizations are no longer acceptable in this time in history." Udall laid the blame evenly on the government, the industry and the UMW. He said the union "must bear a heavy responsibility for this."

Tony Boyle was also present at the crowded, lengthy conference in the Interior Department's cavernous auditorium. He had a full retinue of fellow officers and attendants to hear his speech, which was by far the longest and loudest of the day. Boyle devoted most of his talk to a defense of the UMW's role in seeking mine health and safety legislation. He reviewed the entire history of coal mine safety laws, crediting the UMW with the passage of all of them. He repeatedly singled out the 1966 measure bringing the small mines under the jurisdiction of the

1952 law as an important achievement. Again Boyle had praise for Consolidation Coal: "I said before and I say again that this coal company that had this recent explosion—unfortunately so—was the only coal company in 1966 that aided and assisted the United Mine Workers of America in our effort to get safety legislation passed." Boyle, of course, did not mention that Consolidation had few, if any, mines that were affected by the 1966 amendment since most of its operations were large. Nor did he mention the fact that the company stood to gain from whatever adverse economic impact the amendment had on the small mines and that the UMW, likewise, was glad to see the pressure applied to the small operators, most of whom were non-union.

When the UMW *Journal* came out three days later, most of its coverage of the mine-safety conference was devoted to Boyle's statement and to that of John Corcoran, President of Consolidation. The issue carried excerpts from Secretary Udall's remarks, but his comment about the UMW deserving part of the blame for coal's poor safety record did not appear. Despite the recent disaster and the sharp criticism the industry was getting for its profit-conscious ways, the *Journal* devoted three full pages to long, optimistic reports about coal's economic position by two top coal executives.

For Stewart Udall, the mine-safety conference was an opportunity to speak frankly about a situation that had troubled him throughout much of his administration, but one that he had not succeeded in doing much about. Although he never mentioned it publicly (one writer charged that he had shown more concern for California Redwoods than for coal miners), Udall had sought repeatedly to overhaul the Bureau of Mines from the time he took office in the Kennedy Administration. His first step had been an effort to remove the head of the bureau, Marling J. Ankeny, and its safety director, James Westfield, both of whom he felt were unsuited to the kind of program he had in mind. Udall expected that the coal industry would be opposed to these changes, but in an administration that owed a major political debt to labor and to the coal miners of West Virginia for their support in the state's crucial Presidential primary, Udall doubted the industry opposition would be a problem. Four years later, however, as Lyndon Johnson took office for his first full term, the same men were still on the job. Udall's reform program had run afoul of a powerful lobby, quite unlike any he had ever dealt with before. The lobby was the National Coal Policy Conference, brain child of John L. Lewis, which combined the political muscle of the UMW, the major coal producers, the big utility companies that use coal, and the coal-carrying railroads to lobby the Federal Government jointly for the economic betterment of coal. The desire of a Cabinet Secretary for health and safety reforms was no match for this industry-union combine, and the NCPC went over Udall's head repeatedly in both the Kennedy and Johnson administrations to see that the men it wanted in power in the Bureau of Mines stayed there.

After Farmington, the strange solidarity of the Mine Workers' leadership with the major coal producers became evident in other ways. As the cry went up for new mine health and safety legislation, Hechler, Udall, and others, including Ralph Nader, advocated a single bill containing provisions dealing with both health and safety. Prodded by Hechler and Nader, the Johnson Administration had come up with a bill not long before Farmington, but it had died without hearings. Now the UMW hierarchy, embarrassed by Farmington and the criticism it brought, was clamoring for legislation. Even the industry's top spokesmen, such as the articulate Corcoran of Consolidation, seemed prepared to accept new regulation without a fight. But both the industry and the union chieftains wanted two bills, one for health and another for safety. Accordingly, the UMW introduced two bills through friendly Congressmen. The union hierarchy explained that an effort to put over health regulations in a safety bill might result in defeat of the whole effort. Hechler argued that the political situation created by the disaster made passage of at least one bill inevitable, so it was better to write as much as possible into it. No one who had been around Washington for any length of time doubted that Hechler was right. But the UMW leadership seemed unconvinced that even one strong bill could be passed. "Just between you and me, I think our safety bill will have to be compromised," a union spokesman told one reporter.

Meanwhile, Hechler introduced a combined health and safety measure that went far beyond anything the UMW or the outgoing Johnson Administration had proposed. Drafted by the Congressman himself at his untidy desk, the bill contained stiff penalties for violations both by the mine operators and the miners themselves. The idea of imposing penalties on the miners provoked a quick negative reaction from Boyle and his associates. Significantly, Corcoran too then came out against penalties for offending miners, although many coal operators had been claiming for years that the miners' own carelessness was the main reason so many of them were killed.

Hechler's bill was stronger than the UMW and Johnson Administration bills in a number of other ways. The Johnson bill provided that "the technical and economic feasibility" of health and safety standards would be considered in drafting them. Hechler's bill said, "The overriding consideration shall be the highest degree of health and safety of the individual worker." The administration legislation provided that if a mine were shut down as unsafe by Federal inspectors, the decision could still be appealed to an existing body called the "Federal Coal Mine Health and Safety Board of Review." While there had been so few mine closings for safety reasons in years past that no one could say for sure what the attitude of this board was, its composition suggested it was industry-oriented. Hechler's bill abolished the board, doubled the penalties for violations contained in the Johnson bill, and had a provision for compensating miners whose mine was shut down for safety reasons not their fault. Its most dramatic proposal, however, was to transfer the administration of mine-safety laws from the Bureau of Mines to the Labor Department. In addition, Hechler got a promise from John McCormack, the gaunt, aged, but still powerful Speaker of the House, to use his influence in seeing that the idea of having two bills was scrapped. McCormack made good.

Hechler introduced his legislation on February 6, a little more than a week after he had made a well-publicized appearance at a miners' rally at the vast Charleston Civic Center. He had read the gathering a letter from Ralph Nader and, with his characteristic showman's flair, produced a twelve-pound hunk of bologna as his answer to the UMW's attitude on health and safety. The miners had roared with laughter. The Nader letter came down hard on the UMW leadership and was enthusiastically received. "The record is overwhelming that Mr. Tony Boyle has neglected his responsibility to protect coal miners," the letter said. It then listed five ways in which Boyle had failed to obtain needed health and safety measures for miners. "The time has come," it concluded, "for you to invite Mr. Boyle to West Virginia and have him exercise his right of replying to these facts. You may conclude that he is no longer worthy of being your leader, that you need new leadership that will fight for your rights and not snuggle up close to the coal operators and forget about the men who are paying the dues and paying the price."

Hechler's activities infuriated Boyle and his associates. His public criticism of them after Farmington, although relatively mild, his appearance at the miners' rally with the scathing Nader letter, and his introduction of by far the strongest mine-safety bill had upstaged and embarrassed them at a time when they were trying frantically to recoup. Hechler was aware that his actions had not pleased the union brass, but even he was astonished at the virulence of their reaction. First came a long letter from George Titler, his erstwhile pal and campaign ally. "You remind me of the new-born bull calf which elects to follow his father rather than his mother and does not realize the mistake until feeding time," Titler wrote. "Stop playing dog in the manger, Ken." The next issue of the UMW *Journal* had a front-page editorial aimed at Hechler and Nader. It began as follows:

"There are some arrogant troublemakers scurrying about—or sending messages to the coal fields these days, trying, for devious motives of their own, to convince the members of the United Mine Workers of America that your union is not doing its job in behalf of health and safety for coal miners.

"The French have a name for such persons. They are called *agents provocateurs*. Agents provocateurs are secret agents hired to incite others to actions that will make them liable to punishment.

"The American labor movement has a shorter and more concise term for such troublemakers. We call them finks. A fink is a spy, a strikebreaker, an informer and a stool pigeon among other things.

"In our book persons who accuse the United Mine Workers and its dedicated International President W. A. Boyle of not doing their jobs in behalf of the health and safety of coal miners are finks.

"Don't listen to them! Don't support them!"

Aside from calling Hechler and Nader "finks" on the cover, the *Journal*'s main editorial was devoted to attacking them for being "instant experts." Hechler was also taken to task for having the longest biographical resumé of any member of the House in the official Congressional Directory. "It takes forty-one lines for him to aggrandize his obscurity," the editorial said, "a sharp contrast to many other members of Congress at least equally well-educated who in addition are outstanding national figures, and who take much less space to tell the voters who they are." In subsequent issues, the *Journal* became more defensive of Boyle and more shrill in its attacks on Hechler.

The Congressman was at first both surprised and disturbed by the harshness of the response. There were about four thousand coal miners in his district. Counting their families, they could be depended upon for as many as twelve thousand solidly Democratic votes in a traditionally Republican district. Although Hechler was serious about making an all-out fight for mine-safety reforms, he did not want to lose the support of the miners' union in the process. His strong stand on the issue was already bringing in outraged letters from the numerous coal executives in his district who had been his friends in the past. If he was making enemies of the industry executives, he would need the backing of the miners more than ever. Yet apart from his concern at the political problems an alienated UMW might create, Hechler began to sense that something was wrong in the organization he had for so long almost automatically considered an ally and a force for progress. After Farmington, he had criticized the UMW's judgment in placing most of its emphasis on wage increases instead of safety improvements. Now he began to suspect that something more than poor judgment might be at fault. When the UMW *Journal's* March 1 issue appeared, Hechler became certain his hunch was right. Opposite the editorial page was a story headed "Ken Hechler's 'Credo' is Revealed," by the *Journal's* assistant editor, Rex Lauck. It dealt with a 1959 article about Hechler published in *Pageant* magazine, which had reprinted his ten aphorisms for Congressional campaigners. Only the *Journal's* version was different.

"In its April, 1959, issue," Lauck wrote, "[*Pageant*] magazine described with Hechler's consent: *How to Get Elected to Congress.*

"The words [below] in bold-face type are Hechler's own ideas, not something somebody else said about him. He advised:

'First you pop off to get attention, regardless of the merit of your ideas.

'Then you pose as the champion of the average man against the "interests."

'Then after you are rebutted, no matter how strong the facts against you, you reply at once as the single, "lonely campaigner" seeking the sympathetic support traditionally given the underdog.

'The truth of your statement or the merit of your argument has nothing to do with your response or your conduct.

'Finally you adopt the imaginary "we" as the shining knight defending the oppressed people against imaginary brutalities of the "interests." '

"That explains much about how this man Hechler operates," Lauck concluded: "Shades of Joe McCarthy!"

Hechler, chortling at this obvious and monstrous distortion of his ten rules, immediately produced two back copies of the Congressional Record as proof of the falsity of the *Journal's* report. One issue of the Record contained Senator John F. Kennedy's speech in praise of the Hechler creed, and the other was the issue in which Senator Hubert Humphrey had inserted the *Pageant* article along with Hechler's ten rules. The Congressman passed out copies of the relevant pages from the Record to the press. Lauck, embarrassed by the snickers of reporters who called to ask about his blunder, claimed he had intended only to paraphrase what he thought the Hechler commandments meant. He said quotation marks had mistakenly been put around his version of the rules because of a misunderstanding with the printer. He even blurted at one point that the error, while unintentional, might have resulted from a "fixation" against Hechler. The *Journal* then ignored Hechler's demand for a correction, although one finally was carried months later. The incident, clearly a triumph for the Congressman, convinced him once and for all that he should fight the Boyle administration, not try to mend his relationship with it. He began to study more carefully the letters that had been pouring in to his office from miners and widows claiming they had been unjustly denied benefits by the Welfare and Retirement Fund. He plunged headlong into an incipient grass roots campaign for black lung compensation in West Virginia, a campaign the union officers were refusing to join. He started digging into the financial reports filed by both the union and the welfare fund at the Labor Department. Everywhere he looked, additional pieces of the puzzle began to fall into place.

While it might seem that Hechler was merely making the obviously sensible political moves, it is worth noting that not a single other coal-state politician chose the course he took. Most of Hechler's colleagues in

Congress rushed to the defense of Boyle and his fellow officers. Leading the pack was Senator Jennings Randolph, a portly, courtly West Virginia Democrat. Randolph served as errandboy for the UMW, introducing whatever legislation it wanted, and since he was the ranking Democratic member of the Senate Labor Subcommittee, which would review the safety legislation, his sponsorship was no small favor. On January 24, after introducing the two UMW bills, Randolph took the Senate floor for a speech defending the two-bill approach and the union hierarchy as well. "Mr. President," he began, "this is to refute those critics of the United Mine Workers of America and of the leadership of that International Union—critics who falsely claim that the men who work in the coal mines lack for adequate union attention to their health and safety needs. They are in error. History will not support such allegations; neither will current events."

After briefly reviewing the legislation he had introduced, the rotund Senator continued in his pleasant, measured tones: "At the time of introduction, I expressed the view that separate bills, rather than separate titles of a single bill, might have been preferable to deal with coal mine safety and occupational health. This view has since been supported informally by representatives of coal industry management and of the United Mine Workers."

Without pausing to reflect on the irony of this union-management agreement on a matter that could be enormously costly to the industry, Randolph went on to warn against passing legislation so tough that it might force some mines to shut down. He ended his speech with these remarks: "Mr. President, officials and representatives of the United Mine Workers—men like President Tony Boyle, Vice-President George Titler, and their assistants—must not be accused of lacking in zeal and effort on behalf of their coal miner members, because this is not a fact. There are no more devoted men to the causes of safety and health—and payrolls—of their members than Tony Boyle and George Titler and their associates and assistants. The proposed coal mine Health Act which I have introduced at their request is but one of the very real manifestations of their fidelity to the men who work in the coal mines."

Over in the House, John Slack, the Charleston Congressman who had quarreled so bitterly with Hechler over the airport issue, was sticking up for Boyle. Earlier, Slack had made an inauspicious entry into the

mine-safety controversy with a pie-in-the-sky proposal that the problem
be tackled not by more stringent regulation but by more research toward making it possible to dig coal from aboveground by remote control. However, when the UMW came to Capitol Hill with its proposals,
Slack was quick to drop his campaign for more research and jump onto
the bandwagon as a co-sponsor of the union legislation. On February
19, he rose on the House floor to make a somber speech in defense of
Boyle. "I am dismayed," he said, "by the trend of recent publicity, by
the callous, heartless, self-promotional antics of the few who have appointed themselves arbiters of mine-safety standards." After urging
quick consideration of the bills that had been introduced, Slack said,
"Meanwhile, let there be a moratorium on silly charges against 'the interests,' and a pause in the finger pointing at UMWA President W. A.
Boyle, Vice-President George Titler, Secretary-Treasurer John Owens,
and their colleagues.

"Let us have law, based on fact, and let us define by law what must
be done. Having passed a good law, we can be confident that Mr.
Boyle, Mr. Titler, Mr. Owens, and the knowledgeable leadership of the
United Mine Workers of America will claim their usual position in the
van of a vigorous drive for safer conditions in coal mining."

When the committee hearings began on the proposed legislation,
Boyle again came in for praise. In the Senate, Lee Metcalf of Montana,
normally a battling liberal, appeared to introduce Boyle. "We in Montana are very proud of Tony Boyle," he said. "We are proud of the fact
he came from Montana, we are proud of his achievements. We like to
read about him in the paper when he is speaking for and in behalf of
the coal miners. . . . We don't have very many coal mines [in Mon-
tana] any more. . . . But Tony is still speaking up for mine safety . . .
a fighter for the workers."

During the House hearings a similar scenario was enacted, with
Montana Congressman Arnold Olsen doing the honors. By his lights,
Boyle was a "good and longtime friend . . . a dedicated representative of the nation's coal miners . . . who has devoted his adult life to
fighting for his brother miners."

Despite the encomiums, Boyle was apparently unsatisfied that his
name had been cleared. The Senate Labor Committee was first to hold
hearings on the mine-safety bills and Boyle was its first witness. He
appeared in high dudgeon, accompanied by an entourage that included

his wife, his brother, Titler, Owens, Lewis Evans (the one-man safety division) and assorted other functionaries and publicists.

As the hearing was about to begin, Justin McCarthy chatted amiably with a group of coal executives seated in the audience. "Can we run you against a Congressman from West Virginia whose name will remain unmentioned?" he asked one of them. "I think I could beat him," said the coal man, as his companions chuckled. "Anybody could," said McCarthy. "The whole organization is lined up against him."

The hearing began, and the testimony was vintage Boyle: loud, threatening, often incoherent, rambling, but above all, long. For two hours, the auditorium of the New Senate Office Building echoed with the sound of Boyle's voice while the bemused Senators sat mostly in silence. Although the testimony included an explanation of the provisions of the union's legislative proposals, it was devoted primarily to a defense of Boyle as a safety advocate and to an attack on his critics.

"I speak, I believe," said Boyle, as he was getting warmed up, "with some authority of what black lung might be, because my father died from black lung long before I ever heard anything about these overnight experts on black lung. I held him in my arms while he died. My mother's two brothers died from black lung. . . . I feel quite keen about these instant experts who now tell this President and who now tell the public, and who now rant and rave around the country, and these dogooders that cry from Congress and where have you, about how sympathetic they are. Where were they when I needed them, Where were they when my predecessors needed them?

"For years it has required guts, and plenty of guts in order to speak up for the maimed, the broken, and the deceased coal miners who have gone to other fields long before the time of those publicity seeking, self-appointed saviors who would mislead and deceive the membership of the United Mine Workers of America. . . .

"I will get a bologna, too," he blurted in reference to Hechler's appearance in Charleston, "and I will stuff it down somebody's throat, if necessary, if they keep on. . . . We didn't get any donations, we didn't get any help, we didn't get any assistance from these bologna experts. I didn't know he was a bologna expert until the other day, didn't know he existed. . . .

"We find in the great state of West Virginia men who have been suffering for twenty and thirty years with black lung, who have been agitated by others, by outsiders, so to speak, to lead a fight against this union, and lead a fight against anyone for their own political expediency.

"And we will correct that. Don't think we won't. We are not forgetting it overnight. And they won't say, like they did yesterday, that the bologna, and I am talking about one of your Congressmen who has never been in a coal mine, who said that, 'The bologna can go for Tony Boyle up there.'"

Through all of this, Hechler sat in the audience by himself smiling sweetly, except during Boyle's obvious references to him, at which time he laughed out loud.

"Sure," Boyle went on, "he had a crowd of listeners. Do you know who they were? People who had contracted black lung disease before I was born. And I am responsible for it? I am responsible for it because they got black lung?

"Where was he when I was trying to get it corrected a few years ago, down in the Truman administration, getting me fined or getting my union fined $4 million.

"I will tell him when I meet up with him. Don't think I won't. . . . I will meet these overnight experts, too, who never saw a coal mine and know everything. I want to say this. You wanted to know who these experts are. These experts who are running around, who are not dry behind the ears yet, who know all the answers to automobiles, they know all the answers to the Food and Drug Administration Bills.

"The other day I listened to him on TV. I took time out to listen to him. Now he accuses the medical profession and the surgeons of this country of electrocuting their patients. He wants something done about it.

"I will tell him, too, when I see him, physically, mentally, in the alley, or anywhere he wants to see me."

At this point, Senator Harrison Williams, the New Jersey Democrat who was chairman of the committee, interrupted. "I conclude the last described individual is Mr. Nader. Am I right?"

"Absolutely," said Boyle. "I guess that's his name. I don't know him. I have never met him. He has never been in a coal mine. He has never come to see me. He has not asked me anything about coal mines. He is not an expert."

Said Williams, "I, too, had concluded he was not knowledgeable about mines. But now you have put us in a position where, in equity, we should bring him on and compare decibels."

Williams' wisecrack was not noticed by Boyle, who was extremely agitated and immediately went after Hechler again. "According to one newspaper article that I read, and I have the article, Congressman Hechler read a letter to the black lung people, that contracted black lung before I was born, not knowing that my father died, my uncle also died, my grandfathers died from black lung, and I have a special interest in black lung; he reads a letter from Mr. Nader that says that the coal miners of this country should replace this President Boyle.

"Let me tell him I have news for him. Out in our Denver convention in September, last September, over two thousand delegates in attendance elected by the rank and file membership to represent them at that convention, and it is more democratic than the Congress of the United States, because every resolution comes to the floor of that convention, they are never killed in committee, they are discussed on the floor of the convention, and that is why I say it is more democratic than the Congress of the United States, we discussed every resolution and every man has a right to protect his resolution.

"And there was a bushel basket full of resolutions out there wanting this president to violate the constitution of his union by having the delegates at that convention elect him for life.

"Maybe Mr. Hechler would like to read that to the black lung people down there. If he wants a copy of the proceedings of our convention, we will give it to him. I rose and said to that delegation:

> I don't want this delegation to elect me here for life.
> I want to face the rank and file in every state and every county and every hamlet in this country from Alaska to Alabama and from New Mexico to the state of Pennsylvania. I will meet them and I will face them.

"Then Mr. Nader thinks I ought to be replaced.

"In addition to that I did something else for your edification, Mr. Chairman. This same group of over two thousand delegates were insistent that this president's salary be doubled over what was paid to my great predecessor and myself. I again rose and objected, and told them that I would not accept it."

While Boyle spoke, Justin McCarthy hovered about the witness table snapping pictures of him. He then sat down on the floor facing Boyle

and leaned against the semicircular wooden dais where the subcommittee members sat and continued to photograph his boss throughout his
testimony. When Boyle was finished and stepped down to join his companions seated across the front row, they rose as one—except for the
huge Titler, who appeared wedged into his seat—to congratulate him
and shake his hand.

Perhaps the most dramatic incident in the opening rounds of the
mine-safety controversy came shortly after the Nixon Administration
took office. Not long before he stepped down, Stewart Udall, Secretary
of the Interior, had finally gotten the kind of man he wanted to head
the Bureau of Mines, an unusually direct, forty-two-year-old career
government man named John F. O'Leary. In the aftermath of the
Farmington disaster, O'Leary, who had been in office only a month,
gathered his top advisers around him and determined the most aggressive safety program the bureau could possibly undertake under current
law. He then officially banned the practice of notifying mine operators
of imminent bureau inspections and initiated a stepped-up program of
spot inspections. In the month after Farmington, six hundred such inspections were made, compared with fewer than 150 during the whole
previous year. During this period, the bureau's authority to shut down a
mine judged to pose "imminent danger" to miners was invoked about
two hundred times, compared with only 129 in the entire year before.
Moreover, O'Leary made no secret of the kind of changes he was trying
to bring about. "I got together with technicians and attorneys," he told
an interviewer, "and we took the law out to its extremes, something that
had never been done before." O'Leary also said he thought the Bureau
of Mines had previously been "designed for production economy and
not for human economy, and there is going to have to be a change of
attitudes on that."

It did not take long for O'Leary's actions to make him some enemies.
In mid-February, word leaked out that he would be replaced by the
Nixon administration, although his job had not been one which
changed hands with the arrival of other Presidents. The decision appeared motivated by two things. First, the Republican administration,
starved for patronage after two terms out of power, was cutting a wide
swath through the bureaucracy to make room for the party faithful.
Second, the mining industry, working through the White House staff,

was putting the pressure on for O'Leary's ouster. Either way, it appeared to be a major behind-the-scenes triumph for the coal industry in its efforts to soften the impact of the Farmington disaster. The UMW at first took the news of O'Leary's impending ouster with indifference. "O'Leary is basically an oil man," said Justin McCarthy. "He doesn't know much about the coal industry one way or another." McCarthy's complaint was the same one the industry executives were making. Asked why the union didn't intercede for O'Leary on the basis of his aggressiveness on mine safety, McCarthy explained that their efforts might fail and end up making it difficult to work with the new bureau chief.

Hechler, however, immediately took the House floor for a speech castigating the administration for its still unannounced decision. The Congressman said O'Leary's ouster would be "a kick in the teeth for the thousands of coal miners who daily run the risk of being gassed, burned, buried or trapped in the mines. . . . I urge every coal miner, every coal miner's widow and every coal miner's youngster whose father was killed or disabled in the mines to write to President Nixon and urge that John F. O'Leary stay on the job."

Hechler's remarks received considerable publicity because the Farmington disaster had made the coal industry a hot subject for newspapers and television. Soon afterwards, five of the widows of the Number 9 disaster came to Washington at Hechler's invitation and visited Interior Secretary Walter J. Hickel to urge him to keep O'Leary on the job. Statements on O'Leary's behalf began to pour in from Capitol Hill. Even old Speaker McCormack spoke up for O'Leary at Hechler's request. Later, Representative Roman Pucinski, a well-known Democrat from Chicago, embarrassed Hickel at a House hearing by lecturing him on O'Leary's virtues and urging that the director be retained. Within a week after the first newspaper stories about O'Leary's impending dismissal appeared, the man the Nixon administration had picked to succeed him withdrew his name. Finally, when it began to appear that the administration would keep O'Leary indefinitely, the UMW finally put out a statement supporting him.

While the Boyle Administration struggled with the mine-safety issue in Washington, a related controversy had been simmering in the West Virginia coal fields. When it boiled over in February, the union officers were in for their biggest embarrassment yet. The drama had many protagonists, but one who repeatedly upstaged the others was Dr. I. E. Buff, an abrasive, irrepressible West Virginia heart specialist who succeeded by sheer doggedness in making black lung a household term in every corner of the state's coal fields. This was no small achievement, for the steep terrain of the southern Appalachian mining region had not only isolated it from the rest of the nation, but divided the region itself into hundreds of tiny communities secluded from each other. Only the ubiquitous television set and, to a lesser extent, the UMW *Journal,* succeeded in penetrating these remote mountain hollows and tiny valley towns to bring in an awareness of life beyond the hills.

But if television brought a vision of the rest of America to the southern coal fields, its only effect was to beckon the youth of the area to leave. It could not change the region itself, which centuries of isolation and economic privation had made as distant from the rest of the country in culture and politics as it was in miles.

Wacky, fundamentalist religious sects flourished. For example, it was common in some churches, even in Charleston, for worshipers to handle snakes. Authority for this practice was cited in the sixteenth chapter of

St. Mark in which Christ is quoted as saying, "These signs shall follow them that believe: In my name shall they cast out devils; they shall speak with new tongues: they shall take up serpents. . . ." In churches that did not engage in snake-handling, some pastors were known to go into trances and begin "speaking in tongues." Glossolalia, as it is known, led to the dismissal of two successive ministers at one church by the non-believing congregation. In 1969, West Virginia was considering reinstating the death penalty, which had been abolished several years before; the leaders of the movement to restore capital punishment were ministers, one of whom said he was willing to "pull the switch myself." Another, a Baptist, said that not only should criminals be put to death, but so should incorrigible children, homosexuals and persons possessed by "familiar spirits." He cited a variety of passages in the Old Testament as authority. "I believe in Biblical demonology today as much as in Biblical times," he said. "Numerous miracles of Christ involved the casting out of evil spirits. . . . These spirits are very real things. . . . I don't believe we can improve on God's laws. God is perfect and cannot give an imperfect law. . . ."

Faithhealers and evangelists of all kinds found West Virginians receptive. One of the most popular, Dr. Gilbert Holloway, told his audiences that the secret of health was deep breathing. "When you inhale," he would say to his heaving congregation, "you bring a great supply of VLF, or Vital Life Force, into your bodies." Holloway, also a seer who predicted George Wallace would win the presidency, said all humans are surrounded by an aura of magnetism—"a bipolar magnetized field. The negative force is provided by your physical body, and the indwelling soul consciousness provides the positive magnetic force. This is particularly sustained by breathing. . . ." He said people who became ill were simply demagnetized.

Although the state school system was so retarded that sixty-seven communities still depended on one-room schools, the big debate on education in the state was not over improving the facilities, but over sex education. At the height of the controversy, a magazine was put out by members of a Presbyterian Church for the purpose of denouncing what they called the "sinister . . . diabolical . . . pornorgraphic . . . atheistic . . . immoral . . . subversive . . . Communist-inspired" teaching of sex in the schools. "The teaching of sex without the teaching of sin is the work of Satan," the magazine said.

The Bible-belt beliefs that made West Virginia prime territory for evangelists and revivalists of all sorts were also a major factor in the political career of the state's most successful politician, Senator Robert Byrd. Byrd was a coal camp orphan and the foster son of a miner; he had worked around the mines himself for a time, and had made it to the Senate by a combination of brains, guts, and non-stop work. He was a fastidious, almost delicate-looking man who tended his political fences with more care than perhaps anyone in Washington. No letter from a constituent was too unimportant for an immediate reply, no meeting in his state too small for him to attend. Early in his career he regaled audiences with his expert fiddle-playing, but this was about as close to having a good time as he ever got. On occasional Sundays, Bob Byrd could be found at the pulpit of some West Virginia church, delivering a hard-hitting, old-fashioned sermon complete with rhythmic hand-clapping. Byrd was a conservative whose political credo was closer to that of a deep-South segregationist than a labor-state Democrat, but his personal popularity was so great that he was virtually invulnerable on issues. Byrd was by no means the only politician in the region who tried to establish a following based on personal appeal rather than political position, but he was easily the most successful.

Politics is a favorite pastime in the mountains. The hoopla and excitement of the election season provide relief from the dreary monotony of life in the region. West Virginians turn out in force for rallies and speeches, and they enjoy chewing the fat with the local politicos. But the campaigns are essentially popularity contests rather than issue-oriented exercises in democracy. Thus a legislator from the coal fields can go to Washington or Charleston and make it easier for the coal companies to lay waste the mountains and kill or maim countless miners—and still be handily re-elected. The labor unions in the state exert some influence on their traditonally Democratic members, but the union leaders cannot be counted on to "deliver" a vote for a certain candidate. John L. Lewis found this out the hard way in the presidential election of 1940, after he had wangled an endorsement for Wendell Willkie from the union convention. The miners then proceeded to vote almost to a man for Franklin Roosevelt, who occupied a place in their pantheon of heroes equalled only by that of Lewis himself. Even today, it is common to find pictures of Lewis and Roosevelt hanging side by side in older miners' homes.

People in Appalachia are known for their shyness and xenophobia, but they are nonetheless subject to captivation by a glamorous and personable public figure. John F. Kennedy proved this in 1960 when he won a key victory in the West Virginia presidential primary. The voters regarded him, not as a well-heeled smoothie trying to con them into supporting him, but as an important, rich man who cared enough to come to West Virginia to get to know them. Although they are bashful, benighted, and pessmistic, the Appalachian coal miners and their families are not cynical. Once their friendship and loyalty is won, it is of the most enduring kind. No miner would ever vote against Roosevelt or Kennedy, nor betray Lewis and the UMW by crossing a picket line. But at the same time the miner gave allegiance to the men and institutions that have been his benefactors, he was equally faithful to a host of other politicians and organizations that did their best to see that nothing changed in Appalachia. Thus a people who lived on land rich in mineral wealth and natural beauty remained dependent on what they could earn by hard labor, or could eke out from a paltry pension— while absentee corporations made huge profits by desecrating the landscape to take away the wealth that lay beneath it.

Coal miners asked little besides friendliness of the men they elected to public office, and in the southern mountains, they got even less. Political corruption was institutionalized in West Virginia. It got so bad during the regime of Governor W. W. (Wally) Barron, from 1960 to 1964, that nearly everyone in the administration was indicted by a federal grand jury, Barron included. Twenty-one state officials were charged with felonies ranging from bribery and conspiracy to tax evasion. Although the governor got off, ten men were convicted, including Barron's life-long best friend and law partner, who was sentenced to four years in jail for his part in a huge bribery scheme. Later it developed that Barron's acquittal was bought by a $25,000 payoff to the jury foreman. Both the ex-governor and the jury foreman were then convicted and sent to jail for twelve years. Although the Barron scandal was the worst in the state's history, rotten politics had been a tradition for years. The 1960 census, for example, found there were seven thousand more persons registered to vote than there were eligible adults. In Mingo County, along the Kentucky border at the heart of the southern coals fields, there were 30,331 registered voters, but only 19,879 were eligible. Four years later, there were more voters than persons eligible

in twenty-nine of the state's fifty-five counties, and by 1968 the dispro-
portion existed in thirty-three counties. The files of the Charleston
Gazette contain envelopes stuffed with clippings on the subject "election fraud" going back to the 1940s. It was taken for granted.

In this blighted political atmosphere, where corruption was the by-
word, and issues second to personalities, it is hardly surprising that the
state's principal industry had long been able to work its will. In 1952,
according to legend, John L. Lewis convinced newly elected Democratic Governor William C. Marland to ask the legislature for a modest
but nevertheless unprecedented tax on the production of coal and other
minerals. The proposal was but a first, halting step toward correcting
the imbalance between West Virginia's vast mineral wealth and its
chronic shortage of funds for public roads, schools and other projects.
As elementary a reform as the tax might have seemed, it was more than
the coal operators were willing to stand. And it was to the industry, not
the public, that most legislators felt their strongest allegiance in the
crunch of a controversial issue. At the time, the coal industry virtually
controlled the Charleston *Gazette,* which was the leading Democratic
newspaper, and the paper went after Marland with a vengeance. The
highlight of this campaign was a cartoon depicting the state capitol
with John L. Lewis's head in place of the dome. The Democratic-
controlled legislature got the message and rebelled against Marland.
Not only was the coal tax defeated, but virtually every other proposal
the governor made went down the drain. The state senate even glee-
fully rejected his executive appointments. Marland's promising term
was turned into a nightmare. When it was over, he was unable to make
a living practicing law in the state. He ended up driving a taxi in Chicago.

The coal industry was no more gentle with West Virginia's environment than it was with William Marland's career. Its best known rav-
ages were, and are, caused by strip-mining—the process by which
the surface soil is torn away and cast aside so that the coal can be
gouged out by huge steamshovels. In the mountains, this is devastating.
Whole hilltops are shaved off and tossed down the side, covering the
area with grey, barren, rocky debris. When the rains come, the run off
from the strip-mined area is heavily acidic and sulphurous. It pollutes
streams and turns them a copper color. It kills plant life as it runs off

the hillsides. By 1965, strip mining had laid waste 192,000 acres in West Virignia, and had polluted 755 miles of streams.

Deep mining, while not as well known for environmental mayhem, has been even more destructive in West Virginia. The slate and other refuse separated from coal after it is dug is simply dumped on the mine site. Throughout the steep mining regions of West Virginia, there are whole mountains, hundreds of feet high, composed of huge, grey, smoking heaps of slag. In West Virginia, the Bureau of Mines has counted 213 burning refuse piles, and there are hundreds of others that are not burning. They have a hideous appearance and, when they are smouldering, give off noxious gases; these banks also contribute to water pollution when storm water carries off the slag. A much greater source of pollution, however is the drainage from inside the mines themselves. In the nation as a whole, about six thousand miles of streams are continuously polluted by the acid drainage from underground mines, most of them coal mines and a great many of them in West Virginia. Added to these problems is that of surface subsidence. The Interior Department has estimated that nearly two million surface acres above bituminous coal mines in the United States have caved in to some extent. This has not generally occurred near population centers, but the Bureau of Mines has listed Fairmont, West Virginia, as a danger spot for subsidence.

In a state where industry can wreck the scenery and disrupt the ecology to get at the mineral wealth, most of which is acquired at bargain prices, it should come as no surprise that a workers' disease could reach epidemic proportions before anyone began to say anything about it. But by the time Lorin Kerr made his memorable address on black lung to the UMW convention, Dr. Buff had already began to pound away at the theme that the disease was rampant and that thousands of miners afflicted by it were not receiving workmen's compensation. Since Buff was a member of the state Air Pollution Control Commission, he had enough status for his allegations to be quoted in the newspapers. By September, he was in the middle of a debate with the administration of Governor Hulett Smith, Barron's successor. "There are forty thousand miners in West Virginia," Buff would say, "and twenty thousand of them have pneumoconiosis. Why haven't these men gotten some compensation?" The state compensation department's records showed that only four victims of pneumoconiosis had ever received compensation—and in all four cases the awards were made posthumously to their families after autopsy evidence had been submitted. Nevertheless, the compensation commissioner, a Democratic party regular named Cletus Hanley, insisted that the disease was covered. His dispute with Buff was aired in the Charleston *Gazette*, which, under new management, had become the state's most liberal voice. Nonetheless, the *Gazette* sided with Hanley and the governor. In an editorial at the height of the dispute, the paper urged that Buff "forget about black lung and workmen's compensation." His repeated assertions were "both tasteless and unprofitable," the editorial said. Such reactions were typical of the response Buff's early statements received, but he was undeterred. The day after the *Gazette*'s editorial appeared, Buff was back in print again, insisting that coverage of the disease under West Virginia's law was "a fantasy." He said Hanley "does a lot of talking, but ninety-nine percent of the doctors in the state know that black lung is not covered, although this disease has become recognized for what it is since 1960. Coal dust is a killer." When the UMW's new contract was signed several weeks later, Buff was again in the headlines. "For a few pieces of silver," he said, "the health and welfare of the coal miner was sold out completely." He called Boyle's explanation that no black lung prevention program was negotiated because such a program was contained in legislation before Congress "pure folly."

Despite the attention Buff had been getting in the newspapers, he knew that he wasn't reaching the majority of the coal miners who lived in remote parts of the mountains south of Charleston. Early in November, however, he got what he thought was his best opportunity to get his message to a mass audience. WHTN, a television station serving both Huntington and Charleston, agreed to do a half-hour Saturday night broadcast on black lung. Buff and a representative of a mine equipment supply company would appear with one of the station's newsmen as moderator. Although the show was simple in format, Buff felt that it would have considerable impact when it was broadcast November 9. He showed sections of ruined lung tissue and explained his ideas about black lung—how to recognize it and what could be done to prevent it. The equipment supply man gave a rundown on the various kinds of safety gear that could be used underground to help miners avoid exposure to the deadly dust.

Within days of the broadcast, Buff discovered that the audience of coal miners he had hoped to reach had not been as large as he thought. Miners he knew who lived in parts of the state served by the vast network of TV cable systems that carried WHTN's signal into remote parts of the mountains reported that the station had been blacked out from about fifteen minutes before the black lung documentary went on the air until after it was over. The station received similar reports. Buff immediately suspected that the state's coal companies were responsible. Stephen Young, president of the West Virginia Coal Association, had taken Dick Richmond, the newsman who moderated the show, to lunch prior to the broadcast in an effort to talk the station out of putting it on the air. The station refused, instead offering the association equal time to present its views. The offer was never accepted.

Angered by the blackouts, Buff went to Washington to complain to Nicholas Johnson, the activist member of the Federal Communications Commission. Johnson watched a taped replay of the show and expressed concern about the incident, but said there was little the FCC could do. Buff was never able to prove what was behind the suppression of the show, but this did not keep him from pushing his theory about it. The coal companies, he said, had long cooperated with the numerous small cable concerns by using their payroll checkoff systems to pay miners' cable bills. The cable outfits therefore owed the coal industry a favor which was called in at the time of the Buff black lung documentary. Whatever actually was behind the show's sabotage Dr. Buff was never again frustrated in his efforts to get across his ideas about coal miners' dust disease. Eleven days after the broadcast, the Number 9 mine at Farmington blew up and put the coal industry and its health and safety problems into the forefront of the news. Buff skillfully exploited the publicity that followed the disaster. He lambasted the coal industry in a manner not heard since the heyday of John L. Lewis and won the respect and admiration of thousands of coal miners in the process.

Isidore Erwin Buff, the son of an itinerant coal-field tailor, came to the role of activist late in life. For most of his career, he was part of the Charleston establishment, a well-known cardiologist with a lucrative practice. Many of his patients were coal miners referred to him for treatment by their employers. A number of people in Charleston who knew him took a cynical view of his new activities. They claimed it all started

in 1965 when his wife left him for another man. But Buff could produce
newspaper clippings that showed him speaking out on air and water
pollution as early as 1963. His appointment in 1967 to the state Air Pollution Control Commission, which was undoubtedly deeply regretted
later by Governor Smith, gave Buff the platform he needed to be heard.
A few months later, he accused the governor of fear of "political dynamite" in failing to act on a critical pollution problem in a river near
Charleston. The Charleston area, Buff declared, is the "filthiest place in
the United States."

A slope-shouldered, paunchy man of sixty with thinning silver hair
and a double chin that crept over his shirt collar, Buff did not look the
part of medical crusader, and sounded even less like one. His nasal
voice had the abrasive twang of a courthouse politician from the deep
South. But he had a flair for colorful phrasemaking and a knack for
keeping his opponents off guard with his accusations. Though he usually struck a grim pose, his comments could be outrageously amusing.
In a television interview in Washington, for example, he blasted West
Virginia's Senator Jennings Randolph for his stand on mine safety. Randolph, said Buff, had been "caught with his pants down." After a pause,
he added, "and his zipper won't work."

As Buff told the story, his concern for the lung problems of coal miners grew out of his practice as a heart specialist. "They would send
these men to me after they had collapsed in the mines," he said. "They
were supposed to have an acute heart attack, but I would examine
them and find they had lung failure. Heart attacks are not covered
under state workmen's compensation, but lung problems are. I would
tell these company doctors the men had lung trouble, but they wouldn't
believe me. I was getting tired of it. There are literally thousands of
coal miners in West Virginia who think they've had heart attacks who
have never had one. They are denied insurance and they are denied
workmen's compensation. And they are denied employment. They are
what I call 'false derelicts' thrown upon the population. The reason for
this is that once a man is labeled as having heart disease by a doctor, it
is almost impossible to convince anyone otherwise."

Of course, as Dr. Kerr pointed out in Denver, there was nothing new
about black lung. The British had recognized it as a major hazard of
coal mining for twenty-five years. Yet, as Buff began to speak out, it
was only begining to receive serious attention in this country, and many

doctors, particularly those in the coal fields, had wildly inaccurate notions about it. Two days after Buff's television broadcast, for example, Dr. Charles Andrews, provost of Health Sciences at West Virginia University, said in a speech in Charleston that cigarette smoking was the key factor in miner's lung disease. "Coal dust may add to the difficulty," he said, "but cigarette smoking is perhaps the most important factor."

Coal worker's pneumoconiosis is caused by the inhalation of extremely fine particles of coal dust, which in modern mines are stirred into the atmosphere in huge quantities. When the particles accumulate in quantity in the lung, they begin to break down its ability to transfer oxygen to the bloodstream. The result is chronic shortness of breath and, in the more advanced cases, bronchitis, emphysema, and heart failure. The condition is not only incurable, but progressive. It gets worse even if a man stops working in a dusty area. The medical confusion about the disease is partly a result of the similarity of its symptoms to those of silicosis, a common miners' lung ailment for generations. Silicosis is caused by the inhalation of fine particles of rock dust and it causes the same type of shortness of breath and lung failure as black lung. But there is one important difference. The lung damage of silicosis is easily detectable by X-ray, while the X-rays of a man seriously disabled by black lung may show only minimal damage. Because of widespread ignorance about black lung, most miners would apply to the state workmen's compensation board for benefits for silicosis. They were turned down by the thousands when their X-rays failed to show disabling silicosis. By the time they realized that they had been getting faulty medical advice, it was frequently too late to reapply for benefits for pneumoconiosis because the state law had a statute of limitations on disease claims. In most cases, however, the miners never realized they had applied for benefits for the wrong disease. They simply took their disabled bodies back into the hills. Too often, they returned to work in the mines to make a living.

Buff was getting nowhere in his effort to gain official recognition that black lung disease was an occupational epidemic whose victims got neither proper medical attention nor workmen's compensation. Time and again, state officials would explain that the West Virginia compensation law covered all occupational diseases and all a miner had to do was show that he contracted an ailment at work in order to receive benefits. Nevertheless, the coal towns of the Kanawha Valley around Charleston were full of breathless miners, some of them unable to work, who had never received a dime in compensation. To them, their families, and the miners who knew them, Dr. Buff became an instant hero. They wrote letters to him. Some came to see him at his office in Charleston to tell their stories. Others telephoned him. Encouraged by this reaction, Buff began to go into the coal towns to speak to small groups of miners. At first, it was lonely, tiring work. At nights or on weekends, he would get into his tiny red Datsun and take the main highway out of Charleston, turning off onto twisting mountain backroads past grey board-and-batten shanties and the carcasses of automobiles, finally stopping at some ramshackle meeting hall or schoolroom where a motley assembly of wheezing coal miners was waiting for its unlikely messiah. His speeches were not masterpieces of rhetoric. He used no text, just whatever came to mind. But Buff had impact. "All you men are going to die of black lung," he would sometimes begin. "Not tomorrow, not next week, but maybe in five or ten years. But you've got it." Coupled with this blunt bad news was a scornful attack on the mining industry and the state's medical profession.

In mid-September, a group of miners in Fayette County, southeast of Charleston, announced they were starting their own drive for compensation for black lung. Elsewhere, similar ideas were taking root. Joe Malay, an able veteran miner from Clifftop, in the highlands of Fayette County at the eastern edge of the southern coal fields, went to see James Leeber, one of the UMW's district representatives. Malay took a delegation of concerned miners with him on the trip to District 29 headquarters in Beckley, the principal town in southeastern West Virginia. After a three-hour meeting in which the men urged Leeber to press for improvements in the state compensation law, Leeber refused. In Boone County, just south of Charleston, a similar delegation, led by miner Ivan White from a place called Twilight, called on George Burnette, the union's compensation lawyer at District 17 headquarters in Charleston. The answer was the same. The law was good enough.

While Buff was beginning his missionary work among the miners around Charleston, a twenty-five-year-old anti-poverty worker from Buffalo was carrying a similar message to the miners in the fields around Beckley, sixty miles southeast of Charleston. His name was Craig Robinson and he was a modest, bashful young man who listened more than he talked, and who turned crimson at the slightest hint of praise. He wore bluejeans and plaid shirts, kept his hair short and drove around the mountains in a battered Pontiac sedan. To look at him, one would never know he wasn't a native of the area. His unassuming manner and his refusal to try to dictate to the miners had earned him hundreds of friends in the coal communities around Beckley. "We had been having meetings with disabled miners," he explained, "trying to determine what in the law needed to be amended. We knew a lot of these breathless guys that couldn't get any money and we wanted to know how this could be." Robinson was helped in this effort to draft legislation by Richard Bank, a lawyer who, like Robinson, worked in the government's Volunteers In Service To America (VISTA) program. In addition, Robinson had been reading everything he could find about pneumoconiosis and relating what he learned to the miners. In his patient, unaggressive way, Robinson had given a short but thorough briefing on the disease to hundreds of miners, when he stopped at their homes and talked to them. In November, Robinson and Bank went to a meeting in the small city of Montgomery, along the Kanawha River southeast of Charleston, to hear Buff. "We were amazed," Robinson said. "He was saying all the things the VISTAS had been saying for years. We were ecstatic." Simultaneously with Robinson's and Bank's low-key spreading of the gospel, related efforts were in progress in other parts of the mining region. Molly Marshall, an anti-poverty organizer in McDowell County, next to Mingo along the Kentucky border, and Bruce McKee, a VISTA in Logan County, just north of Mingo, brought small groups of miners to the meetings organized by Robinson.

One of the chief sources of Robinson's information about black lung was a chest specialist at the Appalachian Regional Hospital, one of those formerly operated by the UMW welfare fund. The doctor, Donald L. Rasmussen, a pipe-smoking redhead with a beard and a flat-top that made him look like a lumberjack, had examined about three thousand miners in his laboratory and had quietly become the nation's leading authority on coal workers' lung disease. He was a mild-mannered man, slightly absent-minded, who inspired the same kind of trust and respect in the coal miners that Craig Robinson did. He knew better than any man in West Virginia what was happening to coal miners with lung problems that didn't show up on an X-ray as a disabling stage of silicosis. He had examined them by the hundreds in his laboratory. On

countless occasions, he had certified men as disabled by pneumoconiosis only to have the State Compensation Commission rule that the men
were not entitled to a dime. For even if a miner could convince the
board of three doctors who ruled on such claims that he had pneumoconiosis, the prevailing belief was that, except in its most advanced
stages, the disease was benign. Rasmussen had seen scores of these men,
their lungs literally riddled with dust damage, return to the mines to
inhale more of the deadly dust and to die sooner rather than later. With
his associates at the hospital, pathologists Werner A. Laqueur and
Hawey A. (Sonny) Wells, Rasmussen had been trying to make his findings about the epidemic known throughout the medical profession. But
he found that old ideas were not easily erased, even in the face of the
most overwhelming evidence and with a quarter-century of British experience and research to draw upon.

In 1964 and 1965, the U.S. Public Health Service had joined in the
black lung research effort at Beckley. Rasmussen and his associates
were put on the government payroll and they divided their time between hospital work and research. Additional equipment was added to
Rasmussen's laboratory and considerable progress was made in deter-
mining the prevalence of the disease. In 1966, however, Senator Byrd
arranged for the federally funded research project to be moved to the
state university medical center at Morgantown. It was a change that
sounded like progress, but it proved to be a giant step backward. The
doctors at the Morgantown laboratory, which was impressively named
the "Appalachian Laboratory for Occupational Respiratory Diseases,"
went about their work with none of the feeling of urgency that had
prevailed at Beckley. After two years and an expenditure of $2 million
in public funds, the Morgantown team had examined fewer than a hundred miners. The group was led by a highhat, uptight Britisher named
Keith Morgan who did not hesitate, despite his limited research, to
sneer publicly at the conclusions reached by the group at Beckley,
whom he seemed to regard not as partners but as competitors.

There was, however, no disagreement between the two laboratories
on one point: coal worker's pneumoconiosis was a widespread, poorly
understood occupational ailment in America's coal mining regions. But
Rasmussen and his associates went further. They argued that black
lung could be disabling in its early or "simple" stage. The Morgantown
doctors argued that the disease was a crippler only in its advanced or

"complicated" stage, when it could usually be detected by X-ray. Since the vast majority of afflicted coal miners had "simple" pneumoconiosis, this dispute was of enormous significance. The Beckley group held that huge numbers of men were seriously impaired by the disease in a stage that was extremely difficult to diagnose with absolute certainty. They argued for diagnosis based on a variety of tests, including X-ray, but placing equal reliance on breathing and exercise tests and other indicators. If a man who was impaired had worked in the mines for several years and if his other symptoms were consistent with black lung disability, they contended he should be judged to have the disease—given the benefit of the doubt, in effect. The Morgantown group would have none of this. Morgan argued that the X-ray should remain the deciding test. By implication, he even accused Rasmussen of saying that men with normal X-rays could have black lung, a monstrous distortion. What Rasmussen actually said was that although he had never seen a disabled miner with a normal X-ray, the seriousness of the condition was often not accurately reflected by the X-ray. Literally millions of dollars in compensation payments rode on the outcome of this debate. Meanwhile, of course, most doctors in the coal fields operated on medical notions that made Keith Morgan and his group seem positively futuristic. Nervousness, fear of mining, cigarettes, malingering, and "compensationitis" were the accepted causes of breathlessness in miners who didn't have silicosis.

Six years of trying to help coal miners overcome the abysmal ignorance of most doctors and state officials had stirred in Don Ramussen a feeling of quiet outrage. Retiring and politically moderate, he had nevertheless reached a point where he delighted in reading about the colorful Charleston heart doctor who was harrying the authorities about the black lung epidemic. And although Buff was hardly precise in his homey descriptions of the disease, Don Rasmussen responded to his campaign much as Craig Robinson had. "I shuddered at what he said about the disease," Rasmussen said, "but I couldn't help but admire what he had to say about what was wrong in the mines. It was exciting as hell."

Dr. Rasmussen was joined in his ardent feelings about coal miners by his wife, Jeanne, an attractive woman in her mid-thirties who shared her husband's ability to communicate with the mountain people. She divided her time between her two children and a career as a freelance photographer-journalist. She was fascinated by the Appalachian culture and spent many days in the bleak coal towns around Beckley taking stark pictures of life around the mines. Her studio was a storehouse of cartridge tapes of interviews with miners and their families, many of whom she had met through her husband's work at the hospital. Taken together, her collection of photographs and tapes was an extraordinary documentary of life in the mining regions.

When the mine at Farmington exploded, she was assigned to cover the story for the famous West Virginia weekly *The Hillbilly*. While at the scene, she met many of the reporters who would later return to the state to cover the events that followed the disaster. During this period, Jeanne Rasmussen's knowledge of journalism and her rapport with the mountain people became a key element in the amount and quality of the news coverage. The writers and television crews relied upon her as a source of background information, a guide, and someone who could introduce them to the normally suspicious miners and make sure their interviews were fruitful.

Late in November, following the Farmington explosion, Dr. Rasmussen was invited by Joe Malay to join Dr. Buff in a presentation on black lung to a group of miners at the community center in Clifftop. For Buff, it might have been just another in his series of talks on the subject. But the Farmington disaster and his meeting with Rasmussen, whom he had known only by reputation, gave the session special significance. The disaster had made the health and safety problems of coal miners a hot subject in the press and the Clifftop meeting hit the papers all around West Virginia. Buff did his best to make the most of it. "Coal miners are signing their own death warrants by working in the mines," he told the gathering of about fifty men in the red brick meeting hall, "Fifty percent have black lung, thirty percent have it to a lesser degree and the other twenty percent will get it." Rasmussen couldn't match Buff for drama and sensationalism, but he added an element to the meeting that Buff could not give it—authority. Rasmussen was an expert and Buff was not, and all Buff's efforts to date had been hindered by that fact.

Just over a week later, on the eve of the Interior Department's conference on mine safety, Buff and Rasmussen got together again. This time, the scene was the Hay-Adams House hotel, two blocks from the White House, in Washington. Dr. Hawey A. (Sonny) Wells, the pathologist who had worked at Rasmussen's side at Beckley from 1964–66, was also on hand. He was a voluble, pop-eyed man of thirty-two, with curly blond hair, who looked a little like Buck Owens, the famed country and western singer. His autopsies had made a major contribution to the Beckley research team's effort to establish the prevalence of coal pneumoconiosis. After leaving Beckley in 1966, he became director of the chest laboratory at a hospital in Johnstown, Pennsylvania, and divided his time between research and teaching at the medical school at West Virginia University in nearby Morgantown. His wife, Margaret Ann Staggers, a good-looking brunette and the daughter of West Virginia Congressman Harley Staggers, was also a doctor, but despite this fact and despite his proven ability, Sonny Wells's ambitions lay outside the medical profession. Somewhere along the line, he had been bitten by the political flu, and the cause of miners' health and safety, for which his concern was deep and genuine, provided an opportunity for him to play doctor-politician. It was Wells who had first interested Ralph Nader in black lung and he had appeared several times in Washington to testify for various occupational health and safety proposals. The events at Farmington, created a better climate for such action, and Wells was determined to see this cause through to a successful conclusion.

At the meeting in Dr. Buff's hotel, the three doctors agreed to work together to press for improved conditions in the mines. Wells hit upon the idea of forming a letterhead organization to make the trio seem a more formal organization. Thus, the "Physicians for Miners' Health and Safety" was born. Dr. Buff became chairman, Dr. Rasmussen the secretary and Dr. Wells took the title of "coordinator." Jeanne Rasmussen was named press representative. Although the group's officers were its only members, Wells told those who asked that the organization had about twenty-five members from all over the coal fields. He rationalized the prevarication by saying privately that he knew the group could get more members if it ever needed them. As it turned out, three were plenty. Coal mining was all over the front pages and every news broadcast contained developments in the controversy. During the next several weeks, Buff was besieged with invitations from coal miners throughout the state to speak to meetings on black lung. He accepted them all, scheduling as many as four each weekend and taking his new partners with him wherever he went. Rasmussen and his wife also began to hear from miners eager for the doctors to talk to groups in their communities. The doctors became what one television reporter later called a "traveling medicine show." It was an apt phrase. Buff would usually begin a meeting by citing some shocking statistics of dubious authenticity about the prevalence of the disease. In his rambling lectures, he would castigate the state's doctors, the coal industry, and the various agencies of state and federal government. He would show slides of ruined lung sections (some of them displayed upside down). His most appalling exhibit was a human lung, completely blackened with coal dust, which he carried around in a plastic sack. Rasmussen would follow with some authentic information, which was usually too arcane for most audiences. But the miners listened with rapt attention nevertheless. Then Wells took his turn. His favorite gimmick was to produce a section of autopsied lung. "Here is a slice of one of your brother's lungs," he would say, and then snap it into dusty flakes, like a potato chip. Wells's talks were laced with rabble-rousing rhetoric and calls to political action. The miners loved it all and roared their approval, particularly when one of the doctors would ask, "Where has your union been all this time?"

The audiences got larger as time went on. The television networks, especially ABC, came into the state to cover some of the meetings. *The New York Times* and *Washington Post* sent reporters into the mountains to follow the crusade. After each meeting, Buff would supply the wire services and the major regional newspapers that had not been present with a rundown on what occurred, usually placing heavy emphasis on what he himself said, and sometimes grossly overestimating the size of the audience.

In January, as the campaign continued to pick up steam, another ad-hoc organization was born. Its main organizer was Woodrow Mullins, a cheerful miner who in 1954 had been diagnosed by a doctor as having a disabling degree of silicosis. At the time, however, the men in the union district office urged him not to apply for compensation because there was an agreement between the union and a number of West Virginia coal companies that the company could fire a miner who received a compensation award for disabling silicosis. This was a boon to the companies because silicosis, like pneumoconiosis, usually worsened. If a miner was still on the job, he would be entitled to further compensation. In West Virginia, the compensation payments came from a fund supported by the companies and their premiums were set in proportion to the number and amount of awards made to their employees. Thirteen years later, virtually breathless, Mullins was examined by Dr. Rasmussen in Beckley. The diagnosis was pneumoconiosis but the compensation commission would not accept it and Mullins was left unable to work in the mines, with no way to support his family. Understandably, he became an early admirer of Dr. Buff.

On a Saturday evening early in January, Mullins led a delegation of miners from the Kanawha Valley to see Paul Kaufman, a Charleston lawyer who had been a state senator and a gubernatorial candidate. Although he was out of politics, Kaufman had been the leader of the tiny liberal wing of the state's Democratic party and had for years been urging reforms to end the domination of the state by what he called an "unholy alliance" of out-of-state corporations and prominent local politicians. The legislative session had begun and although the UMW had finally indicated that it would seek a black lung compensation measure, no bill had appeared. The miners asked Kaufman to help them draft legislation. He said he would not only draft legislation, but would act as their lobbyist in getting it passed if they could pay him enough for the necessary time to do the job. He agreed to begin the project if the miners could raise $2,000 as a starter. The next night, Mullins and the group that had met with Kaufman gathered again, joined by about ten other men from various local unions in the area. The meeting was held in the city hall, located above the firehouse in the bleak riverside city of Montgomery. The group could not agree on a plan of action, and the meeting broke up after considerable bickering, an apparent failure.

Part of the reason for the disagreement at the meeting was a feeling among some of those present that independent action on the part of the miners would lead to trouble with the UMW hierarchy. Several of the men argued that since the union had promised to introduce a bill it would be unwise to take any action that might be interpreted as an effort to undercut the official policy of the organization. These fears were well grounded. One of the most serious accusations in organized labor, and one which had often been made against dissidents in the UMW, was participation in a "dual" movement. The UMW constitution provided that a member could be expelled for joining any organization deemed "dual" to the UMW. Loss of union membership meant loss of job and of pension and hospital benefits. It was a punishment few members were willing to risk.

On the street outside the city hall, after most of the miners at the meeting had departed, a few lingered still trying to figure out a way to organize a fund-raising drive to press for the kind of legislation they wanted. One of them, Ernest Riddle, a husky, balding veteran miner who worked at the Allied Chemical Company's vast Harewood Mine at nearby Longacre, suggested the group form an "association." Such a loose organization, he said, could not be considered a dual union since it could be established for a single stated purpose, enactment of a black lung compensation bill. Although Riddle's proposal could not have overcome the objections of the men who were most worried about offending the union hierarchy, those men had left. The plan was quickly agreed upon by the handful who remained. They decided to call themselves the West Virginia Black Lung Association. The street-corner caucus then picked officers from its own number. Charles Brooks, a mild-mannered black man who was president of the local at the Carbon Fuel Company mine at Winifrede where Mullins had worked, was elected president. Ernest Riddle became treasurer. Later that night, Brooks called Kaufman and asked him to go ahead on the strength of the association's promise of a fund drive. The same night, another of the association's charter members, Lyman Calhoun, called a friend of his, Arnold Miller, and asked him to help the group raise money. He could not have asked a better man.

Arnold Ray Miller, president of the 192-man local at the Bethlehem Steel Company's mine at Kayford, was an exceptionally alert and articulate man in his forties who would long since have become a district or international officer in most other unions. He was personable and soft-spoken, and his white-grey hair and clear-eyed, keen expression gave him a distinguished appearance. He wasn't a big talker or a braggart, but his fellow miners knew him as a man who could be counted on to do anything he said he would do. That night, Miller told Lyman Calhoun he would help the Black Lung Association. Within days, Miller had raised $1,000 at a special meeting of his own local and had convinced the members of two other locals to put up a total of $550. Meanwhile, Calhoun's local voted to contribute $1,000 and Mullins' and Brooks' local agreed to come through with an equal amount. The Black Lung Association was off to a good start.

The newly formed association and the three doctors immediately found common cause and the meetings addressed by the doctors also became fund raising sessions for the leaders of the black lung group, which shared the platform. By mid-January, these meetings were occurring with rapidly increasing frequency and the attendance was steadily improving. The idea that miners might be able to do something about getting compensation for their lungs was spreading fast through the coal counties at the southernmost tip of West Virginia. These counties, Logan, Boone, McDowell, and Mingo, had both the most mining and the most poverty, misery and environmental damage in the state. It had been a long time since anyone had stirred things up in these remote and dismal hamlets and the ferment over black lung was making the local establishment nervous. Union officials in the area did what they could to tamp things down. But their efforts only made matters worse for them and the harder they tried the more volatile the situation became.

Late in January, the doctors took their program deep into Mingo County, heart of the region where the Hatfields and McCoys had shot it out years earlier, and an area notorious for the squalid political machine which had long maintained dominion over local affairs by massive election fraud. The meeting was held at Matewan, a narrow strip of a village crisscrossed by a wide swath of railroad track serving the huge Island Creek Coal Company mine at nearby Red Jacket, the principal source of employment in the town. It had once been a busy place, but the shrinking coal industry had left it a dreary town of grimy board-and-batten shanties lining the edge of the railroad tracks, with nothing that could even be called a business center. Nevertheless, the town occupied a special place in West Virginia history. Matewan was the site of one of the main events of the savage union-industry struggles in the early part of the century. During a strike in 1920, the operators had imported a brigade of hired thugs from the infamous Baldwin-Felts Detective agency to evict the miners from their company-owned houses. After they had done their dirty work, they lingered unarmed in the main street of the town, waiting for a train to take them back to Bluefield, where the agency's headquarters were located. A group of strikers, led by Sid Hatfield, the Matewan chief of police, ambushed the posse of "mine guards," as they were euphemistically called, and shot ten of them dead in the street. The volley of gunfire poured forth from upstairs windows, rooftops, and other vantage points along the street. The victims included two brothers of Thomas Felts, co-owner of the hated detective agency. The murderous mob celebrated its slaughter by whooping it up in a drunken frenzy around its victims and continuing to pump slugs into their bodies. The "Matewan Massacre," as it was known, along with other incidents of violence, earned the county the sobriquet of "Bloody Mingo."

Mingo County is also famous in labor annals as the birthplace of the despised "yellow-dog" contract, which was first used by the Red Jacket Coal Company, precursor of Island Creek, shortly after the massacre in Matewan. The company required all its non-union employes to sign contracts disavowing any association with the UMW. The union was locked in a violent struggle with the mine operators in its effort to organize the area. The miners who had chosen to join up were almost perpetually on strike to achieve recognition. The "yellow-dog" contract spread rapidly throughout the southern coal fields and it enabled the companies to obtain injunctions against any union activity at their mines. When the Supreme Court upheld the court orders, the United Mine Workers was dead in southern West Virginia. The miners who had chosen to side with the union throughout the struggles prior to 1920 were left unemployed and defenseless. The coal operators again ruled the region as principal landlord and virtually the sole employer. In his account of West Virginia's four major mine wars, *Bloodletting in Appalachia* former State Attorney General Howard B. Lee tells what happened once the "yellow dog" contract took hold:

"As a bitter aftermath of those strikes, yellow-dog contracts and injunctions and in the years between 1920 and 1925 no fewer than fifty thousand men, women, and children were evicted from their homes in southern West Virginia. They found shelter under cliffs, in tents, and in improvised shacks built by the union. Year after weary year, they lived and starved in those unwholesome surroundings. Malnutrition and unsanitary conditions increased the death rate to appalling figures, especially among the children. But there was no relenting by the coal barons. To many of them, their hungry, protesting workers were pariahs, or outcasts, to be starved until hunger forced them to return to the service of their masters. In the end, hunger won, and the workers slunk back to the mines, with hearts filled with hate and their minds embittered by the memory of the wrongs they had suffered."

With the passage of the Wagner Act in 1935, the yellow-dog contract became only a memory and the United Mine Workers was able to organize the mines in southern West Virginia. But as Dr. Buff and his company took their campaign into the region, they found that once more the hills were filled with men who were angry at the way they had been treated, not only by the coal operators, but by the UMW and the government as well.

These were men like Billy Hutchinson, a humble, slightly-built man who lived near Matewan. He had been a willing worker during the decades he had spent in the coal mines. Now, however, Hutchinson was totally disabled at the age of forty-nine. His lungs were so damaged that he could barely utter a sentence without pausing to catch his breath. His back was supported by a brace. His troubles had begun twelve years earlier when he began to experience shortness of breath. He paid little attention to it until he became unable to lie down at night because of searing pains in his chest. He was able to get only a few hours of sleep, kneeling in bed with his head resting on a pile of pillows. His ailment was diagnosed as a disabling stage of silicosis by one reputable doctor, but the UMW lawyer who handled his case insisted he also be diagnosed by a second doctor, a member of the state's Silicosis Medical Board, which had been established to rule on silicosis cases only. This doctor said Hutchinson did not have silicosis, but offered no suggestions as to what might have caused his illness. When Hutchinson returned home with this news, his wife insisted this diagnosis must have been a mistake. She urged him to go back to Charleston to be re-examined. His first trip had been paid for by the union welfare fund, but the fund made no allowance for more than one examination. "I didn't have any money," he recalled, "no way whatsoever to get back for this return appointment. So I didn't know nothing else to do and I said, 'Well, I'll just have to go back in the coal mines and try it. If I fall dead, well, I'll just fall dead, that's all. I'll just have to try it.' So that's when I went back and kept on trying to work. I'd get an hour or two's sleep, get up and go on to work. I'd go two or three hundred feet and stop. Then I'd go two or three hundred more feet and stop, several times before I would get to my job. Many times, things got to looking so blue to me that I'd think I was just about gone.

"But I would go on into the mines and do the best I could to perform my day's work. And many, many days I would just about smother to death in the mines. You'd come in contact with rock dust and coal dust and this bad, musty air in a worked out place. You'd get so weak you

couldn't raise your shovel full of coal. These mine inspectors don't realize about what accumulates in the mines and the dust that settles. You
have to crawl through this dust on your hands and knees and you begin
to weaken down. . . ."

Hutchinson put in four more years in the mines under these trying
circumstances until one day his back was injured when he was pinned
against a shuttle car while loading coal. He nearly smothered before he
was able to free himself. "I was hurting awful bad," he said. "The fellow that run the motor came around and he said, 'Are you hurt?' And I
said, 'Yeah, I'm hurt pretty bad.' He said, 'You want me to take you
outside?' I said, 'I don't know. Let me rest a little while and I'll see if I
can finish my shift.' I went ahead and I think I loaded maybe a car and
a half of coal the rest of that shift. The next day I got to hurting so bad
I went to the hospital and they kept me in there 25 or 26 days with
weights on my legs and feet. Then I went on home."

Billy Hutchinson was partially crippled and he sought workmen's
compensation for his back, but received only a small award. When he
tried to reopen his case, the union lawyer refused to help him. The
result was that Hutchinson tried to go back to work in the mines. "I
didn't want to be a burden to no one," he said. He worked twenty-one
shifts, but couldn't go on. He was never paid for that final month. "I've
tried several times to get them to pay me for it, even just part of it so I
could get some medicine," he said. "They tell me they'll put a check in
the mail but I've never got nothing."

The meeting at Matewan was held in the gymnasium of a dingy, red-
brick high school. About 250 miners showed up, most of them suffering
from various forms of lung trouble. It had been a long time since anyone had taken a serious interest in these men and their problems. They
seemed overwhelmed by the idea that three doctors would troup the
mountains without pay to help them understand what was making
them short of breath and why they couldn't get compensation for their
illness. The session was organized by Elmer Brown, a disabled miner
who was president of a nearby local at Delbarton. He had been a patient of Dr. Rasmussen and had become a stalwart in the Black Lung
Association. Arnold Miller had sought him out a few weeks earlier and
asked him to help distribute copies of the Pennsylvania black lung compensation law, which the association was using as a model to draft its

own legislation. Brown was a bald man of fifty-one with a benign, man-in-the-moon look about him and a heavy mountain accent which made "it" come out as "hit" and "went" sound like "we-int." He shared the platform on the stage with Earl Stafford, another black lung victim who was president of his local. Stafford was a slender, thoughtful man with glasses and an alert mind that earned him the respect of the miners. Alongside the doctors and the rank-and-file leaders sat the kingpins of the local power structure. There was State Senator Noah Floyd, the political boss of Mingo County, who for years had done his best to see that the old gang stayed in control by using his power as chairman of the Senate Elections Committee to bottle up election reform legislation. Seated with him was Harry Artis, the local high-sheriff, and Elza Johnson, a field representative in the county for the UMW, who hit it off just fine with the local politicos. The attendance was held down somewhat by the fact that Island Creek was working its mines on Saturday for the first time in several years.

The doctors gave their familiar presentation, with Buff in rare form with his rabble-rousing rhetoric. He laid about him on subjects ranging from the schools ("The coal companies are suppressing your brains; they don't want you to have a good education; the schools are terrible") to the Rockefellers and the Mellons ("These billionaire families didn't build West Virginia—you miners did—and now they are letting your health be wrecked"). He tied into the prominent statehouse politicians, accusing them of being captives of the coal industry. The miners roared their approval. Elza Johnson apparently felt he should try to take some of the steam out of their reaction. He took the floor after the doctors had finished.

"The only way we're going to get any bill passed has already been stressed," he told the group. "The senator from this area has already expressed his support for the best possible bill you can get out. The Mine Workers has already produced a bill which all the local unions have been sent. . . . I urge each and every one of you to support the Mine Workers bill. . . . Now we don't want the tail to wag the dog all the time and we've been the dog a long time. We don't want to start being wagged by the tail . . . and of course, I'm telling you if you leave the cigarettes off you'd have better lungs, too. . . . Now, if you're gonna talk about lungs, you'd better talk about all the things that is hurting us. . . . And I think we ought to be plumb fair and frank and I don't think all the politicians is bad fellows, either. . . . I don't think we ought to sit and talk about our elected officials unless a man can prove that they're doing a bad job, and I'm just a little bit afraid we're playing unfair with our elected politicians. . . . You know, I read a little article in the Mine Workers *Journal* which is typical of some of the things we used to have: it says, 'Buddy, push the car out . . . it's too dangerous to put the mule in there.' So we know us coal miners went through a lot, but we fare better today than we ever fared before. . . . That little old law is not agonna do you any good without the Mine Workers, and fact is, you ain't gonna get no law without the Mine Workers. . . . So the Mine Workers, and all labor in this state has introduced a bill . . . a good bill in my opinion . . . and if we got any better, we'll support that too. . . . So I thank all of you for your attention."

Johnson sat down to a chorus of boos and Dr. Buff took the floor. "I'm very pleased at what you say," he said, "but let me tell you something. Actions speak louder than words. Remember that. Action is louder than words." This comment brought strong applause. The miners had been in no mood for what Johnson had said, and their anger was heightened by the fact that they didn't like him much anyway.

As Buff took his seat, Earl Stafford stood up. Ordinarily he was a calm, easygoing man, but he too was infuriated by Johnson's words. "My name is Earl Stafford and I'm a coal miner," he said angrily. "I've mined coal with Mr. Johnson, and things *is* pretty good . . . for fellows like Mr. Johnson. He's not up here digging coal now. He's not up here eatin' this coal dust. He was a good man at one time, I'll say that. . . . He may be a good man in a way yet. *But he lacks about ten ton of weighing a nickel.*"

Stafford's words brought the fury of the audience to a crescendo. The building shook with cheering and loud hand-clapping, while men in the balcony stood and shook their fists at Johnson, shouting insults. Johnson got up and said, "Now, if you want to get personal, we can do that too . . ." but he was drowned out by the roars from the angry crowd.

Elmer Brown took the floor to try to calm things down. One man was restrained as he tried to approach Johnson with a knife. "Gentlemen," Brown said, "this meeting was called for the purpose of trying to get a black lung bill up there in Charleston. There is some of us fellows who has worked awful hard at it." But the angry crowd was still shouting at

Johnson. "Now wait a minute . . . hold it a minute, boys. That's not right. Not right. . . . I'm a man who's fought a long time for the coal miners and the things that goes on in the coal mines and I appreciate seeing anybody get their rights every now and then, but this is the wrong place and the wrong time to do it. The things we want is a black lung bill passed up there that will take care of these coal miners who are disabled and knocked out, such as this man right here [he pointed to a man on the front row] who has never received nothing in his whole life and is ready to go in his grave.

"The bill that we want is to see that these men who has spent their lives as a human man, who has worked all up and down these roads and carried guns and laid out all night. They fought for it, let's give it to them, and this thing of people raising their voices when it's not necessary, we never called this meeting for that purpose at all. I thank you." This appeal calmed the irate audience but Johnson was still jeered as he stalked out, accompanied by high sheriff Artis.

As the black lung drive continued to gain momentum throughout the state, the establishment was trying frantically to slow it down. In mid-January, the Cabell County Medical Society, meeting in Huntington, solemnly passed a resolution condemning the doctors for "inciting the miners." The resolution was based on a report presented by Dr. Rowland Burns, who often was a paid witness for coal companies in compensation cases. There was "no epidemic of devastating, killing, and disabling man-made plague among the coal workers," Burns said. The society's resolution asserted that pneumoconiosis was usually "a condition compatible with reasonable health." It criticized the doctors' "alarming appeals based upon evidence open to serious question."

Ten days later, the Kanawha County Medical Society, which included Charleston doctors and numbered Buff among its members, passed a similar resolution. This one attacked "the activities of those in the medical profession who have unduly alarmed and have incited a number of those employed in the coal industry without first having presented scientific documentation of their findings." This was not Buff's first brush with the society. In May of the previous year, one of its committees sought to suspend him for his public utterances. Buff foiled this move by refusing to appear before the group to face the charges unless the meeting was open to the public. The society's rules forbid making such a proceeding public, and a stalemate resulted. When the black lung resolution was passed, Buff replied that both the Kanawha and Cabell County measures "uphold the point of view of the vested interests."

Far from hurting the doctors' cause, both these medical society condemnations were a big help, for they almost immediately backfired when the federal government expressed strong official concern about the disease. The same day the Cabell County Medical Society took its action, the Secretary of Health, Education and Welfare, Wilbur Cohen, answered an appeal from Ralph Nader with a letter that called pneumoconiosis "a significant occupational health problem" and a "disabling and tragic condition." Cohen ordered that an eight-point program be undertaken to advance the Public Health Service's slow-moving research into the problem. The effect of Cohen's announcement was to put the Federal Government on record in support of the doctors, and to call attention to an earlier estimate by the Public Health Service that pneumoconiosis "affects conservatively more than a hundred thousand soft coal workers."

Following the tense rally at Matewan was a huge convocation at the cavernous civic center in Charleston. It was at this meeting that Nader's letter attacking Boyle was read to the crowd of about three thousand by Hechler. The Congressman also displayed a sign that he described to the chuckling miners as a "secret message" from the policy-making council of the West Virginia Medical Association, which had met in the city the same day. "Black lung is good for you," the poster read. Hechler then produced his most celebrated prop, the twelve-pound loaf of bologna. The audience whooped with laughter. Hechler ridiculed proposals for further study of the black lung problem which he said could drag on for "five, ten, or fifteen years, and by that time either the problem will go away or your lungs will go away."

The mass meeting also heard speeches by the three doctors, by Warren McGraw, a fiery young state legislator from the southern coal fields, and by Paul Kaufman, who had finished drafting the Black Lung Association's legislation and had arranged for it to be introduced in both houses of the state legislature. He urged the miners to accept no substitute for the Association's bill. "Doctors can't agree on what black lung looks like under a microscope," he said. "We have to have a bill that says if a miner has worked in the mines two years or more and contracts lung disease, he is entitled to compensation." After Nader's letter was read, the gathering cheered through a resolution calling on Tony Boyle to come to West Virginia to support the Association's cause. After Buff had given the final speech, and got a standing ovation, the group adjourned to the steps of the Capitol Building not far away, where Sonny Wells led them in prayer for "a solution to human crisis in the kingdom of coal."

The Charleston rally was a big success, well attended, well publicized, and filled with the melodrama that seemed to give the movement its impetus. And this was a movement in every sense of the word. The Black Lung Association had no members, actually, except its officers. Instead, it had adherents and contributors who went about their chores on an ad-hoc basis. The meetings never had an agenda. Instead, Association officers usually consulted the doctors and Kaufman and then figured out some general plan of action or subject for discussion. These would then be put to the meetings in the form of resolutions or offered informally as suggestions, and would be accepted as policy depending upon how enthusiastically they were received. The Charleston rally marked the first time that elements of the movement from different parts of the coal fields were gathered under one roof, so that there was danger of disagreement or factiousness. Nothing of the sort occurred. Instead, there was a strong sense of conviviality and common purpose that seemed to be strengthened by the universal feeling of gratitude the miners had for the doctors. "We just can't let these doctors down," was a feeling that was frequently expressed at the meetings, and that was invariably greeted with applause and shouts of "Amen" and "That's right" from those assembled. By now, the miners had begun to appear with some of the typical accoutrements of a political campaign or movement. Many wore their white hard hats with skulls and crossbones emblazoned on each side. Others wore large red and black buttons with the numbers "78–4" printed on them. These referred to the seventy-eight men killed at Farmington and to four who had died in a flooded mine at Hominy Falls, West Virginia, six months earlier. An often repeated slogan of the crusade became: "Seventy-eight, four, how many more?" In addition, there were cut-out cardboard discs with black skull and crossbones and the words, "Stop Black Lung Murder!"

The Charleston rally, with the Nader letter, the challenge to Boyle to come to West Virginia, and the determination and solidarity among the miners that it demonstrated, seemed to infuriate the UMW hierarchy more than any previous event. The union officers responded with their crudest attempt yet to deflate the movement. They raised the dreaded charge of dual unionism. The seriousness of this accusation cannot be overestimated. John L. Lewis had used it ruthlessly in the days prior to passage of the Landrum-Griffin act to suppress dissent among the rank and file. In 1940, a miner from Lewis's home local in Springfield, Illinois, who headed a group called the "Autonomy and Self-Government Committee" that was pushing for the election of district officers, dared to oppose Lewis for the union presidency. At the convention in Cincinnati that year, Lewis had the challenger, Ray Edmundson, denied his seat and appointed a three-man committee to determine if he were guilty of dual unionism. Two days later, the convention ruled him off the ballot, and a short time later the International Executive Board convicted him and his supporters of dual unionism and kicked them out of the organization. It was a lesson that remained vividly clear to many veteran miners.

On January 29, three days after the Charleston rally, a letter went out to all local unions in District 17, which encompassed the Charleston area, the Kanawha Valley, as well as much of the mining area to the south, including Logan and Mingo counties. The letter instructed the members to get behind the UMW-sponsored legislation. Then came this paragraph:

> No doubt you are aware of the self-appointed group which is now sending letters to all local unions, not only in West Virginia but in Kentucky and Virginia, soliciting funds to pay an attorney $10,000 they are alleged to have hired to prepare a compensation bill. As working members of District 17, you are now paying an attorney to handle your legal affairs, under the compensation law, and some of the best legal minds in West Virginia had a part in preparing the UMWA bill, as stated above. Therefore, your local union has no authority to donate money from the treasury, to some unknown group which, in my opinion, is dual to the UMWA, to be used for any purpose they see fit.

The letter was signed by R. R. Humphreys, the aging president of District 17. The part about local unions lacking authority to donate money to the Black Lung Association was nonsense. Local unions have considerable independence and sovereignty under both the law and the union constitution. However, as UMW conventions clearly show, the union officers did not have any strong compunctions about the legality or constitutionality or their actions.

The Landrum-Griffin Act supposedly outlawed the kind of arbitrary action taken in 1940 by the Lewis administration against the autonomy activists. But many union members still felt they could trust neither the law nor the UMW constitution to deter the international officers from doing as they pleased. At the same time that Humphreys mailed his ominous letter to the miners in District 17, an incident was shaping up, just across the border in eastern Kentucky, that provides a clear example of the reason many miners felt such mistrust. The President of District 30, Carson Hibbitts, a devout Boyle supporter, was preparing to take action against a militant and popular local union president who had been a nuisance both to the district office and to the coal companies, often for the same reason. His name was John Thornsberry, but everyone around the tiny town of Melvin called him "Big Jim." He was a tall, broad-shouldered man with a leathery, ruddy face and short grey hair, who spoke in a rasping voice that made him sound older than his fifty or so years. Like Arnold Miller and others in the Black Lung Association, Thornsberry was an authentic leader among the rank and file, who would long since have been elected to international office in most other unions. He was the president of the huge thousand-man local at the Island Creek Coal Company mine in nearby Wheelwright, one of the largest mines in the state. Thornsberry had angered the district office by his actions during a wildcat strike that occurred while he was off the job suffering from lung trouble. The strike started in sympathy with a walkout at a nearby mine and it happened while big George Titler happened to be in the area. Titler was summoned to help end it. A meeting of Thornsberry's local was called so that a back-to-work vote could be taken. Thornsberry showed up at the meeting unexpectedly and got the floor. "Boys," he said, "these men are trying to take over my job, which is presiding over this local union. As far as I am concerned everything about this meeting is illegal and I hereby declare the meeting over." Thornsberry walked out and nearly every miner left with him except for a handful whose coziness with the company and the district officers had earned them the sobriquet "company sucks." Thornsberry then sent a small group of miners loyal to him back into the meeting to make sure Titler and company did not get a quorum and vote through a back-to-work resolution. Hibbitts was furious. On February 17, Thornsberry got a letter from the district president. It began as follows:

> It is necessary for the district organization to remove you from the office of president of local union 5899 because of violation of section 28, article 14 of the Constitution of the United Mine Workers of America and because of your failure to carry out the instructions of the international and district organizations.

If he had not been ill, Jim Thornsberry would have fought the district's action. But his lung problem appeared to be serious and he was afraid he would lose his medical benefits from the welfare and retirement fund if he made more trouble for the hierarchy. So he stepped down.

The section of the union constitution which Hibbitts had cited provided that no one could be eligible for local office who was "not employed in or around a coal mine, coal washeries, coke ovens or other such industries as may be designated as approved by the international executive board." Since Thornsberry was sick, he was deemed not working and the clause was invoked against him. Of course, the hierarchy had for years systematically ignored the six hundred or more locals composed *entirely* of inactive miners despite another section of the constitution requiring that a local be made up of ten or more men "working in or around a coal mine, etc." Hibbitts' action also flew in the face of another clause which required charges against local officers to be "first lodged with and prosecuted before the local union of which the alleged offender is a member." Not only was there no trial in Thornsberry's case, there was not even any notice of the charges.

If Humphreys had not waited as long as he did to raise the dual unionism charge, it might have had considerable impact. But the black lung activists had gone too far to be turned back. Too many miners had enlisted in the cause and, as many of them put it, "They can't kick us all out." So Humphrey's letter succeeded only in further convincing the aroused men that their union leaders were against them.

During the first week in February, the legislation drafted by the Black Lung Association was introduced in both houses of the West Virginia legislature. Delegate J. E. "Ned" Watson, chairman of the House Judiciary Committee, announced that six hours had been set aside on

February 11 for a special hearing on the bills before a joint meeting of the judiciary committees of both houses. It was an unprecedented amount of time for a single subject. Seven bills had been introduced on the subject and a variety of medical experts were expected to testify, including Dr. Jethro Gough, the Welsh chest specialist who was considered the world's leading authority on coal miner's lung disease. But if the legislature appeared ready to take major action on the black lung issue, there was little reason to hope it would enact anything even faintly resembling the law the Black Lung Association wanted.

The principal sticking point in the legislation the Association wanted was a so-called "presumptive clause." Under it, any miner with black lung symptoms after a few years underground could be presumed to have contracted the disease in the mines. This would eliminate the necessity of proving that the disease was work-related and thus overcome one of the main legal tactics employed by the coal companies to defeat compensation claims. The second controversial part of the Association's legislation was a liberal definition of pneumoconiosis that did not make the X-ray the last word. These clauses and others as well were certain to meet with stiff opposition from the industry and from the doctors who took its side in the debate.

Although things had changed a bit since the days when King Coal ran Governor Marland out of the state, it was still unwise to bet against the coal industry in a political fight it wanted to win badly, especially if the underdog did not have the support of a labor union. The coal industry had its key men in strategic positions throughout the political structure of West Virginia. Much of its lobbying was done by the prestigious Charleston law firm of Jackson, Kelly, Holt, and O'Farrell, which was considered the most politically influential law firm in West Virginia, and with good reason. Its partners included the clerks of both the House and Senate judiciary committees, which would pass upon the black lung legislation. It was the job of the clerks, of course, to interpret the various bills for the committee members and their recommendations could spell the success or failure of a piece of legislation. The firm also included Thomas Potter, the state Republican chairman, who was a member of the House of Delegates and was on the Judiciary Committee. More important than these men's jobs, however, was the size and experience of the firm. Its members had been operating in the hallways and backrooms of the Capitol for years. Some had served in the legislature. They were well-known and capable. They knew all the pitfalls and shortcuts involved in getting things done. And when they were representing the West Virginia Coal Association or one of their other coal industry clients, they had something else going for them—the traditional attitude of the West Virginia body politic that what was good for coal was good for the state. It wasn't a concept that everyone went around talking about. It was accepted as obvious, a part of the conventional wisdom of the state.

Of course, the legislature had some members who were more imbued with this concept than others. Such a man was House Judiciary Chairman Watson who, although he had no visible ties to the industry, happened to be the great-grandson of the founder of the Consolidation Coal Company. Another such man was a delegate, Harry Pauley of McDowell County, a coal operator considered one of the most reactionary men in the legislature, but someone who was regarded by many of his colleagues as the man to consult about issues involving coal. In the Senate, the industry could expect a sympathetic ear from Tracy Hylton, a Democrat from Wyoming County, a major coal area, who was a coal operator himself and vice-chairman of the Senate Committee on Mines and Mining. Others likely to take the corporate viewpoint were Lloyd Jackson, a drilling contractor and natural gas producer who was President of the Senate, and Carl Gainer, an oil company distributor who was a member of the Judiciary Committee.

The miners' chances of pulling an upset against this lineup might have been greatly improved by the assistance of the state's most promising young liberal politician—John D. (Jay) Rockefeller IV, the Secretary of State. Rockefeller, who was considered certain to be the next governor, had come to West Virginia to work in the poverty program and stayed to launch a political career as the only Democrat in his famous Republican family. After serving one term in the House of Delegates, Rockefeller made the race for Secretary of State in 1968 at the age of thirty. With his remarkably attractive wife, Sharon, daughter of Illinois Republican Senator Charles Percy, he campaigned tirelessly throughout the state for over a year. Standing six feet, six inches, with the distinguished good looks that seem to come naturally to the children of old money, Rockefeller was an enormous hit with the state's starstruck voters. As they had done with John F. Kennedy eight years earlier, the mountain people gave this newcomer affection instead of suspicion. He was elected by a two-to-one margin. This impressive display of vote-getting, coupled with the fact that everyone knew he had the resources to mount a high-powered campaign for himself and his friends and against his political opponents, gave Rockefeller influence in state affairs far beyond the rather limited responsibilities of his office. Most of the black lung activists expected he would be strongly on their side. But this was not to be. Nothing was heard from him until the Charleston rally, which he attended and to which made a $5 contribution. It was a gesture that seemed insulting to many of the miners. As Woodrow Mullins later put it, "I saw coal miners there with five little ragged kids who gave five dollars."

On the eve of the legislative hearing on the black lung bills, a stormy meeting was held in a conference room of the Daniel Boone Hotel in downtown Charleston. The UMW's George Titler had been dispatched to his home state to try to quench the fire of the upstart miners' movement. He organized the meeting in an effort to convince the black lung dissidents to drop their drive and support the union's bill—a general workmen's compensation reform measure drafted with the active assistance of the state AFL-CIO. Titler was joined at the session by George Burnett, the union's workmen's compensation lawyer, and James Leeber, one of its lobbyists. Representing the Black Lung Association were Kaufman, Dr. Rasmussen, Arnold Miller, and Charles Brooks. Also present was the eminent Dr. Gough who was accompanied by Dr. Murray Hunter, medical director of the Fairmont Clinic and one of the men most responsible for Gough's appearance at the hearing. The meeting began with Kaufman and Burnett reading their respective bills, and it quickly became an argument over which was better and stood the most chance of passage. At first it seemed that an agreement might be reached but the negotiation foundered over a provision sought by the miners abolishing the existing Silicosis Medical Board. This three-doctor panel was regarded by the miners hopelessly ignorant of pneumoconiosis and they wanted it abolished in favor of a new and better qualified Occupational Disease Board, which would review all disease cases. The UMW-AFL-CIO measure proposed merely to give the old silicosis board jurisdiction in black lung cases along with a new name. During the course of the debate, Dr. Gough felt compelled to speak up several times in favor of the Black Lung Association bill, and the wording of his comments made it clear that he was under the impression that Burnett was a lawyer for the coal companies. The meeting ended with no agreement and left the rebellious black lung activists as far apart as ever from their union officers.

The West Virginia State Capitol is a majestic building that belies the shabby brand of politics that has so often been practiced in its broad marble corridors and elegant chambers. Finished in 1932, the $10 million, buff limestone structure is part of a U-shaped complex of state buildings that occupy sixteen well-manicured acres on the banks of the Kanawha River at the edge of downtown Charleston. The building is modeled on the national capitol, long and rectangular with a bright blue and gold dome in the center. There are marble porticos at the top of long Roman stairways leading to both the front and rear entrances to the rotunda. The plush, red-carpeted Senate chamber is on the west side of the building with the larger but somewhat less luxurious House chamber at the opposite end of the hallway. Because a large crowd and an unusually long list of witnesses were expected, the House chamber was set aside for the hearing on black lung legislation.

Scores of miners jammed the galleries for the marathon session. Many of them wore their hard hats, and the buttons and signs that had appeared at the civic center rally were everywhere apparent. A few miners carried signs that said, "No law, no work," and a new button was inaugurated. "Tax coal," it said. Adding to the dramatics was a black coffin which a group of miners carried around in the corridor outside the chamber. In the hallways, others sang songs that echoed through the building. Inside the hearing, the audience cheered whenever a favorable witness scored a point and laughed triumphantly when one of their adversaries had trouble fielding a question. Most of the testimony was couched in such technical medical terminology that it was lost on both the legislators and the audience. But there were a few highlights that everyone understood.

One of these occurred after Dr. Rowland Burns of the Cabell County Medical Society had testified and was being questioned by Warren Mc-Graw, the young legislator from Wyoming County who had taken the miners' side. Burns had not impressed the Black Lung group with his Medical Society's resolution condemning the three doctors, and there was little in his testimony to change their minds. They were delighted when this exchange occurred:

MCGRAW: Dr. Burns, I would like to ask you a rather personal question and I believe it would be in order. I am rather curious to determine how much you have been paid by the coal association to testify in their behalf. [Laughter, applause, cheers.]

DR. BURNS: If you will ask my wife. . . .

CHAIRMAN WATSON: If the gallery desires to hear the rest of this testimony, they will remain quiet.

DR. BURNS: If you will ask my wife and if you will ask my associates who work for me and the people and the time that I have lost in my practice, I have not been paid near enough. I can't tell you exactly what I've been paid, but I've been paid for my opinion and for my time. . . .

Aside from giving the partisan audience something to cheer about, Burns's inept reply, with its acknowledgment that he was a paid witness, discredited him and his position in the eyes of the legislators. This gain for the miners was probably offset by the performance of Dr. Buff, who was regarded as a publicity hound and a crackpot by most of the legislative old guard. Buff had the chamber darkened for his testimony, which was accompanied by a series of slides showing lungs in various stages of deterioration from coal-dust damage. When a badly blackened and punctured lung section appeared on the screen, Buff gave this narrative in his scornful, twangy tones:

This is a black lung. It don't work. It is half-dead. Let's not use fancy terms we don't understand. Let's call hardening of the arteries hardening of the arteries instead of arteriosclerosis. . . . Who are you trying to fool? This is a black lung. I don't care whether it is scientific or not. But ninety-nine percent of the people don't know what you are talking about when you say pneumoconiosis. They don't even know how to spell it. This is dust around an artery in the lung. Look at it. There are some people that says this is just mechanical obstruction, it's nothing. . . . I want to say that General Benecort in 1794 addressing the Continental Congress said, 'Figures don't lie, but liars figure.' I want you members of the committee to remember this because this is a bunch of humbug. It was paid for by the West Virginia Coal Association. . . .

Don Rasmussen's testimony was different. It seemed to impress the legislators. After his prepared statement stressing the high percentage of disability from lung problems among coal miners compared with the rest of the nation's work force, Rasmussen introduced two disabled miners. "I would like to introduce to you," he said, "two coal miners who actually have the frustrations of many more miners in West Virginia: Mr. Evans."

> EVANS: I am a forty-eight-year-old coal miner. I worked in the coal mines twenty-eight years, equivalent to about thirty on extra duties and I became sick on December the ninth, 1966. I haven't been able to recover for many reasons and I have misery in my chest and I have difficulty breathing and I cannot bend over to do any good at all, my breath will be cutting off and I am not able to do any types of work.
>
> RASMUSSEN: How much smoking did you do, Mr. Evans?
>
> EVANS: I am not a cigarette smoker or a tobacco user.
>
> RASMUSSEN: Have you applied for workmen's compensation benefits?
>
> EVANS: I have applied for workmen's compensation benefits during the time I was drawing social security disable benefits, the only thing that I have to survive on now, and I was granted a complete, perfect bill of health by the Board of Directors in the Workmen's Compensation.

A second miner introduced by Rasmussen explained that he also had been turned down for compensation. He was asked if he had difficulty breathing. "Yes, sir. I do. It's practically all the time that I can't hardly breathe and I get so weak from it, it seems like it just pulls me plumb down, night and day." Had he ever smoked?, he was asked. "Not as I can remember. I never smoked a cigarette in my life, a whole cigarette."

Dr. Rasmussen seemed to make a strong impression, and his testimony received strong corroboration from several other highly qualified witnesses, including Dr. Gough. The first was Dr. Eugene Pendergass, known as the "Dean of American Radiology." Most of his testimony was highly technical, but under questioning this point came through with clarity:

"Do I understand that you feel that X-ray is a necessary tool, but not necessarily conclusive," Pendergass was asked.

"Yes, sir, that's exactly it," he replied.

This opinion, of course, was in line with Rasmussen's view that the X-ray could not be depended upon for diagnosis of disability in pneumoconiosis cases and it could hardly have come from a more authoritative source. The same view was expressed by Dr. Leon Cander, head of the University of Texas at San Antonio's Department of Physiology and Internal Medicine, who had previously examined scores of coal miners in Pennsylvania. "I would like to emphasize," he said, "the terribly important fact that it is exposure to the coal dust that is the important thing. If you do not see significant changes on the X-ray, this should not surprise us too much."

Most of Dr. Gough's testimony was couched in medical language too recondite for the committee or the audience. There was one critical point that caused Rasmussen to rejoice, although it was missed by nearly all the legislators. Dr. Gough said, "So this simple pneumoconiosis is not necessarily a fatal disease; but it's a disabling disease." It was on this issue that Rasmussen and most of the rest of the medical community, particularly Keith Morgan and his Public Health Service team from Morgantown, had their sharpest differences, and here was the world's leading authority on miners' lung disease stating his unequivocal agreement with the Beckly group. One legislator understood its importance clearly. He was Ivor Boiarsky, a dour, impatient millionaire bank president and lawyer who had recently been elected Speaker of the House of Delegates in a close race with Watson. Boiarsky, nicknamed "Sweet Ivor" because of his perpetual frown and unpleasant disposition, had not been inclined to be sympathetic to the miners' clamor for changes in what was generally considered a liberal workmen's compensation law. But he was intelligent and honest and, while no flaming liberal, could be counted on to act on conviction. He considered Buff and Wells "eccentrics," but thought Rasmussen was "a cut above," as he put it. "At the hearing," he later said, "it became apparent that these people had a case. It's a damned dangerous occupation and it seemed that this disease was hard to prove and I began to think that maybe the presumption should be changed." Boiarsky's conversion was an important victory for the miners, and one that they had no way of knowing they had won, for Boiarsky kept his thoughts to himself. In West Virginia, the Speaker of the House appoints all committee chairmen and also selects the members of the conference committees which iron out differences between legislation passed by both houses on the same subject.

Contributing to the speaker's change of mind was the fact that Keith Morgan did not make a good showing on behalf of his research group from Morgantown. Tense, rigid, with a dignified British manner that suggested arrogance, Morgan seemed to be struggling to retain his composure throughout much of his testimony. He was unable to disguise his dislike for Buff and the Beckley group, which scarcely lent credibility to his insistence that he was an objective scientist with no axes to grind. "I would like to suggest to you before any firm legislation comes out that you consult some impartial group to advise you on the facts," he said. "I don't think today's display has been impartial and I'm not selecting one particular side or the other. I can only—well, I'll forget that part. [Laughter] I'll only say—on second thoughts I won't. . . ."

Later Morgan was questioned closely by Odell Huffman, a freshman delegate from Mercer County, a coal region along the Virginia border. Huffman had done considerable homework, and tried through his questions to establish that even small amounts of coal dust could seriously damage the lung. This was an effort to destroy the myth that "simple" pneumoconiosis was, as many West Virginia doctors thought, a benign condition. The question Huffman posed to several of the medical witnesses was deceptively tricky but no one tripped over it as badly as Morgan. Huffman asked if coal dust retained in the lung "in less than suffocating quantities" was injurious. "That is a very difficult question," blurted Morgan, as the audience burst out laughing. Morgan then proceeded to give an inconclusive answer. During all of this, Huffman had in front of him an American Medical Association publication that contained an article citing Dr. Gough as authority for the very position he was trying to get Morgan to embrace. Before confronting Morgan with it, Huffman questioned him on whether this obviously respected publication was authoritative. Sensing that he was about to be mousetrapped, Morgan tried to avoid being led any farther. "You will agree," said Huffman, "that this is recognized in your field as being a source of information and authority on diseases. Is this correct?"

"Sometimes," said Morgan. "Sir I have very few principles [laughter], but one of them is not to answer hypothetical questions. The questions you are asking me are equivalent to saying do I beat my wife. The answer, of course is yes. . . ."

At this blooper, the miners in the gallery exploded with laughter that drowned out the rest of Morgan's answer. Huffman continued to bore in, finally cornering Morgan and getting him to endorse the portion of the medical journal article which Huffman had quoted for the record. He then put the original question to Morgan again, knowing that the doctor had to answer it affirmatively or contradict himself. Again, Morgan tried unsuccessfully to worm free.

"And you agree, then," said Huffman, "that coal dust of itself, pure carbon coal dust, is injurious to the lung when taken in less than suffocating quantities?"

The miners chuckled wickedly at the question, knowing that Morgan was trapped. "Sir, I answered that," the doctor said. "It produces respiratory impairment and it produces, in some instances, well—I don't know what to say. . . ."

"I want you to say what you were about to say, Doctor," said Huffman sweetly.

"Well, I would like to ask you to define a suffocating quantity," Morgan said.

"Doctor," said Huffman with an edge of sarcasm, "I would prefer that you use language with which at least you are quite familiar. In your own terms, and elaborating upon it as you may wish, you may accept the word 'suffocating' and explain it however you may wish, but it is you and not I that is expected to answer questions on this occasion."

"Sir," said the beleaguered Morgan, "I have done my best to answer them honestly. The answer to that is that any form of coal dust should be averted where possible, but I don't think it is going to gain any useful end. The absolute way of preventing any inhalation of coal dust is to shut down every mine in West Virginia. . . ."

Now Morgan had made himself look foolish and biased as well. The legislation at hand dealt with compensation, not dust suppression and the issue of mines closing was not remotely relevant. That this was a matter of major concern to Morgan when he was under rigorous questioning tended to lend credence to Buff's charge that the Morgantown research team was too cozy with the industry. Huffman could have gone farther in his questioning, but the job was clearly done.

For all the confusion, the hearing was considered a victory by the Black Lung Association. Even the Charleston *Gazette*, which only a few months earlier had been urging Dr. Buff to shut up, editorialized the next morning about the need for action. "Pneumoconiosis as an occupational disease has been brushed under the rug for too long," the editorial said. "The time is long overdue, in our opinion, for the West

Virginia Legislature to see that justice is done in this particular problem." House Judiciary Chairman Watson promised that his committee would report a bill early the next week. It was a promise the miners took literally. When the following Monday passed with no bill reported, they became restive.

On Tuesday, a week after the hearing, there was still no bill. There was angry talk at the mines. These men were both suspicious of the legislature and, at the same time, naive enough about it to expect promises to the public to be kept with punctuality. On Wednesday, the miners' uneasiness was abruptly translated into mass action. A dispute between a group of miners and their superintendent at the East Gulf mine not far from Beckley had led to a wildcat strike on Tuesday. When the leaders of the four hundred to five hundred men who left their jobs were asked the reason for their action, they said it was because of the legislature's delay in passing a black lung compensation bill. By late Wednesday, the strike had spread to fourteen other mines in the area, and the misstated rationale of the original protest had become the accepted cause of the growing wildcat. By the weekend, twelve thousand miners were off the job in five counties and the strike was still growing.

The leaders of the Black Lung Association were caught short. A strike had always remained the miners' ace in the hole, but playing it before it was certain which way the legislature would move seemed rash and premature. A jittery Ken Hechler released a statement in Washington, declaring that "I don't believe that endless, bitter, and disorganized strikes and walkouts will either solve the problem or result in good legislation." This only made things worse, because it seemed to many miners, and to the three doctors as well, to have the aroma of betrayal. In Charleston, Paul Kaufman was careful not to endorse the strike, calling it a "mistake," but coupling this with a pointed explanation that the miners felt the legislature was too industry-dominated to be trusted to produce a fair bill unless pressure was applied. At the Capitol, House Judiciary Chairman Watson was trying to milk the adverse public reaction to the strike for all it was worth. "If you look real hard," he said, "you will see that people on the federal payroll are behind it. The same kind of rabble rousers who have been causing all the other problems of which we're all aware for a great number of years. . . . If you want to know who I'm talking about, I'm talking about VISTA workers. They tell these people, 'you strike, you demonstrate,' and we'll get a benefit. But do they really care for the welfare of the people of the state?" This was the familiar, political line, blaming outside forces for local strife. It had been used countless times before in West Virginia and it had usually worked. But this time, Watson would find the miners had not needed VISTA workers or anyone else to tell them what to do, and that they didn't take kindly to being told they did. A more moderate reaction came from Speaker Boiarsky, who told members of the Black Lung Association, "I promise you a bill will come out. I won't promise you it will be as strong as you would like, or as weak as the coal operators would like. I think it will be a reasonable compromise."

On Saturday, meetings were held across the strikebound southern section of the state. At some, there was talk of sending roving pickets out into the northern coal fields to close the mines there. At other gatherings, the men talked of a massive march on the Capitol. Among the leaders of the movement, there was consternation. The strike had started unexpectedly and spread spontaneously. Now the issue had been forced and they had to decide on some course of action. Encouraging the strike would risk public opprobrium that might enable the legislature to claim it was being blackjacked and to refuse to pass any bill. But urging the miners to go back to work was equally risky. For one thing, it might not work. This would destroy the solidarity that had been the movement's strength. If the men did go back, the movement might just fizzle out thereafter, taking the heat off the legislature and opening the way for a weak bill. It was a knotty dilemma. A rally had been scheduled for Sunday afternoon in the tiny, worked-out coal town of Affinity, not far from Beckley. As the three doctors met at the Rasmussen home that morning, they knew their movement was facing its first crisis.

The narrow back road that leads to the old frame union hall at Affinity was lined with parked cars for nearly a mile when the doctors arrived. The building itself was already filled to capacity. Men were sitting on window sills and standing six deep in the rear of the hall. Dozens of others, unable to squeeze in, crowded around the windows outside to hear the meeting. Still more were grouped in knots in the dirt parking lot, which was crammed with cars. It was a dreary, chill, February day, but there was no sign that the weather had dampened the spirits of the miners. They shouted friendly greetings to the doctors as they made their way toward the building from their distant parking spots. As they entered the hall and edged through the crowd to the tiny platform at the front, a cheer went up. The doctors had set out for the meeting with no clear idea of what course they would urge the men to follow. But the size and mood of the crowd made it clear that there could be no backward steps.

It was an extraordinary meeting. The huge attendance made it necessary for each speaker to climb out a rear window to repeat his remarks to the overflow crowd waiting outside. Buff began with a characteristically demagogic appeal to the miners' pride, telling them what contempt the coal executives and the politicians had for them. "At the joint Judiciary Committee hearing," shouted Buff in his abrasive nasal tones, "they didn't want dirty old coal miners sitting on the first floor. Oh, they let three or four sit there, but the rest they put upstairs. Back-door business." Buff urged the men to fight for their version of the black lung legislation, telling them it was "the only answer." He finished by saying, "Are you slave or free? If you want to be free, from now on you go in the front door, no more back doors."

Don Rasmussen spoke next. He explained why the Judiciary hearing had been a scientific triumph for the miners' cause. The men listened intently, grasping his general message if not the specific medical details. By the time Sonny Wells got the floor, the crowd was warmed up.

"I didn't counsel this strike," said Wells, his youthful face a picture of determination, "and I didn't advise it. But in my judgment there's never been a strike that's more justified. [Shouts of "that's right," "amen," cheers.] You can call it a police action if you want to, or vacation, or sick leave, or blue flu [laughter]. But I'll tell you, you've heard of what we used to call the double shaft, well, you've had the triple shaft [more laughter, cheering]. You're not only getting it from your legislators and the companies, but I want to know where is the union? Where is the leadership. . . ."

At the mention of the union, a few men shouted "yeah" and "amen," but as Wells tried to continue, the reaction spread. Men jumped to their feet shouting angrily in agreement with Wells. The uproar continued for several moments before he could resume.

"Mr. Titler told me personally that he was behind this legislation all the way. Now what does all the way mean? You've come out all the way. You've done everything you can do [shouts of "right," "yeah," cheers]. Now where is he? That's what I want to know [more cheers]."

Ted Stacy, a local member of the House of Delegates, followed with assurances that a bill would pass soon. He got polite applause. Next came Warren McGraw, the fiery young delegate from Wyoming County whose questioning had forced Dr. Burns to admit his financial relationship with the industry during the legislative hearing. McGraw, a good speaker, had supported the miners from the start and they knew it.

"I was advised on the floor of the House on Friday, for public consumption, that by Wednesday the chairman of the Judiciary Committee expects to deliver to the floor of the House of Delegates a bill covering black lung. Now, I hope this is so. At least it was said publicly and I'm not saying anything to you that hasn't already been said. And I'm not applying any pressure, as I have been accused of attempting to do, and as you are accused of doing now. But, gentlemen, if it's pressure that it takes, then, by God, put it where it counts. . . ."

McGraw delivered this punch line with flawless timing and it brought the men to their feet, roaring their approval. When the noise died down, McGraw went on, with a slight twinkle in his eye.

"As Dr. Wells said, I haven't counseled with you on your strike. I'm not saying to continue it or discontinue it. But I'll tell you this. You never got anything without asking for it and without flexing your muscles."

The doctors and McGraw made good speeches, but those that seemed to move the miners most were given by their fellow workers, particularly Charles Brooks, the mild-mannered Negro who headed the Black Lung Association, and Ernest Riddle, the organization's treasurer.

"After hearing such good statements from the more educated people," Brooks began quietly, "it's hard for me to speak to you. . . . This is the first time that the coal miner has ever come out and asked for anything. Everything that you've ever got in the past years your union has said, 'Well, let's help our fellows out there in the field that's feeling hungry.' But this time the coal miner is asking for something for himself. So, as Mr. McGraw just stated, if it takes pressure to get this done, put pressure where it belongs. Now, as President of my local union, I can't tell my men to strike. You know that. But if it takes pressure, put it where it belongs. Now if you men want to go on vacation, I'm with you a hundred percent. Every man from my local union can tell you that. If you're wrong and you think you're right, I'm still with you."

Brooks' remarks drew a combination of laughter and loud applause. He was followed by Ernest Riddle. A short, stocky, bald man whose rimless glasses seemed out of character, Riddle could not write a coherent letter. But like many of his fellow miners, he could be remarkably eloquent in speech. "We have a Constitution," he said, "which backs us up in expressing our freedom of thought, either by tongue or by pen. And we would especially appreciate it if each and every one would take the time to write their Congressmen and their legislators down here. Call 'em on the phone. Keep 'em up at night if you have to. But write them and ask for their support. Now, I got here late. Incidentally, I couldn't get in here for close to a mile on account of the traffic [laughter]. I didn't know there were so many people back in here [more laughter]. We appreciate every bit of support, we appreciate everything we see today. And we know that everybody that's got a father—each and every one of you—when Dad comes home in the evening and he can't breathe, you know what's a hurtin him ["yes, sir," "that's right"]. And a woman that's living with a man and seeing him slowly die, nobody has to tell her. Nobody has to explain to them babies what was wrong with Daddy that he couldn't get his breath at night. Some of you were little then, and maybe you've grown up now, and you know what was bothering Dad.

"Living in what is supposed to be a civilized country, a country that's capable of sending missiles around the moon and taking snapshots of it, a country that's capable of sending a little machine, landing it on the moon and sending radio signals to it to tell it what they want it to do, which size do you want to take a sample of, picking it up and taste it, see what it is. But we can't define black lung. There's something wrong somewhere, boys [laughter, clapping, shouts of "amen"].

"Men, to make a long story short, I appreciate seeing all of these men out here today in support and expressing your appreciation for these doctors. I've only got an eighth grade education. I ain't got much to lose, buddy. They done wore out everything that I have. These coal companies done wore out everything I have and what they ain't wore out they plugged up. Now, I think there is a time and a place for everything, as the Bible says, and I think we have come to the crossroads where we must take a stand and put up a fight for what is ours, what is justly ours. I thank every one of you [prolonged, loud applause]."

Aside from the enthusiasm of the crowd of more than 1,200, there were other signs that the miners intended to see their cause through. Both Wells and Rasmussen mentioned House Judiciary Chairman Watson's comments attributing the strike to the VISTAs. The miners snickered sardonically. When the meeting ended, no resolutions had been passed, no formal plans made. But general agreement had somehow been reached that there would be a mass meeting at the Civic Center in Charleston on Wednesday, possibly to be followed by a march on the Capitol. Most of the men felt that this would be the time, if no bill had appeared, to appeal directly to the newly inaugurated Republican Governor, Arch Moore, for action, since he had promised to press for black lung compensation in his first message to the legislature.

In the brief interlude between the Affinity rally and the planned mass gathering in Charleston, the strike continued to spread, with more and more of the mines in the northern part of the state closing down. The coal operators tried frantically to get the men back to work. Full-page newspaper ads were taken, urging the miners to "respect the terms of the contract" and calling on the UMW leadership to get the men back on the job. Nothing could have been more futile. The strike was far beyond the reach of any appeals from the coal companies and it was not likely to be stopped by pressure from the union hierarchy, which had had a major role in causing it, but no role in leading it.

Dozens of striking miners crowded the corridors of the Capitol and jammed the galleries on Monday and Tuesday. They hovered outside the closed doors of the House Judiciary Committee and buttonholed its members as they came and went. More than once, alert miners caught members of the committee giving misleading reports on what was happening as the black lung bill was being debated. The miners were getting information from maintenance men who entered the conference room to clean up and overheard the discussion. Most of the Capitol maintenance crew were former coal miners. Their sympathies were with the strikers.

On Tuesday, Ernest Riddle barged into Governor Moore's press conference demanding to know why millions could be spent on welfare but not enough on black lung. Moore, taken aback, replied that he was deeply interested in the miners' cause. "That's the reason we voted for you," retorted Riddle. Moore said he felt the miners were in "good hands" on the black lung issue.

The same day, another group of miners met with Judiciary Chairman Watson and demanded to know if he had any financial interest in the coal industry. Watson told them that his family once had, but that he had none himself.

By late Tuesday, the strike had idled about thirty thousand men, nearly three-quarters of the state's miners. Officials said nearly half the mines in the northern part of the state had closed. Busloads and carfuls of men, women, and children headed for Charleston Wednesday morning for the rally, scheduled for two in the afternoon.

When the meeting began, more than two thousand persons were present, including Representative Hechler, whose first reaction to the strike—urging the men to go back to work—had caused many of the men to regard him with suspicion. Hechler won them over, however, by acknowledging that he had been wrong. He contributed a $1,000 check to the Black Lung Association. "Don't forget," Hechler said, "I'm the original 'fink' labeled by the national United Mine Workers leadership because I suggested the UMW wasn't doing enough to help you. By the way, how much is the UMW leadership doing to help you with this strike?"

"Nothing!" roared the crowd.

This was not the only sign of bitterness toward the union leaders. As the meeting broke up, amid pledges that the strike would continue until a satisfactory bill was passed, the miners grouped outside the Civic Center to march on the Capitol. Many of the men had brought their children with them. One boy wore a sign which read, "My daddy is a coal miner. He needs protection." Others wore the familiar "78–4" buttons and had their hard hats emblazoned with a variety of slogans. Some carried signs denoting the number of their local union. As they began their slow, four-abreast procession through downtown Charleston to the Capitol, they waved their signs and shouted and whistled to passers-by, many of whom returned the greeting. Along the wide stretch of Kanawha Boulevard, which runs the length of the city next to the river, the men were hailed from upstairs windows by hundreds of well-wishers.

The procession seemed jovial until it passed the impressive red-brick converted residence that served as District 17 headquarters of the UMW. There was no sign of life in the building as the miners approached. No one was at the windows to watch the marchers pass, and the shades were drawn. A few miners shouted epithets as they passed; others shook their fists. The cry was taken up down the line, and produced a chorus of angry shouts and gestures as the procession passed the building. But there was no visible reaction.

By the time the miners approached the Capitol, Governor Moore was waiting for them. He knew they were coming. Indeed, many of them had visited the Capitol earlier in the day to check on the progress of their legislation. Their continuous mass presence had already provoked some grumbling among the regular lobbyists who were not used to competing with crowds of rank-and-file citizens for the attention of the legislators or the choice seats in the galleries. One was overheard complaining that, "I don't think you can push the legislature this way." This comment sparked an exchange with another man, who replied, "Who's doing the pushing? These are the people and these legislators were elected to serve the people."

Another prime topic of conversation in the Capitol corridors was Delegate Watson's charge that the strike was started by the VISTAs. Black Lung Association President Brooks's response to a newsman's question about it was, "He is a liar. VISTA people have nothing to do with it." Added another miner, disgustedly, "Watson thinks we miners don't have any sense. He thinks we are a dumb bunch."

Arch Moore, a stocky, fleshy man with white hair and a booming voice, addressed the miners from a rostrum set up on the Capitol steps. He told them he was sympathetic to their cause and promised that if no black lung bill passed the legislature, which then had only a week to go, he would introduce one of his own during a special session he planned for the summer. Moore, however, had misjudged the mood of the men. His promise was greeted with angry shouts of "No, no, we want it now." He then protested that he had no vote in the legislature and could only wait upon action by the Senators and Delegates, an explanation regarded skeptically by many of the miners, who knew well the importance of pressure from the governor in enacting legislation of any kind. The governor concluded the impromptu meeting by proclaiming, "If this matter is paramount in your minds, it is also paramount in mine."

By late that afternoon the House Judiciary Committee had reported a black lung bill. At first it was hailed by some legislators as a triumph for the miners. But Paul Kaufman quickly spotted numerous loopholes and decided the bill was full of mischief. In some ways, he concluded, the measure left miners worse off than they were under the existing system. It required, for example, that a man have worked ten years in the mines in order to be compensated for any kind of lung disease. Under the existing law, a miner who could prove he had silicosis could be compensated regardless of how long he had worked in the mines. The bill also limited compensation to men who inhaled dust, thereby removing the possibility of an award for lung disease caused by smoke, fumes or other underground elements which could contribute to the deterioration of the lungs.

That night in his office, Kaufman met with the leaders of the Black Lung Association, a number of its most active members, and the three doctors. He stood on a chair in the crowded waiting room and gave the group his analysis of the bill. They were shocked and angered. Dr. Wells became so upset that he grabbed his coat and stalked out of the meeting, declaring the bill a lost cause. Kaufman, however, urged a more rational approach. He proposed trying to have the bill amended significantly on the House floor. This would require the consent of the mighty House Rules Committee, which was normally reluctant to allow a bill to be rewritten on the floor. Although deeply discouraged and outraged by the House action, the group agreed to let Kaufman try his plan.

The next morning, the Association issued a statement denouncing the bill. "By mistake, mischief, or malice," it said, "the House of Delegates Judiciary Committee has turned out a workmen's compensation bill that does credit only to the West Virginia Coal Association. This atrocity is an insult to the miners who have worked hard and sacrificed much to obtain decent legislation." Not surprisingly, the coal association was busy pretending the bill was disastrous for the industry. Stephen Young, the youthful vice-president of the association, told reporters the bill's presumptive clause, which was far weaker than the one sought by the miners, was "extremely dangerous." He blamed the committee action on "irresponsible statements by certain doctors," which he said left the impression that "a black plague is loose in West Virginia."

Kaufman, meanwhile, went to see his friend Boiarsky, who, as Speaker of the House, was also chairman of the Rules Committee. He asked the speaker to allow him to appear before the committee to explain why the miners felt the bill was deficient. Although such dispensations were seldom granted, Boiarsky agreed. Kaufman made a fifteen-minute presentation to the committee which analyzed the provisions of the bill and the reasons the miners opposed it. He urged the committee to allow the legislation to be extensively revised on the House floor. The committee agreed, but Sonny Wells nearly ruined this opportunity when he went before an open meeting of the Judiciary Committee and angrily suggested that its members had been bribed by the coal companies. He said rumors to that effect were widespread and added, "The facts speak for themselves. What has the committee been doing for three weeks? I'm not saying you were bought off. I'm saying the tactics of delay are the tactics of defeat and you'll have to answer for it."

Chairman Watson was furious. He was not mollified by Wells's subsequent remark that "I am a little emotional and probably a little insulting to you gentlemen." Watson angrily asserted that no bill had ever received more attention in his fifteen years in the legislature. He said the miners had been whipped into an emotional pitch by "a few doctors and a bologna-waving Congressman," whose principal concern was personal publicity. Later, he took the House floor to complain that he and other members of his committee had been "taunted and badgered on all sides."

Nevertheless, when the black lung bill reached the House floor the following day, Friday, a host of amendments were passed making it a near replica of the legislation the miners' group had introduced. The only amendment defeated was a measure to restore to miners their right to sue their employers for injuries caused by gross negligence. This would have drastically changed the entire concept of workmen's compensation, whereby the worker trades his right to sue for the right to compensation, regardless of blame. Although the House was in a mood to help the miners, it was not prepared to revolutionize the entire system. When the bill, with all its amendments, came to a vote, it sailed through, ninety-four to one. The lone dissenting vote was cast by John Bobbitt, a doctor, who said before the roll call that he opposed the bill because it would encourage "chicanery" among lawyers and doctors. When he saw the final tally on the electric board behind the Speaker's rostrum, however, he realized that he was all alone in opposition. The miners in the gallery were snickering. He signaled the Speaker that he wanted to change his vote. The official total then became ninety-five to none.

Kaufman and the legislators who supported the miners' cause felt passage of the strong bill by the House was crucial. They had little hope that a measure favorable to the miners would pass the Senate, which was by far the more conservative of the two bodies. Indeed, among the ninety-five who voted for the bill in the House were some who opposed it but decided to avoid political trouble with the coal miners by voting for it in the certain knowledge that no such measure would ever get through the Senate.

The coal operators, aware that the Senate was already deliberating its version of the bill, made a show of outrage at the House action. Up to now, coal association vice-president Stephen Young had been doing the operators' official talking. But for the purpose of denouncing the black lung bill, the president, Quinn Morton, was brought into action. Young had termed the original, committee version of the bill "social legislation." In Morton's eyes, the version that passed was not merely "social legislation" but "galloping socialism." He said the bill "could go down in infamy as one of the blackest days in the industrial history of West Virginia." He added, "It appears to be a classic example of bowing to pressure from mass demonstrators with total disregard for sound reasoning and medical facts. . . . It is a bill founded on sensationalism and irresponsibility, nurtured on emotionalism and passed under a gallery of pressure with total disregard of proven medical facts."

In the Senate, the man with the most to say about the black lung bill was William T. Brotherton, Jr., the chairman of the Judiciary Committee. A short, rotund man with a bespectacled baby face that made him look considerably younger than his forty-three years, Brotherton had been in the legislature since 1952 and was a wily politician. As a gesture to the miners in his Kanawha County district, Brotherton had introduced the Black Lung Association's bill in the Senate. This, as it turned out, had no bearing on his ultimate position on the issue.

Although he was less conservative than many of the other powers in the Senate, Bill Brotherton did not find the mass-action approach of the Black Lung crusaders appealing or convincing. As he later explained it, "The miners said, 'Just pass it and let everyone who has a cough get paid. Then they'll do something about safety.' There was a threatening attitude. It reached the point where some of the legislators thought they might be bodily harmed." Brotherton felt that the publicity and the strike had created a supercharged political atmosphere in which many legislators were being railroaded into going along with the miners without waiting to see if they were right. To assure that this did not happen in his committee, Brotherton held a special closed-door hearing on miners' lung disease with the three members of the State Silicosis Medical Board. It did not matter to Brotherton that these doctors had shown abysmal ignorance of pneumoconiosis for years and that they had examined countless afflicted coal miners who were mistakenly applying for silicosis benefits and turned them down without ever realizing they had a serious lung impairment. Brotherton was personally devoted to two of the doctors, William Stewart and James Walker, who had seen him through a successful bout with cancer; understandably, he had high regard for their judgment. "Dr. Walker and Dr. Stewart are friends of mine," he later said. "They're my doctors."

Walker and Stewart convinced Brotherton and most of his committee that the presumptive clause considered so important by the miners was unwise. Pneumoconiosis is diagnosable, the doctors contended, and compensation awards for it should not be based on presumption. "My feeling on the legislation evolved from the doctors on the compensation board," Brotherton said. "And their attitude was that the only way you could diagnose pneumoconiosis was by X-ray. The House bill would have meant that if a man had been in the mines ten years and he was coughing, he had pneumoconiosis and you didn't need a doctor's diagnosis." Although Brotherton knew it might be politically costly to oppose the miners on so explosive an issue, he was convinced they were wrong and he disliked their tactics. He resolved to see that the legislation reported by his committee conformed to the advice of the doctors he had consulted in secret.

The black lung bill that the Senate Judiciary Committee brought to the floor, was radically different from the House version. The definition of pneumoconiosis, loosely written in the House bill because of the difficulty of making a foolproof diagnosis, had been tightened to make an X-ray the key factor in recognizing the disease. And the presumptive clause, although it required a man to have worked only two of the past ten years in the mines, was nonetheless tied to a precise diagnosis and was therefore virtually worthless in the eyes of the miners. Senator Neal Kinsolving attempted to amend the bill on the floor, but his move, while applauded by miners in the gallery, was beaten twenty-eight to five. The Judiciary Committee version then passed, thirty-four to nothing.

The Senate action came on Wednesday, and while it was no surprise to the miners, it was still a blow, because the legislative session was now nearly over. It would end officially at midnight Saturday. Three days were precious little time to iron out the gaping differences in the House and Senate versions of the bill. The miners were discouraged but still determined. Said one, as he descended the stairway from the gallery where he had watched the Senate vote, "Okay, let the Senate mine the coal."

The next crucial matter was the makeup of the five-member conference committees appointed to represent each house. The Senate committee would be led—and undoubtedly dominated—by Brotherton. Although there was a possibility that a couple of Senators friendly to the miners' cause might be appointed, little help could be expected from them because their assigned task in the conference would be to uphold the Senate version of the bill. The only hope was that the House committee would be strongly on the miners' side. The job of appointing the House committee fell to Speaker Boiarsky, who announced after the Senate vote on Wednesday that he would make his choices the following day. He was under heavy pressure. The coal industry by this time had its best lobbyists on the job. Among them were H. Laban White, who had been Speaker of the House before Boiarsky but who left the legislature to make an unsuccessful race for Congress. Afterwards, he returned to private life. Another key industry agent was Julius Singleton, also a former House Speaker, who had become the chief lobbyist for the West Virginia Coal Association. In addition, the association's top two officers, Young and Morton, plus other staff lawyers and lobbyists from individual companies, had been sent to Charleston to put out the fire. As Cleo Jones, the mild-mannered Republican delegate from Kanawha County who was to play a key role in the conference, later put it, "We were really bombarded by lobbyists. I never knew the industry had so many. They were just all over the place." Boiarsky got separate dinner invitations from six lobbyists on Wednesday. He turned them all down.

For Ivor Boiarsky, the decision on the conference committee appointments was one of the toughest of his first term as Speaker. A lawyer and bank president who cherished orderly, businesslike procedure, he did not want it to appear that he was stampeded by public pressure and fuss into going along with the miners. Yet he was personally sympathetic to their cause and had been convinced by the medical testimony that their position was essentially right. Kaufman was urging him to appoint Robert Nelson to head the conference committee. Nelson, a Democrat from Huntington who acted as Ken Hechler's administrative assistant when the legislature was out of session, was on the Judiciary Committee and had been the sponsor of the Black Lung Association Bill as well as one of its most persuasive advocates. The coal operators, on the other hand, wanted Chairman Watson to head the committee. Boiarsky resolved this dilemma by deciding to name neither to the committee. "I had a judiciary chairman who was known to be friendly to the coal operators," Boiarsky later explained, "and another member of the committee [Nelson] who was a top protagonist for the miners. I agonized for a long time. I felt I should name a strong committee that would represent the House position."

Boiarsky's choices could hardly have been more surprising. All were freshmen, except Republican Cleo Jones, a second-termer. The chairman was Robert Dinsmore, a twenty-nine-year-old member from Morgantown, who was the youngest of the five. "Dinsmore was a first-termer," Boiarsky explained, "but he is bright and I knew he was like me and would agonize over the bill." He summoned the five to his blue-carpeted office off the House floor. "I'm not going to tell you what to do," he said, "but I hope that you will uphold the House position. Before you sign the conference report, come in and tell me."

Paul Kaufman was disappointed with the choices. Why hadn't Boiarsky chosen Bob Nelson and Warren McGraw? he wanted to know. Ned Watson and the coal operators were also displeased. "The operators gave me hell," Boiarsky recalled. "Watson gave me hell. They said I had stacked the deck."

Although the House conferees favored the miners' position, there was considerable doubt that they could hold the line in a showdown with the more experienced Senate group. A legislative conference committee is essentially an eleventh-hour bargaining session in which both sides trade concessions. The impetus for compromise is the political imperative of reporting legislation of some kind. A politician who can work his will in a conference usually must have considerable experience and the ability to bluff convincingly and make it appear that he is giving away more than he is when he makes a trade.

When Friday passed with no agreement, the tension mounted. Only one day remained in the session. Brotherton and his group showed no signs of yielding. They treated the younger House members patronizingly, taking the attitude that their superior experience entitled them to more say in the bill. The UMW's two lobbyists, fearing that no bill might be reported, were ready to settle for major compromises. Dinsmore, likewise jumpy at the prospect that no bill might emerge, went to see Boiarsky. The Speaker told him to hold out.

Inside the meeting, held in a remote conference room in an upstairs corner of the Capitol, Cleo Jones began to play an increasingly important role. A calm and soft-spoken man of fifty-two, with an appealing twinkle of wit and intelligence in his narrow eyes, Jones had learned much in his two terms in the House. Further, he had high respect for Don Rasmussen, whom he felt "knew more than anyone in this country about black lung."

Jones recalled later, "The Senate strategy—I sensed it immediately— was to give away a much more liberal weekly compensation benefit (a change that would benefit all workers, not just miners). They wanted to trade that for our dropping our presumption clause and our definition of pneumoconiosis. But the Senate underestimated the political situation and the tenacity of the House members."

By late Saturday afternoon, the principal sticking point had become the definition of pneumoconiosis, which was, by any standard, the key to the bill. Just before a recess, Jones typed a proposed definition which seemed acceptable to both sides. It pegged the diagnosis to X-ray evidence or "other physiological change accepted by recognized specialists. . . ." When the meeting reconvened, the Senate conferees indicated they had agreed to Jones's definition and distributed what appeared to be copies of his typed draft of the key paragraph.

The House members were jubilant. They dashed downstairs to the Speaker's office with the news. As Jones examined the sheet the Senators had given him, however, he spotted something. Where his proposed definition had used the phrase "physiological change," the copy in his hand said "pathological change." Because the words look alike and are about the same length the change had been missed by the others, but the difference was crucial. "Pathological change" would have meant scientific evidence of disease, whereas physiological change could mean only impaired ability to function. Under the "physiological" definition, a man with difficulty breathing, chest pains, and other severe symptoms might be found to have pneumoconiosis whether it showed up on X-ray or not. With the word "pathological" substituted, he might need a lung biopsy as proof of his disease. The Senators, using the same typewriter as had been used for Jones's version, had typed up their own definition, spaced it identically and even used three asterisks to punctuate the end of the section, just as Jones had. Then they xeroxed their version and passed it around. It was an extraordinary gambit. And it nearly worked.

"Hold it boys," said Jones in the Speaker's office, "we've been taken."

His elated fellow conferees took a few minutes to grasp what had happened. Boiarsky then sent them back to the conference with instructions to hold out. He knew, and Jones knew, that the Senate, having passed the more conservative bill, was at a disadvantage in the conference, since a failure to report legislation could more plausibly be blamed on the Senate than the House.

Moreover, catching the Senators in their attempted deception gave the House conferees a certain psychological advantage in the ensuing hours of negotiation. Several minor points that had seemed lost in other sections of the bill were resolved in the House's favor. But when a recess was called at ten P.M., there was still no agreement on the definition of pneumoconiosis. As they were leaving the room, Jones, bluffing, said to Dinsmore in a voice loud enough for the Senators to hear, "Well, I guess there's nothing else we can do but to go down to the floor and ask the governor to call a special session." At this point, no one could be certain what the consequences would be if the legislature failed to act. Every mine in the state was closed and there had been no sign that the forty-three thousand miners were weakening in their resolve. The coal association was claiming that the strike had already put a number of smaller companies out of business. It seemed possible that, if there were no bill, the strike might continue indefinitely. So when the House group again met with Boiarsky, his instructions were simple: "Hold on, they'll buckle."

There were still a number of onlookers in the House gallery at 11:50 when Dinsmore rushed into the chamber, the conference report in his hand. A definition of pneumoconiosis had been agreed upon which allowed *either* pathological or physiological change to be the principal evidence of the presence of the disease. This was an outright victory for the House, which cared not at all what else was included as long as physiological change was valid evidence. In addition, pneumoconiosis was defined to include a variety of miners' lung ailments, including silicosis and black lung. All claims for these diseases would be handled by the old Silicosis Medical Board, to be renamed the Occupational Pneumoconiosis Board. The bill raised the maximum weekly compensation benefits from $47 a week to $52, which, while still low, was an improvement. And it provided for further, automatic increases tied to the cost of living. The presumptive clause required the miner to show that he had been exposed to coal dust for ten of the past fifteen years and had a lung disease "consistent with a diagnosis of occupational pneumoconiosis." If he could do this, it would be presumed he contracted the disease on the job. This was a major step forward, for the chief tactic the companies used to fight compensation claims was to question whether the claimant had got the disease on the job. Since it was hard to prove the presence of pneumoconiosis to begin with, it was doubly difficult to show it was work-related. Perhaps the sweetest language in the bill from the viewpoint of Don Rasmussen and those who had taken his side in the medical controversy was the following: "X-ray evidence shall not necessarily be held conclusive inasmuch as it bears upon the absence or presence of occupational pneumoconiosis."

Boiarsky had just finished putting into the House record a routine communication from the Attorney General when Dinsmore arrived. The Speaker had been careful to get all other important business out of the way so that any last-minute agreement on the black lung bill would be assured of a vote. One of the delegates asked that the discussion of other business be suspended so that the conference report could be acted upon. The Speaker, who had been on the floor to present the letter, took his chair for the vote. By now, of course, its passage was a foregone conclusion. It went through, ninety-three to nothing, with minutes remaining in the session. Moments afterwards, word came from the Senate that the bill had passed there also.

The miners, still suspicious of Governor Moore, held a rally at Beckley Sunday afternoon and resolved not to go back to work until the bill was signed into law. On Tuesday, Moore signed it and the strike was over.

The strike, the first ever started by the miners for purely political purposes, had lasted three weeks and closed the industry. The legislation it produced was not all the miners wanted. It retained, for example, the same medical board, although with a new name, to rule on their lung disease claims. But the bill went much further than any knowledgeable observer of West Virginia politics had thought it would. The prevailing assumption had been that the black lung issue would be referred to a study committee and quietly buried. Instead, the legislature had enacted the most liberal workmen's compensation statute of its kind in the country.

The sudden political activism of the coal miners that accompanied its passage had plainly scared many state legislators who had long consid-

ered the miners apathetic and gullible. As one state senator was overheard to remark, "From now on, the question will be 'Where were you
when the miners went out?' And anyone who doesn't have a good answer will be in trouble." More important than what the crusade might
have taught the politicians, however, was what it taught the miners
themselves, about politics, their own potential strength, and their union
leadership. The taste of triumph had led many of them to ask themselves, "If we can do this, why did we have to put up with things as
they were for so long?" The answer, of course, was that most miners
had assumed that their union leaders were looking out for them. Yet
when they responded to the hierarchy's call to action on black lung at
the 1968 convention, the union officers took no interest. When the drive
gathered momentum anyway, the officers tried to discourage it, even
raised the issue of "dual unionism" against its participants. When the
miners went out on strike, they found the union joining with the operators to get them back to work.

For years, many West Virginia miners had been disappointed with
their union officers. But faith and trust in the United Mine Workers was
so ingrained in them that they refused to believe there was anything
profoundly wrong with the organization. Many of them thought that
the problems were in the district offices, perhaps the fault of a single
district officer. Few believed there was real corruption or coziness with
the hated coal operators. Only among the retired and disabled, who felt
they had been cheated by the welfare fund, was there alienation matching that found among the miners of Pennsylvania and Ohio. For most
West Virginia miners, the process of alienation had only begun. But the
Farmington tragedy and the black lung uprising had greatly acceler-
ated it. Among the more intelligent miners—the natural leaders—the
feeling was virtually unanimous that something was terribly wrong
with their union. Their success in the black lung movement had convinced them they could do something about it, particularly since it was
1969, election year in the UMW.

The black lung uprising made a strong impression in Washington, where the legislators with the most to say about mine safety were, almost to a man, from the coal fields. In the Senate, West Virginia's Jennings Randolph was the ranking Democrat on the Labor and Public Welfare Committee, which had jurisdiction in the issue. Randolph also had the number-two spot on the committee's General Labor Subcommittee, to which the various mine health and safety bills were referred. The subcommittee chairman was New Jersey's Harrison Williams, a handsome, Ivy League liberal, who was expecting a tough battle for reelection. Williams' alcoholism had become such an open secret that he had been forced to admit it publicly and to promise to take the cure. He was on the wagon and eager to put his mark on a piece of significant legislation to bolster his sagging prestige. But he knew he would have to defer often to Randolph on mine safety. The West Virginia Senator had a great political stake in the matter and his support would be needed when the bill came before the full committee, where Randolph outranked Williams.

In the House, mine safety was the province of the Education and Labor Committee, headed by Carl Perkins, an easygoing but shrewd politician who represented the coal fields of eastern Kentucky, just across the border from Ken Hechler's district. The subcommittee handling the mine-safety bills was presided over by John Dent, a short, heavy-set man with the bearing of a maître-d'. Dent hailed from the coal regions of southwestern Pennsylvania.

By the time the miners' strike began, the general assumption in Washington was that the Farmington disaster had provided sufficient impetus for some kind of legislation on mine safety. The issue had been dormant for seventeen years and even industry spokesmen were admitting that coal's safety and health record was abominable. When hearings began in the Senate, the National Coal Association's officers went on record in favor of strong legislation. The only question seemed to be how tough the legislation would be when it finally passed.

The coal industry did not risk much by publicly speaking in favor of new regulations, however costly they might prove to be. Mine disasters had forced Congress to act before, but in every case the industry had succeeded in opening gaping loopholes into the bills and rendering them economically harmless. What matters in legislation is not what is said publicly, but what is done privately. Mine safety is an arcane and complicated subject. Outside of the industry itself, there are few experts, except for the timid people in the Bureau of Mines whose reflexes have chronically been pro-industry. Thus it had always been relatively easy for the coal industry to convince politicians in Washington and elsewhere to change an occasional "must" to a "may" and thereby make meaningless key sections of mine safety bills. The lesson of the past was that, after the publicity and clamor that followed a major mine disaster had subsided, weak legislation could be passed off as strong and few would realize the difference until years later.

Certainly the top officials of the coal industry must have thought the same pattern would repeat itself in the wake of the Farmington disaster. The explosion had clearly shocked the nation and it therefore was good public relations to speak out for a stronger safety law. But sooner or later the hubbub would die down and they would be able to go to work on the toughest parts of the bills under consideration. The UMW might be more diligent this time about pressing the miners' side, but the union had not been an effective lobby for years and was unlikely to become one overnight. Successful lobbying requires expertise, political savvy, and persuasiveness. Tony Boyle had none of these and the two men registered as lobbyists for the union didn't have them either. For the coal industry, it remained to wait until the noise abated and the spotlight of publicity was focused elsewhere.

The Congressional deliberations on mine safety progressed routinely for several months. Exhaustive hearings were held by both the House and Senate. The witnesses ranged from Boyle, to the three West Virginia doctors, to small coal operators ready to resist any new regulation. The UMW imported Dr. Jethro Gough from Wales to testify on black lung. Subcommittee members from both houses visited Britain for a first-hand look at mining there. Field trips were also made to mines in Pennsylvania, and Senator Williams even went to Czechoslovakia with Dr. Buff for a tour of coal mines. All of this, of course, was done with maximum fanfare, which provided little clue to the intentions of the men who would ultimately determine the shape of the legislation. In May, however, Senator Randolph showed his hand when he added still another bill to the half dozen or so already under consideration in the Senate. His action would have gone virtually unnoticed were it not for the vigilance of Ralph Nader.

For Jennings Randolph, the mine-safety issue was a devilish political problem. The coal industry was West Virginia's principal industry, the miners its principal voting bloc. His course, therefore, was fraught with political danger. He couldn't afford to alienate either side. Unlike his colleague Robert Byrd, Randolph had considerable authority in the committee handling the legislation and he was thus unable to emulate Byrd by staying as far from it as possible.

So, in public, he hedged. At sixty-seven, Randolph had been in and out of Congress since 1932 before being elected Senator in 1958. He had an old-fashioned political style that was formal to the point of stuffiness. Where some other politicians tried to be hard-hitting and controversial, Randolph sought to be soothing. He spoke in pleasant, measured tones, always striving to smooth over disagreements, to dispel controversy. He was known as a liberal but, in fact, it was difficult to be certain where this master of equivocation stood on many issues. If he asked a witness a tough, leading question at a hearing, he would invariably follow with an explanation that such questions were necessary for the record, and were not a reflection of his own views. He said he was for mine safety, but he didn't want to close down mines with unreasonable regulations. He introduced the UMW's bills, but at the same time defended the industry and praised its executives. But when he introduced a bill of his own on May 12, after the hearings ended and presumably based upon conclusions drawn from them, he gave himself away. The event itself went largely unnoticed. A few brief news stories quoted the Senator as calling the bill "a workable compromise" among the various positions that had been staked out on the issue.

Five days later the Randolph bill exploded on the front pages. The news was that Ralph Nader had written the Senator a five-page letter castigating him for his action and analyzing the bill in painstaking, devastating detail. Nader, of course, had become a national figure whose accurate muckraking, flashy phrasemaking, and crusading image gained him wide publicity for his revelations and accusations. His letter to Randolph was as strongly worded as any he had written.

Randolph's bill, wrote Nader, "clearly displayed, officially and meticulously, what your true intentions have been all along as the sickening tale of mine-inflicted hazards and disease unfolded to a startled American public. You chose coal over the miner; industry over the working man and his family. In a word you have betrayed your constituency. . . ." The letter said Randolph had been inspired to introduce his "notorious bill" by Stephen Dunn, President of the National Coal Association. Nader said the bill contained "more than forty separate weakening provisions, as compared with the scarcely adequate Administration bill."

"Coal mining," said Nader, "is the most dangerous occupation in the country in the category of trauma and far and away the most hazardous in the category of disease. Black lung strikes at about fifty percent of the working miners to a significant degree, often ending in death. The misery and the pain were brought to the Senate hearings. You saw miners in such pain, you saw an actual black lung [from an autopsy], you heard the testimony of experts abstracting the anguish and the bodily destruction of these cruelly depleted human beings who rely on you to represent them. Why have you forsaken them? Why was your introductory statement on May 12 so full of emphasis and concern over the industry's property and costs and so deprived of attention to the miners' health and safety? Why was this statement larded with false prophecy about the devastating impact of the safety and health legislation on the industry? The coal industry has never faced a more expansive and profitable present and future. . . . What conceivable reason, therefore, can there be for a U.S. Senator indenturing himself to an industry that exacts such a costly price from the working miner? What of the right of the miners to have their physiological integrity protected by adequate investment in safe and healthful working environments by operator-corporations?

"Few Senators have the opportunity during their career to identify themselves so closely with so significant a legislative program relating to their citizens back home. When they do, their choice is lives over property surplus in corporate coffers. Whatever course you choose to take from this time on, Senator Randolph, will be well-recorded history. For the invisible Senator has become visible. . . ."

Nader's analysis was on target. Randolph's "workable compromise" was an outright capitulation to the industry. The bill, for example, abolished all civil penalties for safety violations. It retained with expanded powers the Federal Coal Mine Health and Safety Board of Review, an appeals board for decisions by the Bureau of Mines to close unsafe operations. The panel had long been dominated by industry men. At the time, three of the five members, including the chairman, were closely associated with industry management. Instead of vesting power in the Bureau of Mines to promulgate new regulations when time and technology made them necessary, the Randolph bill would have required that Congress make all changes—a procedure almost unheard of in industrial safety regulation. His bill had no requirement for underground toilets, thus, as Nader put it, "leaving the miners to relieve themselves as if they were packhorses." Under the administration bill, miners would have medical examinations every year. Randolph's bill changed this to every other year. His bill had no requirement for underground lighting or underground explosion shelters. It proposed a weak standard for reducing dust in the mine atmosphere. The only injuries that had to be reported under Randolph's bill were "lost-time" injuries. This opened the way to inaccurate statistics because miners frequently avoided missing time with minor—and occasionally major—injuries. Said Nader, "In the Administration's and Representative Hechler's bills, injuries are injuries."

Nader caught Randolph off guard. His analysis of the bill was factual and left the Senator with no way to reply to the substance of the letter. Nader had only made an educated guess as to who had actually inspired the bill, but apparently he guessed correctly in naming Stephen Dunn, because Randolph refused to comment on the matter. "Now is not the time to discuss how I drafted the bill," he said. Several days later National Coal Association officials acknowledged a major role in drafting the bill. Nevertheless, it had been introduced as Randolph's own, not—as in the case of the UMW health and safety measures he had introduced—as legislation put forth by request.

Randolph never actually responded to Nader's charges. He attempted a reply of sorts about a week later in a memo to his colleagues on the subcommittee. The memo was released to the press. "I was a target of Ralph Nader's shadowy operations last weekend," Randolph said. He insisted that he was not wedded to his bill and added some criticism of Nader's methods, but said nothing of the substantive issues in the Nader letter. He noted that Nader had declined to testify before the Senate. "I did not ask Ralph Nader for advice. Neither did Mr. Nader offer any advice to me before the fact—only criticism and vilification after I introduced my post-hearing version. . . ." Randolph said the letter was released to the press before he, the Senator, had received it. "It was not until Sunday afternoon that a member of my staff found the signed original in a public corridor of the fifth floor of the New Senate Office Building outside a door to my offices. It was contained in an unsealed envelope, without return address . . ."

So the Senator had been able to muster no more of a reply than a few derisive comments about how the letter had been delivered. He must have known that this would not wash. He immediately began to back away from his bill, saying, "This merely puts another approach before the subcommittee. I have never said I was for any certain bill. . . ." Several weeks later, he did something few politicians, especially powerful old-timers like Randolph, ever do. He admitted he was wrong. In a letter, which was made public, to Interior Secretary Hickel, Randolph said, "Some of the provisions of bills I have introduced would be interpreted as being less effective for coal mine health and safety than existing law. I will not continue to advocate such provisions. They are mistakes."

The entire affair was a political nightmare for Randolph. He had been caught red-handed doing the bidding of the coal operators at a time when the coal miners in his state had gone on an unprecedented strike and begun to show other signs of a new militance and political awareness. Now he could make no false move on mine safety or the damage would be worsened. Instead, he would have to bend over backwards to make it seem he was really looking out for the coal miners all along, a development of immeasurable importance to the internal politics of the Senate labor committee. Subcommittee Chairman Williams, who was sympathetic to the miners, wanted to bring out a strong bill to enhance his tarnished reputation. His problem had been Randolph. Now that Randolph had gotten himself into this political jam, Williams' job was much easier.

Ralph Nader had entrusted the task of keeping an eye on the progress of the mine-safety controversy to Gary Sellers, a thirty-two-year-old former government lawyer who was one of five Nader had hired to help him run the Center for Study of Responsive Law. The Center, financed by foundations and private contributors, was the home base each summer for the teams of college students imported by Nader to investigate the bureaucracy. The first study by "Nader's Raiders," as they were known, was a devastating critique of the Federal Trade Commission which created a sensation and forced the FTC to take a more aggressive role on behalf of the American consumer. Now, Nader was channeling youthful talent and energy into a host of other areas. One of these was occupational safety—long a pet subject of Nader's— and he picked Sellers to help lead the project. Sellers came from the Bureau of the Budget, where he had worked in the natural resources division for four years. He was an authority on coal mining technology. A short, intense man with shaggy hair and rumpled suits, Sellers went about his tasks with single-minded devotion to the cause and to Nader. It was he who read and analyzed the Randolph bill.

Later, Sellers was instrumental in convincing Phil Burton, a liberal Democratic Congressman from San Francisco, to take a personal interest in the mine-safety issue. Burton, a burly, noisy, Irishman who liked to pad around his office with his shoes off and his tie loosened was known on Capitol Hill as an abrasive but effective legislator. Burton was on the Education and Labor Committee, as well as its General Labor Subcommittee headed by Representative Dent. He was one of a number of restless, capable House liberals who liked to get involved in issues of no direct interest to their constituents. His theory was that, once an issue is joined, a member with expertise can have great influence. Burton had the interest, Sellers the expertise. They began to work closely together. Later, Sellers was put on Burton's staff at a nominal salary so that he could have access to the closed-door committee meetings when the bill was being drafted.

At the same time, a similar arrangement was made between Ken

Hechler and an ex-Interior Department lawyer named David Finnegan whose zeal on mine safety and other issues had cost him his job on the staff of the department's General Counsel. Hechler hired Finnegan and gave him one assignment: do whatever was necessary to see that a strong mine-safety bill was passed. Since Hechler was not on the committee or subcommittee considering the bills, Finnegan could have no official entree to them. But he was easygoing and tireless. He made himself useful to the committee staffs in both the House and Senate. Since he was exceptionally knowledgeable about mining and familiar with the inner workings of the Bureau of Mines, his advice was welcome. Eventually, he was acting as a full-time unofficial advisor to both committees.

The placement of Sellers and Finnegan in such strategic spots was an important asset to Hechler, Nader, and the other reformers. In the past, the industry's assertions on technical points in legislation had gone unchallenged. Usually, they were supported by the Bureau of Mines. But with Sellers and Finnegan behind the lines, everything the industry spokesmen said was subjected to expert scrutiny. Time and again, the arguments of industry lobbyists were rejected by the committees in both Houses. Had Sellers and Finnegan not been present, the members and their staffs would undoubtedly have gone along with the coal companies because they would have been incompetent to dispute their contentions. Of course, the political climate created by the Farmington disaster and the black lung strike made most members less willing to yield to industry pressure than they might otherwise have been. And those, like Randolph, who were willing to work behind the scenes for the companies found that their actions quickly became public knowledge. Although Hechler could take no part in the committee's deliberations on the legislation, he put enormous pressure on committee members with his constant public statements urging strong legislation and criticizing each weakening proposal advanced by the coal men. He was kept informed of progress by Finnegan and Sellers. Although most of Hechler's remarks were not nationally publicized, they were carried by the newspapers and other media in the coal regions, which meant they reached the constituents of such men as Perkins, Dent, and Randolph, making it much more difficult for them to go along with any dilution of the legislation.

While Nader's primary concern with the coal industry was safety and health, which fit into his overall preoccupation with public safety, he was appalled at the United Mine Workers leadership. His first impression of the union was that it took little interest in worker safety. He found, for example, that despite its great wealth the UMW maintained only a one-man safety division. It had pressed for no new safety regulations since 1952. As early as March, 1968, months before Farmington, Nader had publicly criticized the union's safety efforts in a letter to Interior Secretary Udall. The response from Boyle was a letter to Udall which spoke of the UMW's "acclaimed knowledge and skill which it alone possesses" in mine safety. Nader also began reading the UMW *Journal,* and was amazed at its unsubtle glorification of Boyle and his lieutenants. Letters from miners began to appear in the mailbox of the downtown boarding house where Nader lived. Many had complaints about the Welfare and Retirement Fund. Others spoke of undemocratic union procedures. Little research was required for Nader to establish that there was something to these grievances. A quick check of the public record showed that up to $70 million of the Welfare and Retirement Fund's assets were stored in non-interest-bearing checking accounts in the National Bank of Washington, which the union controlled by its ownership of seventy-five percent of the bank's stock. It was also a matter of record that the Boyle administration permitted no elections in most districts and that legal action to prevent this practice had been bogged down for years. The public reports required by the Labor Department also revealed that a host of relatives of the top officers were on the payroll, several drawing huge salaries, and that the union had lifted $850,000 out of the treasury to establish a full-salary retirement program for the top officers. With this much visible to anyone willing to look up the records, there could be no telling what might lie below the surface. Although reforming labor unions was outside Nader's usual province of public safety and consumer protection, he regarded the UMW as a special case. He saw it as a potentially powerful instrument of progress that had deteriorated into an autocratic nest of corruption and collusion with management. Safety reforms, he felt, would mean little without a strong union to see that they were enforced.

At a Senate hearing on banking in March, five months after the Farmington explosion had put coal and the UMW in the news, Nader made headlines with charges that the union's bank loaned money to coal operators. He said the UMW's relationship with management was "probably the closest in our economy." He ticked off particulars about the pension fund's no-interest deposits, the measly pension ($1,350) available to a miner, and the full-salary plan for the top UMW officers.

Late the following month, he wrote a six-page letter to Senator Ralph Yarborough, chairman of the Senate Labor and Public Welfare Committee, urging a Congressional investigation of the union. Nader knew there was little chance that Yarborough, a staunch labor ally, would start such a probe, but the letter was a vehicle to get his new charges against the union into the press.

"The continuance of the black lung epidemic over the years without attention, prevention, or remedy," said Nader, "parallels another disease—that afflicting the United Mine Workers of America leadership.

"Reports coming from coal miners and delegates at the 1964 and 1968 UMWA conventions indicate irregularities and violations of both the UMWA Constitution and the labor laws. There are at least four hundred 'bogey locals,' as they are known, composed either entirely of pensioned miners or without the required number of active miners (ten) under the Constitution of the Union. Convention proceedings have involved shouting down of dissenters and wholesale violations of the union's own procedures. Some delegates from locals have never been heard of by members of the local. . . . The UMWA cultivates close ties with the coal industry while perpetuating a remoteness and nonresponsiveness with its rank and file that is staggering in its scope. UMWA leaders regularly meet in secret with coal corporation executives and the Bituminous Coal Operators Association to decide about various degrees of inaction on coal mine health and safety. . . . Keeping the rank and file member in the dark is the function of the UMW *Journal* which comes out twice a month in an attempt to show miners that the leadership cares for them. The *Journal* is filled with repeated extended praises of the union leaders, particularly its President, W. A. Boyle. Next come the sorrowful descriptions of mine disasters due to conditions so long ignored by these leaders. Then a few recipes for the ladies. . . . The *Journal* brooks no dissent from its members. There is no space for letters to the editor, even ones correcting clear falsehoods. Articles disagreeing with the union leaders' policies are not permitted. In its style and content, the *Journal* is the classic prototype house organ of an autocratic system. This is a most serious matter inasmuch as the

Journal is the chief communication link with and between the union membership. . . . The union itself appears infected with mismanagement, padded payrolls and nepotism of the most pristine variety. For example, the UMWA President, W. A. Boyle, has his brother and daughter on the union payroll. R. J. Boyle, district president, Billings, Montana, a member of the Executive Board, is listed at a salary of $25,000 plus $8,975 for expenses for the year 1967. Antoinette Boyle, listed as an Attorney, receives a salary of $40,000 plus expenses in 1967 of $3,288. This $40,000 salary equals the salary of the Vice-president of the Union. . . . While it is incumbent upon all individuals to be good to their children, it is fair to ask what Miss Boyle does to earn this salary. The same inquiry can be put to the work of R. J. Boyle. Consider the scene at Billings. The UMW office in Billings is composed of four small rooms with only one lady—not Miss Boyle—in attendance. From all appearances, neither Miss Boyle nor R. J. Boyle have much to do with this office. . . . Anyone who has talked with union members in the coal mining regions receives clear impressions of overwhelming dissatisfaction and resentment against Mr. Boyle and other union leaders. The mass coal miner safety movement in West Virginia, in clear disregard of the leadership, is evidence that the miners are at the limits of their patience. . . . No political pundit is needed to predict that if a free election were held, Mr. Boyle would be doing very well to receive twenty-five percent of the vote. . . ."

At the same time, Ken Hechler was stepping up his attacks on the UMW, particularly on the management of the welfare fund, which he called "inadequate, inconsistent, and in fact incredible." He put extensive excerpts from letters from coal miners about the fund into the Congressional Record. He revealed that 145 employees of the fund made more than $10,000, thirty-seven getting $20,000 or more. He questioned the size of the salaries in view of the revelations about the fund's investment policies. He added his voice to the call for a Congressional investigation.

Nader's letter to Yarborough received great publicity. The *Washington Post,* for example, splashed it eight columns across page two with a story that focused on the charges of nepotism. Less than a month later, Nader wrote a similar letter detailing other charges. It was sent to John L. Lewis, now eighty-nine and enfeebled, at his home in Alexandria, Virginia. It urged the old man, who still was chairman of the board of trustees of the welfare fund, to come out of retirement to save the union. As with the Yarborough letter, Nader knew his request had little chance of being met. But the appeal to the aging giant of the labor movement was dramatic and the story was big news in the coal fields and Washington. Simultaneously, newspapers, some of which had ignored the UMW for years, began to take a closer look. Stories appeared giving a general—and invariably unfavorable—assessment of the organization.

Surely, it must have appeared to Tony Boyle, insecure and volatile as he was, that his whole world was coming apart. For years the UMW had operated in relative obscurity, virtually without criticism. The only criticism he could remember went back to the days when John L. Lewis was regularly excoriated for his extreme militance. This, of course, was better than praise in the eyes of a labor leader. Now Boyle was being accused on all fronts of failing his members, of cheating them, and of collusion with the coal operators. And the criticism came not only from a group of malcontents among the rank and file, but also from a Congressman, a nationally respected safety crusader, and leading newspapers. In West Virginia, there had been signs of large-scale discontent among the members. They had shut down the coal industry in defiance of Boyle, booed his name, and cheered when he was criticized at their meetings.

Boyle did not take the criticism lying down—not in an election year. One candidate, a northern West Virginia miner named Elijah Wolford, had already announced he would run against Boyle. Steve Kochis, the rough-hewn character who challenged Boyle in 1964, was expected to do so again. So Boyle tried to recoup. Under the guise of a campaign to drum up support for the union's health and safety legislation, Boyle, Titler, and Owens held a series of weekend political rallies in the coal fields. Since they were billed as "health and safety rallies," the trips could be passed off as official presidential duties and paid for out of the union treasury. To make sure the message of the rallies reached those who did not attend, the *Journal* soared to new heights of Boyle boosting. The May 15 issue, for example, had twenty-eight pictures of Boyle in its twenty-four pages. He appeared twice on the cover and facing pages of the issue were devoted to a layout of a dozen pictures from various rallies, with Boyle in the middle of every one. Editorials called for the members to get behind the hierarchy. "You working and retired coal miners," editorialized Justin McCarthy, "in the last international union election in 1964, gave your overwhelming vote of approval to the leadership of President Boyle. Acting on this mandate of support, President Boyle has brought tremendous new benefits to coal miners both in the wage agreement and, indirectly, in improved Welfare Fund benefits. . . . Most UMWA members, we feel it is safe to say, know these facts. So stick with your union; work for it; support your leadership."

At the rallies themselves, the officers found a host of bogeymen to blame for the controversy that swirled around them. In Pittsburgh, John Owens warned solemnly that big insurance companies wanted to "take away from the United Mine Workers of America this Welfare and Retirement Fund." In Charleston, George Titler growled that the big oil companies "who have gobbled up the big coal companies" were out to destroy the UMW and the welfare fund. Other favorite targets of blame were the Communists and anonymous "enemies of labor." The *Journal* went to great lengths to rebut charges against the union published in the Communist *Daily World*, which is one of the most widely ignored publications anywhere, particularly in the coal fields. "Communists Never Give Up; Don't Disseminate Their Lies," warned one headline over a piece by assistant editor Rex Lauck. The article not only squared matters with the *Daily World*, but had strong words for such other well-known publications as *The Militant* and *The Bulletin*.

By May 22, the date of his celebrated letter to John L. Lewis, Nader was deeply involved in another, far more significant effort to change the UMW. In a conversation with a young Washington lawyer, Nader had mentioned that he wished there were someone of stature in the union who could mount a serious challenge for the presidency. The lawyer, Steven Yablonski, replied that his uncle, Joseph Yablonski, a power in UMW affairs for twenty-seven years, was disenchanted with Boyle and might be convinced to make the race. On May 8, Steve Yablonski arranged the first in a series of secret meetings between his uncle and Nader. "Jock" Yablonski, as he was known to the miners in the District 5 area around Pittsburgh, had been an elected member of the union's International Executive Board since 1942. He had served for eight years as District President. Recently, he had been assigned by Boyle to bolster the union's lackluster lobbying team as acting director of Labor's Non-Partisan League, the organization's political arm.

At fifty-nine, Yablonski was comfortably accustomed to life as a labor executive. He was paid $26,000 a year, plus a generous, no-questions-asked expense account. Investments he had made in real estate, stock, and a harness racing track near his home had done well. He lived in a huge fieldstone house on a 365-acre farm near the small village of Clarksville, forty miles south of Pittsburgh. His position with the union had helped make him a power in local Democratic politics. A short man with a powerful build, Yablonski had a craggy, pock-marked face with the large, blunt features so common in American working-class immigrant families. His hair was wiry and grey, his eyebrows bushy. He looked like a coal miner. But his expensive clothes and confident bearing were evidence that he was no mere rank-and-file worker; he had been out of the coal mines and in the union hierarchy for a long time and it showed. Yablonski's fealty to Lewis and, in recent years, to Boyle had gained him much. He was well off, had sent his two sons and daughter through college, and had a secure existence ahead of him. He would risk it all if he broke with Boyle.

But there was another side to Yablonski. For one thing, he detested Boyle, a man he had known but slightly until Boyle became acting-president of the union late in 1962. One of Boyle's first public appearances had been at U. S. Steel's giant Robena mining complex in Pennsylvania after an explosion underground had killed thirty-seven men. While at the scene, Boyle was overheard asking, "Did a trapper boy leave the door open?" Trapper boys, who once manned the doors to mine passages to avoid ventilation interruptions, had not been used for several decades. The remark got around. To Yablonski, knowledgeable, sensitive to the miners' feelings, a man who took pride in his public utterances, such a callous blunder was unforgivable. Then came the pressure in 1963 from the rank and file in his and neighboring Pennsylvania and Ohio districts for a new contract. Boyle nearly provoked a rebellion with his intransigence about reopening the contract. When he finally did negotiate one, he oversold it with inflated claims of seniority provisions and other gains. This set off the wave of wildcat strikes that swept the northern coal fields early in 1964 and led to the effort to reform the union at the Miami convention. After Yablonski watched men from his district being beaten up by helmeted Boyle supporters on the first day, he had threatened to lead his delegation out of the convention if the violence did not stop.

Yet Yablonski worked hard that year to defeat Steve Kochis, the miner from Clarksville who ran against Boyle for the union presidency. At the same time, he secretly supported another rank and filer, Karl Kafton, in his effort to win the seat on the International Executive Board held by Peter Philippi, one of Boyle's men. Karl Kafton was a huge, handsome man with a reputation as a militant and troublemaker without parallel in the northern coal fields. Yablonski gave him $1,000 to finance his campaign which, while unsuccessful, made Kafton as unpopular with the union hierarchy as he had been with the coal companies. The next year, Kafton was one of the celebrated "Bellaire Six," fired after a spontaneous strike over alleged contract violations at Consolidation's huge Ireland mine. Many miners believed the reason Boyle never did anything to have the men reinstated was that Kafton was among them. Kafton and Yablonski were close friends.

During this period, Yablonski was president of District 5, one of only four districts in the UMW where election of all officials was allowed. In 1965, the problem of occupational dust diseases was taken up by the Pennsylvania legislature in a bill to grant $75 monthly payments to miners and other workers with dust diseases who had failed to qualify for other benefits. Coal worker's pneumoconiosis was not included in the bill, however. Yablonski knew the disease afflicted thousands of miners and urged the union's lobbyist, Lester Thomas, to try to have the bill amended to include it. Thomas polled the union's other Pennsylvania officers on Boyle's orders, to get their opinion on the proposed amendment. But they feared the amendment might snag the whole bill and therefore opposed the idea. Yablonski felt the bill was nearly worthless to coal miners without pneumoconiosis included. He told Thomas he would try to have the bill changed on his own. When the bill came up for action on Columbus Day that year, Yablonski went to see Governor William Scranton, hoping to have the amendment attached at the last minute. He reminded the governor that his own conference on pneumoconiosis only a year earlier had recommended an all-out program to deal with the disease. Scranton said such a program could not be included in the compensation bill, to which Yablonski replied that the disease could at least be included as compensable. Scranton agreed. The amendment was proposed, and accepted without a fight. The bill was enacted later the same day. "From that day forth," Yablonski later recalled, "I noticed a terrible apparent difference in attitude, even in manner of greeting, with Boyle." The following year, R. O. Lewis stepped down as vice-president of the union. At the District 5 convention, the delegates voted overwhelmingly for a resolution asking that Yablonski be named to replace him.

All this was apparently too much for Boyle. Later in 1966, he sent a commission of his loyal supporters into District 5 to investigate charges of "maladministration" by Yablonski. Although outsiders who had visited a number of UMW district offices had invariably been impressed with the businesslike management of Yablonski's office in Pittsburgh, the eight-man commission reported to Boyle that there were irregularities. Yablonski was summoned to Washington and told that he would have to resign as district president. If he refused, Boyle would place the district in trusteeship. The Landrum-Griffin Act empowers a union president to suspend democratic operation of a district temporarily in the event of financial irregularities or contract compliance problems. Yablonski felt that if this was ever done in his district—the only major district in the union with full democratic rights—the trusteeship would never be lifted.

The charges against him were highly questionable. For example, the commission said the district had "borrowed" $276,000 from the international union, money which had not been used in the members' best interest. Such so-called "loans" were made to all districts and were nothing more than cash transfers—of the members' money—from one branch of the organization to another. But the Boyle administration liked to label them as "loans," so that it could declare that the borrower district was not "self-supporting," and therefore not entitled to consideration as an autonomous subordinate branch of the organization. Instead, the district would be considered "an administrative arm," and therefore not be allowed the elections required by law for autonomous subordinate units within a labor organization. This contrived theory was transparent enough, but it was the best the union could come up with to explain the undemocratic operation of virtually all its district organizations. Now it was being used to get Yablonski out of office. As he later told the story, he was tempted to defy Boyle. But he knew Boyle could legally slap the district into a trusteeship, which could not be challenged by the government for eighteen months. By that time, he felt, the damage would be done. If he resigned, he would still retain his seat on the International Executive Board and the district would keep its autonomy. So he decided to step down. Obviously, the matter did nothing to improve Yablonski's relations with Boyle. "He will rue the day," Yablonski kept saying privately.

Two years later, when Boyle appeared at the Farmington disaster with praise for the company, Yablonski saw another example of what he felt Boyle had shown at the Robena tragedy six years earlier, namely, that Boyle was stupid and oblivious to the feelings of the miners. "The goddamn man just rants and raves and he doesn't know what he's talking about," Yablonski complained privately. He considered Boyle's response to criticism by Nader more of the same.

Yablonski was intelligent and well-informed, an intense newspaper reader. As a delegate to the 1968 Democratic convention, he had supported the unsuccessful "peace plank" for the party platform advanced by supporters of Senator Eugene McCarthy. He was deeply troubled by the violence at the Chicago Democratic convention, and even went to Grant Park to talk to the young people congregated there. Although Yablonski had supported Humphrey, he did so reluctantly. He had approved of McCarthy's lonesome crusade for the presidency and against the war, which Yablonski also strongly opposed. To Yablonski, Ralph Nader was a man to be admired and listened to. He saw Nader's interest in mine safety—even with its accompanying criticism of the union—as an opportunity to be seized, not as an insult to be virulently countered. He hated seeing the union, which had always been in the forefront of struggles for social change, in a fight with one of the most brilliant and respected young activists of the day.

Moreover, Yablonski's years in the union's upper echelons had not shorn him of his basic unionist instincts. He identified strongly with coal miners, was sympathetic to the point of outrage with their grievances. He had worked in the mines himself and his father had died in a mine accident. During his eight years as the elected president of District 5, miners frequently drove out to the Yablonski farm in Clarksville to talk to him. He would ask them in to the chestnut-paneled den of the square, 175-year-old fieldstone house. There he would listen intently to their problems or simply chat with them about the topics of the day. He usually brandished a cigar as he sat by the huge bookcase built into the cavity in the wall which once was the kitchen fireplace. After he stepped down as district president, the visits from miners were less frequent, but the men still knew that "Jock" was a man they could talk to.

Yablonski was a man of formidable bearing and stern manner with a mercurial disposition. In a bad mood, his gravel voice would roar in anger that was awesome and intimidating. In good spirits, he exuded a rugged, masculine charm and warmth that was enormously appealing. His rasping laughter would fill a room and his eyes twinkled knowingly as he spoke. Few could help but like him. He had been one of John L. Lewis's trusted troubleshooters. Although he had grave doubts about some of Lewis's policies, he revered the old man, loved his combative spirit, thrilled to his rhetoric. He saw himself cast in the same mold: rugged and proletarian, but able, clever, and possessed with the magic of leadership. He loved to make speeches and he made them well. He coupled his deep, husky voice with a keen sense of drama and timing that made his rambling speeches theatrical and absorbing.

For all his personal ambition and dislike of Boyle, Yablonski had gone along with the organization for years. He had worked for Boyle's re-election, participated in the permissive use of union money, kept silent about friendliness with the coal industry. One of his most ardent supporters even admitted that he helped rig the pensioner vote to help Boyle win in 1964. "But he wouldn't steal a vote in the District 5 working locals," the supporter said admiringly. Now that Boyle was in hot water and was making the rounds in the coal fields, Yablonski was called upon to introduce him at rallies. He used all his rhetorical skill to praise Boyle at these meetings, even as he was privately expressing his contempt for him.

Nader, in his meetings with Yablonski, used all his persuasive ability to talk Yablonski into making the race against Boyle. Nader spoke of the "sterility" of organized labor as a force for social progress and the need for a "new politics" in the labor movement. He further indicated he would marshal whatever resources he could to help Yablonski. "There's never been a fight I wanted to win more," Nader said. Although Yablonski had strong reservations about breaking with Boyle, he was tremendously impressed with Nader, who he felt would be a powerful ally, lending legitimacy to his cause and attracting support and the interest of the press. And Nader was not the only one urging

Yablonski to challenge Boyle. His possible candidacy had been the chief topic of conversation in the Yablonski family for months. His wife, Margaret, an intelligent and gifted woman whose judgment Yablonski deeply respected, had urged him to make the race. Mrs. Yablonski was joined in this by their daughter, Charlotte, twenty-five, who had been caught up in the spirit of the miners' movement after Farmington while working in the poverty program in northern West Virginia. Also urging Yablonski to take on Boyle was his brother Leon (father of Steve), who was a UMW organizer in Northern West Virginia. Yablonski's oldest son, Kenneth, a thirty-five-year-old lawyer with a thriving practice in the Clarksville area, wanted his father to stop making adulatory speeches for Boyle but would not go so far as to urge him to try for Boyle's job. The same view was expressed by his younger son Joseph, known to everyone as "Chip," who was a National Labor Relations Board lawyer in Washington. Yablonski had also been visited by a delegation of northern West Virginia coal miners, led by Bill Fetty of Morgantown, a black lung activist, who wanted him to challenge Boyle. Yablonski told them he would think it over.

He was torn. The tradition of absolute solidarity in the UMW went back nearly fifty years. Boyle had dealt ruthlessly with dissenters, such as those who opposed him at the 1964 convention. Could he be expected to be gentler with one of his own lieutenants? Also, it was a secure existence Yablonski would be risking. His family might be endangered. All sorts of roadblocks would be thrown in his way. If he did make the move, he told Nader, he would absolutely require two things: an excellent lawyer to fight the inevitable court battles his candidacy would produce, and good press relations. Nader promised he would do his best to provide both. But after six meetings with Yablonski, the decision was still in doubt.

9

On the morning of May 29, 1969, a bemused group of newsmen gathered in the Pan-American Room of Washington's Mayflower Hotel. They were there to attend a press conference held by a man whose name they did not yet know. The night before, each of them had received a phone call from Ralph Nader, who gave them the time and place of the meeting and told them that a top official of the United Mine Workers had a major announcement to make. The reporters were asked to tell no one else of the event. The air of mystery was heightened by the presence of two well-dressed but hefty young men at the doorway, who carefully checked the credentials of each newsman. Outside of Presidential appearances, such checking is extremely rare in Washington, where the competition for publicity is so keen that most public figures are glad to have anyone attend their press conferences. Had someone other than Nader issued invitations to the session without naming the person involved, it is doubtful that a single reporter would have appeared. Few newsmen want to tell their editors they are on their way to a press conference, but don't know who is holding it. As it was, however, both wire services, the television networks, *The New York Times*, *The Wall Street Journal*, the *Washington Post*, *Newsweek*, *The Louisville Courier-Journal*, and a host of smaller publications were on hand.

The guards at the door were Joseph (Chip) Yablonski and his

cousin, Steve. When the television equipment had been set up, they closed the doors. Jock Yablonski sat down at the table at the front of the narrow banquet room before a battery of microphones and began reading a fourteen-page statement that had been distributed to the reporters.

"Today I am announcing my candidacy for the presidency of the United Mine Workers of America. I do so out of a deep awareness of the insufferable gap between the union leadership and the working miners that has bred neglect of miners' needs and aspirations and generated a climate of fear and inhibition. For thirty-five years I have been associated with the union. I have seen this organization stand as the only bulwark against the oppression and greed of the coal operators and the insensitivity and corruption of government in coal mining areas. I have seen the courage and determination of coal miners and union organizers under the leadership of John L. Lewis against the combined power of industry and government who were determined to break the union's will and return the miners to their subterranean serfdom. . . . In an otherwise harsh and hostile environment, the miners relied on their union, trusted their union and gave their union their undivided loyalty. But in recent years, the present leadership has not responded to its men, has not fought for their health and safety, has not improved grievance procedures, has not rooted itself in the felt needs of its membership and has rejected democratic procedures, freedom to dissent and the right of rank and file participation in the small and large issues that affect the union.

"In recent months the shocking ineptitude and passivity of the union's leadership on black lung disease—not to mention its ignoring this massive disability of its men for years—became apparent to the nation, not just to those inside the union. The leadership's inaction toward obtaining workmen's compensation laws, outside of Pennsylvania, to include payments for black lung disability became apparent to the nation. The abject, follow-the-leader posture of the leadership toward the coal industry became apparent to the nation. I have been a part of this leadership. I participated in and tolerated the deteriorating performance of this leadership—but with increasingly troubled conscience. I will no longer be beholden to the past. I can no longer tolerate the low state to which our union has fallen. My duty to coal miners, as I see

it, is not to withdraw but to strive for leadership of this union, to rein-
vigorate its activity with idealism and to make it truly a union of miners
rather than a union of inaccessible bureaucrats. . . ."

Yablonski outlined an eleven-point platform of reforms which promised, among other things, a major drive for improved health and safety
conditions in the mines, a special convention to establish democratic
procedures in all districts, mandatory retirement of union officers at the
age of sixty-five, a modernized grievance procedure, an increase in the
welfare fund royalty, and elimination of nepotism. As he read his statement, it was evident from his occasional faltering and the misplaced
emphasis in certain sentences that this was not his own work, but that
of Nader.

In the question period that followed, Ben Franklin, *The New York
Times*'s reporter whose probing coverage of the coal story since the
Farmington disaster had been unusually trenchant for *The Times*,
asked Yablonski the inevitable question: why had he so "lionized"
Boyle in speeches at union conventions and elsewhere? "I know how
you have to act in this organization since Mr. Boyle became president if
you intend to stay," Yablonski said. Then he recalled a saying John L.
Lewis had once related to him. " 'When ye be an anvil,' " he quoted
Lewis as saying, " 'lay ye very still. But when ye be a hammer, strike
with all thy will.' Today," Yablonski added, "is the day I cease being
an anvil." The quote, paraphrased from a couplet by the seventeenth-
century English poet George Herbert, turned a potentially troublesome
question into a home-run pitch. The reporters were visibly impressed.
"That's very good," murmured Franklin as he jotted it down.

Yablonski also took pains to point out that in 1931, at the age of
twenty, he had served an eight-month prison term for breaking into a
slot machine to retrieve money he had lost. Yablonski said he was later
pardoned for the offence by the governor, and explained that he
brought it up in the certain knowledge that if he didn't, his opponents
would. Asked about the reasons for the unusual security at the press
conference, Yablonski said, "I'm not naive enough to think that there
won't be much difficulty and I know the lengths they will go to." Yablonski was grimly serious as he made the remark, but the reaction of
the reporters seemed one of puzzlement rather than belief.

Seated at Yablonski's side throughout the meeting was Joseph L.
Rauh, Jr., a man familiar to nearly every reporter in town. A lawyer

and former counsel for the United Auto Workers, Rauh had been deeply involved on the liberal side of local and national politics for years. He was former chairman of the District of Columbia Democratic Party and was a major figure in the Leadership Conference on Civil Rights and the Americans for Democratic Action, of which he was a founder. When approached about representing Yablonski—probably without pay—in the race against Boyle, the former law clerk for Supreme Court Justices Cardozo and Frankfurter replied, "If you came into my office as a paying client, I couldn't take you. But if you're ready to fight to clean up this union, then I'll represent you." Such an attitude was typical of Rauh. A tall, grey-haired man with a ruddy complexion and a broad mouth that seemed always wreathed in a triumphant grin, Rauh was noted for the quaint bow ties he invariably wore to work. In his office, his tie came off, his shirt collar was opened, and he worked in shirtsleeves in an atmosphere of busy informality. He had a deep, somewhat nasal voice that was instantly recognizable, usually in the form of hearty laughter or the salty language with which he would describe his adversaries. His manner was open and friendly, but aggressive and determined. To his admirers, he was a laughing, likeable, indefatigable crusader for the underdog. To his detractors, he was a pushy, abrasive loudmouth of suspicious political sympathies. On the wall just inside his unpretentious office overlooking Farragut Square in downtown Washington is a photograph of him conferring with President Johnson at the White House. "To Joe Rauh, a fighter," says the President's inscription. No single word could better describe him. For although he had personal wealth and considerable ability as a lawyer, Rauh was always ready to join a picket line, march in a demonstration or raise havoc at a stockholders' meeting for a cause he believed in. To the Washington business community and the conservatives in Congress, Joe Rauh was a wild man. They were soon to be joined in this opinion by the top officers of the United Mine Workers.

Besides helping map Yablonski's platform, writing his candidacy statement, and organizing his news conference, Nader also assigned two of his summer "raiders" to work in the Yablonski campaign. One, John Bowers, a bearded University of Michigan law student, went to work in the one-room Washington office Yablonski had rented for his headquarters. The other, Beverly Moore, a young man from Harvard Law School, was assigned to assist Rauh.

At the very outset, Yablonski's campaign seemed to have llmitless potential. It was certainly off to a good start. After the news conference, Nader, who had stood quietly in the rear of the room throughout the session, told a friend over lunch that Yablonski should have no trouble winning if he could raise $100,000. On that spring day, this didn't seem an unrealistic objective. With the UMW's declining reputation, the great publicity recently given the coal story, and the help of such recognized activists as Rauh and Nader, the campaign seemed likely to become a liberal cause célèbre. Yablonski came off well in the extensive news coverage given his announcement, and he got a quick boost from Ken Hechler, who made a speech about Yablonski's candidacy and inserted his statement into the Congressional Record, calling his platform "a veritable Magna Carta for the coal miners of America." Union headquarters was silent.

Yablonski's first hurdle was to obtain the fifty local union nominations needed to gain a place on the ballot for the December 9 election. He had no doubt that Boyle would make every effort to deny him this goal and thereby snuff out his candidacy before it had a chance to pick up the kind of broadly based support it would need to be a serious threat. But Yablonski was widely known in the rebellious southwestern coal regions of Pennsylvania and had always gotten along well with the dissidents across the border in Ohio. If he concentrated his nomination campaign in these areas, he was confident that no matter how hard the Boyle organization worked against him he could win the support of at least fifty locals with little difficulty. This territory was, after all, the birthplace of the insurgent movement in the union, and it had pushed strongly for the hopeless candidacy of Steve Kochis five years earlier. The miners were angrier now and Yablonski was a better candidate. His only concern about the nominations, and it was a mild one, was whether he could gain enough local endorsements to lend credibility to his candidacy in areas where he was not well known. He decided to move at a measured pace at the outset, focusing on his home territory and using a large-scale mailing of campaign literature to attract support in the rest of the coal regions. In this manner he hoped he could assure himself of nomination, avoid "peaking" early and conserve his limited resources for the election campaign itself.

The nomination period was scheduled for July 9 to August 9. On June 2, Yablonski wrote Boyle asking for equal time in the UMW *Jour-*

nal and for the right to use the official membership list to mail campaign literature (a right guaranteed under the Landrum-Griffin Act). A week later, he walked into his office at Labor's Non-Partisan League, a block and a half from union headquarters, to find a letter from Boyle telling him he was fired for neglecting his duties as head of the league, a job he had held just a month. Yablonski was instructed to report to District 5 headquarters in Pittsburgh for reassignment.

On Rauh's advice, Yablonski immediately wrote back that he "rejected" the order as a "political reprisal." He continued to occupy the league office. His letter to Boyle contained a day-by-day itemization of how his time had been spent since his assignment to Washington. Boyle retorted in a June 10 letter that unless Yablonski obeyed the firing order, Boyle might take "drastic measures" to discipline him for "insubordination." At this point Rauh felt Yablonski had made a sufficient show of protest and of his desire to keep his job. He recommended that Yablonski return for the time being to Clarksville. Both men thought there was a possibility that the irate Boyle might resort to violence.

Two weeks later, the International Executive Board met and a resolution was introduced approving Boyle's action in firing Yablonski. Yablonski went to the meeting and tried to read his correspondence with Boyle on the subject into the record but Boyle ruled he was out of order. After the resolution was read, the board members took turns speaking in favor of it. Some of the remarks were hardly diplomatic in view of Yablonski's presence. John Kelly, of Pennsylvania District 4, said, "I think it is time that we fight fire with fire. I believe other steps ought to be taken, and they should be taken as soon as possible. Let this board act on them to make them official, because under no circumstances or in no other place can any individual continue to be paid and refuse to work. I think it is time, with all the adverse publicity that has been given to this issue, that this board take immediate action. If it takes the action of this board to remove membership, to cut salaries, or whatever course has to be taken, I feel it is the obligation of this board to support the International President and the executive officers in doing so."

Equally strong, if less specific, suggestions came from Albert Pass, the board member from District 19, home of the hard hats of the 1964 convention. "President Boyle," he said sternly, "we are not going to leave you and the other officers sitting out in that field and these damn fellows behind the bushes shooting at you, you out there by yourself. By God, we will run them out from behind those bushes." The resolution sailed through. Rauh promptly filed suit in United States District Court in Washington to have Yablonski restored to his job because the firing was a political reprisal.

Meanwhile, union general counsel Edward Carey issued an opinion that Yablonski's request for a mailing of campaign literature should be denied because Yablonski was not a "bona fide candidate," since he had not received the requisite nominations to be given a place on the ballot. Rauh took this issue also to court and quickly won an order for the union to distribute the campaign literature to the membership, at Yablonski's expense.

In the midst of all this came another major event: the death on June 11 of John L. Lewis at the age of eighty-nine. Although it was by no means certain, Yablonski had entertained high hopes that the old man would at some point endorse him for the presidency. Lewis's health had been bad and he had seen few people in his final months; nevertheless, the word had gotten around that he was deeply disillusioned with Boyle. Lewis was quoted as saying that making Boyle his heir was "the worst mistake I ever made." As the criticism of the Boyle administration mounted, he was said to have remarked, "Let them drown in their own slime."

Boyle wasted no time in capitalizing on Lewis's death. With maximum dramatics, he declared a three-day mourning period. The *Journal* published a special issue that, while focusing principally on Lewis, managed to work Boyle in wherever possible, consistently harping on the theme that he was Lewis's protege. Even the lead paragraph of assistant editor Lauck's story on Lewis's death was a quote from Boyle's statement on the matter. On June 23, Boyle had the International Executive Board name him the union's new representative to the board of trustees of the welfare fund. The next day, he met with George Judy, the industry trustee. Josephine Roche, the 83-year-old associate of Lewis who was the third trustee, was hospitalized at the time with a broken hip and was not notified of the meeting. Boyle gave Judy the impression, as Judy later put it, that he had Miss Roche's "proxy in his pocket" and thus was in a position to make whatever decision he wanted on the management of the fund, whether Judy agreed or not.

Boyle said he wanted to raise the miners' pensions from $115 to $150 a month. Assuming he would be outvoted whatever he said, Judy went along—a decision that later cost him his job as President of the Bituminous Coal Operators Association. The truth was that Boyle did not have Miss Roche's proxy—indeed, Miss Roche, who was also the chief executive of the fund, was opposed to an increase in the pension because she felt it would be actuarially unsound. Boyle later denied that he intentionally misled Judy about having Miss Roche's vote. But there was no denying that Miss Roche was never consulted about the pension increase, which a General Accounting office investigation later found had put the fund in danger of insolvency within five years.

The pension increase was of great political importance to Boyle. In a union of fewer than two hundred thousand members, there were about seventy thousand pensioners, who, unlike retirees in other unions, were required to maintain their membership and had full voting rights. Although there had been tremendous ferment in the coal fields over the management of the fund, most of the grumbling came from those whose benefits had been cut off or were never granted in the first place and most of these miners, with no reason to remain members of the union, had allowed their memberships to lapse. The only dissidents among the actual pensioners were those who felt their benefits were too small. A thirty percent increase would go a long way toward changing their minds. Since many of them belonged to the six hundred or so locals of dubious constitutionality which were composed entirely of inactive miners, they were to a large degree cut off from the active miners. They knew little of the issues of health and safety, contract benefits, and grievance problems that had so aroused the working men.

The pension increase was not the only setback Yablonski suffered in June. Four days after he announced, he met with a group of local union leaders in a room at the State House Inn in Springfield, Illinois. After the session, which had not been particularly friendly, Yablonski was talking with a few of the men. He was struck in the neck from behind and knocked unconscious. When he awakened several hours later, he was on the floor of the room. Everyone had gone. His head and neck throbbed and his left arm and hand felt numb. Fearing the attack might be only the beginning, he immediately flew back to Pennsylvania. The next day, he was examined by his family doctor in Clarksville, who told him the blow had narrowly missed a spinal nerve. It might otherwise have killed or paralyzed him.

Yablonski had been scheduled to appear that Sunday at a rally in Shenandoah, Pennsylvania, in the heart of the anthracite coal fields. His injury, of course, kept him at home, but his supporters decided to go ahead with the meeting. By this time, Yablonski had reached accord with the small rank and file organization that had sprung up around the candidacy of Elijah Wolford, the Morgantown, West Virginia, miner who announced against Boyle in March. Wolford had formed a ticket with Elmer Brown, the disabled miner from Mingo County who had been so active in the black lung drive. Brown was to be the vice-presidential candidate with Landell Thornsberry, a good-natured rebel miner from eastern Kentucky tentatively chosen as the candidate for secretary-treasurer. When Yablonski announced his candidacy, it became evident that Wolford's ticket could never win, and that its presence could only hurt Yablonski's chances. So Wolford agreed to drop out and support Yablonski in return for a promised job at union headquarters if Yablonski won. Elmer Brown, a man well known and liked in the southern mountain region where Yablonski was virtually unknown, became Yablonski's vice-presidential candidate. No formal agreement was reached with Thornsberry, but since his place on the Wolford slate had been only an informal arrangement, this did not prove to be a problem.

Wolford and Brown met and drove to Shenandoah together the morning of the meeting. There they met William Savitsky, a former anthracite strip-mine worker who had literally been driven from the industry because of his differences with the coal operators and union officials. Savitsky had been fighting the UMW and the operators for years. He had taken his grievances to the Labor Department and the National Labor Relations Board, but with little success. Although he had found work in another field, he still maintained his union membership and waited for the day when a change might come. He had been asked by Wolford and Brown, shortly before Yablonski's announcement, to organize a rally for them. He arranged to use the auditorium of the old high school in town and contacted the miners he knew in the area who might be interested in attending. Most were either retired, disabled or simply inactive. There were only about four thousand active miners in the region and estimates of the inactive went as high as thirteen thousand. Pensions were paltry and the bitterness of the older miners ran deep. A protest committee had been organized by the pensioners, with a fiery old-timer named Charlie Nedd as its chairman. Nedd was one of the first persons Savitsky contacted as he sought to raise a crowd for the rally. Nedd joined Savitsky, Wolford and Brown on the stage of the dingy auditorium as the Sunday meeting was about to begin.

Fewer than fifty men had gathered in the building. As the hour of the meeting arrived, a noisy throng of men marched in and began to disperse throughout the auditorium. About a hundred of them had placards that read "OUR UMWA TEAM—President W. A. Boyle—Vice President—George Pitler [sic]—Secy. Treas.—John Owens." They shouted and marched around for a while, creating a roar that Bill Savitsky, the chairman of the meeting, knew would make it impossible for the speakers to be heard. Nevertheless, he walked to the podium and asked for quiet. The roar continued, but Savitsky began to speak.

"We are here today to begin a campaign which will give us sadly needed reform and return the union to you, the rank and file members, where it belongs, and where the roots of this organization began. We must take steps to restore the damaged image of a once-great union, which has taken on now an attitude and practice of a dictatorial administration, not answerable to the membership and operating more as an exclusive officers club financed by you. We cannot tolerate a leadership any longer which constantly tampers with the truth and deals in deceit."

This was as far as Savitsky got. Boley Overa, an International Representative, stood up in the front of the room and shouted, "Where do you work? You don't do any stripping. Where do you work?" The crowd noise grew still louder. Elijah Wolford got up and tried to speak, but it was no use. He was shouted down. By now at least two hundred Boyle supporters had come into the auditorium. Most of them were younger than the old men who had come to hear the speakers. Charlie Nedd later related what happened as follows: "I said to Mr. Savitsky, 'Bill, maybe I can quiet them,' because I attended hundreds of meetings with the pensioned miners in Pennsylvania. I know we had hecklers at times, but it was not like it was today. The men who attended these meetings are the old members of the United Mine Workers, men who are crippled with miners' asthma and other wounds that they had received in their work in the mines. . . . Finally I looked and I seen these old men getting fidgety, some going to the side to get out the door and others looking at these fellows with the placards hollering and everything like that. There was only one thing for me to do because I knew if anything would have happened there, somebody would have started something, I don't know what the outcome would be but I know some poor pensioned miner would have been hurt. I got up and gaveled the meeting to adjournment. We adjourned the meeting and we waited for fear that maybe they would work on us. So finally we waited about ten minutes and then the hall cleared out and we went home. . . . And I'll tell you, I was frightened."

Although Boley Overa was the most visible of Boyle's hired hands in breaking up the rally, he was not the only union official who took part. John Karlavage, another international representative, played a major role in organizing the mob. He contacted, by his own estimate, about seventy-five of the men and arranged and paid for the signs they carried.

The incident led to repeated efforts by the Yablonski camp to convince the government to take action against those who broke up the rally. The Landrum-Griffin Act provides that, "It shall be unlawful for any person through the use of force or violence, or threat of the use of force or violence, to restrain, coerce, or intimidate, or attempt to restrain, coerce or intimidate any member of a labor organization for the purpose of interfering with or preventing the exercise of any right to which he is entitled under the provisions of this act." The section carries a $1,000 fine or a year's jail sentence, or both. The government, however, never took action. The Labor Department contended that there was "no evidence of violence," while leaving open the question of whether there was the threat of it. Questioned about the rally later, Karlavage would say, "I have seen Holy Name Society meetings that were noisier than this one."

As Yablonski anticipated, Boyle's strategy was to nip his challenge in the bud by preventing him from obtaining the fifty nominations necessary to place him on the ballot. Across the coal fields, a massive effort was underway to undermine his support and to promote Boyle. Miners in Yablonski's area of Pennsylvania known to support him were approached by district officials and told they had better change their allegiance or face unspecified reprisals. Some were offered jobs on the union payroll in exchange for supporting Boyle. Men were hired for "organizing drives," which proved to be little more than excursions, larded with pep talks for Boyle, lasting a few weeks with a paycheck of more than $2,000. Even before Yablonski announced his candidacy, the hierarchy had been fattening the payrolls of the rebellious districts in Ohio and Pennsylvania with men identified as potential insurgent leaders. They were given jobs as "organizers" or on a so-called "Dust Committee" formed to check mines for excessive dust. Since the contract contained no provision for inspections by any such groups, the men could do little but collect their paychecks and work for Boyle's re-election.

Months before Yablonski announced, other efforts were underway to grease the skids for Boyle's re-election. District 5 President Budzanoski, fresh from a trip to Washington in early February, told a meeting of the four District 5 Board members that he had been given $10,000 in union funds to be used in Boyle's campaign. He instructed the four to draw up four false expense vouchers for $2,000 apiece. The vouchers were supposed to claim the money was needed for an effort to stop the West Virginia black lung strike from spreading into Pennsylvania. The four were supposed to cash the checks they received from District Secretary-Treasurer John Seddon and turn the money over to Seddon for use in Boyle's re-election drive. Two of the board members, Marion Pellegrini and Peter Halvonik, carried out their instructions and obtained and turned back to Seddon more than $4,000 which he stashed in a safe deposit box. Pellegrini and Halvonik, however, were close allies of Yablonski and after he announced his candidacy, the matter was reported to the Justice Department. Word of the incident spread before the money was spent and Seddon was then forced to hang onto it.

The UMW *Journal* continued its Boyle-boosting, never once mentioning Yablonski's candidacy, although it was unquestionably the biggest story in the union in years. The *Journal* even gave Boyle and the UMW West Virginia staff credit for the black lung bill. The *Journal* staff also produced a so-called "Election Bulletin," with help from Budzanoski. The eight-page sheet was labeled "produced, paid for and distributed by friends, associates and supporters of W. A. (Tony) Boyle." The fact was that the sheet was worked on by *Journal* editor McCarthy and others on the staff and that it used the *Journal's* photos, and was thus published partly at union expense. It contained one long adulatory story on Boyle which outdid anything McCarthy had ever written for the *Journal*. Under the banner headline: "W. A. 'Tony' Boyle Runs for Re-Election," the story heaped praise on Boyle for his "truly amazing record." The rest of the publication, which was distributed throughout the coal fields, was devoted to scurrilous articles distorting incidents in Yablonski's life. Throughout, Yablonski was referred to as "Loudmouth Joe." The sheet even ran the mug shots taken of Yablonski in connection with his 1931 prison term. Said one headline, using the number on his chest in the photos, "No. 24786 Shall Not Be UMWA President." A typical story went as follows: "In joining the campaign against UMWA President W. A. Boyle, Loudmouth Joe Yablonski has lined himself up with some very interesting company. The big international oil companies which have bought their way into ownership of much of the coal industry with the 27½ percent depletion allowance they get from the American taxpayers—including coal miners, of course—do not like President Boyle. 'Tony' Boyle steps on peoples' toes, especially when those people are adversaries of the United Mine Workers of America. 'Tony' Boyle believes in protecting coal miners' jobs. So 'Tony' has publicly opposed the tax loophole enjoyed by the oil industry. And 'Tony' is against the importation of cheap foreign residual oil because this takes jobs away from coal miners. . . . 'Tony' Boyle has also come out strongly agaInt taxpayer-financed atomic power plants. And the atomic energy industry does not like him because he stirs up trouble for this multi-billion dollar monopoly. Boyle says atomic power plants, financed with government money, are dangerous, uneconomical and a threat to coal miners' jobs. So the Atomic Energy Commission and its 'sleddog,' the Joint Congressional Committee on Atomic Energy are out to 'get' Boyle. Loudmouth Joe Yablonski, very interestingly, had nothing to say about either the oil industry or the atomic industry when he announced he was going to run for Boyle's job. How come? You can draw your own conclusions."

When the nomination period began in July, the Boyle machine redoubled its efforts to crush Yablonski's campaign. With the power to appoint all the officials in nineteen of the twenty-three UMW districts in the United States, Boyle had a ready-made campaign organization. In districts where he was especially weak, such as in Ohio, northern West Virginia and southwestern Pennsylvania, he had shored up his strength by loading the payroll with his potential opponents among the rank and file. He was perhaps weakest of all in the northeastern Pennsylvania anthracite region, but he had taken a major step the previous March to consolidate his grip there. He combined the three anthracite districts into a single new, "provisional" district and eliminated democratic rule, which had prevailed in two of them. The miners in this area were particularly bitter. The industry was in a steep decline from which it showed no signs of recovering, and the hierarchy in Washington was preoccupied with the prospects of the much larger, much more profitable bituminous industry. The health and welfare fund formed for the anthracite miners had been allowed to deteriorate from rampant nonpayment of the eighty-cent-per-ton royalty. Pensions, originally $100 per month, now were $30 for the lucky miners who qualified. Tales of collusion with the industry were everywhere.

Word of dozens of election law violations began to pour into Yablonski headquarters in Washington from across the coal fields, especially from the anthracite region where the work of the union officials was most intense. The Landrum-Griffin Act requires unions to hold nomination meetings with ample advance notice and in conformity with democratic procedures—such as secret balloting—spelled out in the organization's constitution. But at one regular local meeting in the anthracite town of St. Clair, Pennsylvania, for example, nominations were reportedly opened by a district official without any notice whatever. The thirty or so members present, however, turned out to be overwhelmingly for Yablonski. So the Boyle men tried to close the nominations before Yablonski's name could be offered. When this failed, they refused to allow a secret ballot, called for a voice vote and declared Boyle the winner. At a local meeting in Shenandoah, John Karlavage, the Boyle man who helped break up the Yablonski rally, reportedly got a few of his friends together after most other members—unaware that nominations were to be held—had left. Karlavage then pushed through a vote for Boyle. At another nearby local, where it appeared certain Yablonski would be nominated, Karlavage and another union official stood outside and offered money in exchange for supporting Boyle. When several of Yablonski's supporters entered the meeting shortly before the appointed hour of seven P.M., they found the clock on the wall set forward. They were told that Boyle had already been nominated. Elsewhere, local union meetings were reportedly packed with nonmembers who swelled the pro-Boyle vote. Nominations were held in countless locals without notice. Some Yablonski nominations were declared invalid by rump sessions held after most members had left.

When the Boyle forces in the anthracite region were not busy at local union meetings trying to swing nominations away from Yablonski, they spread around an impressive amount of cash on behalf of their boss. Thousands of dollars were spent by Karlavage, Rogers, and their fellow International Representatives in treating members to drinks and food at local taverns and clubs. They approached dozens of influential local union officers with offers of up to $100 for supporting Boyle. Their records later indicated that more than $9000 of Boyle's campaign funds were spent by district officials in the anthracite region during the nomination period.

While there undoubtedly were many miners who accepted the money they were offered to back Boyle, many also refused. As depressed and dismal as these dying coal towns were, and as hard as the miners' lives and work had been, there was a basic strain of almost naive honesty in many of these men. They come from immigrant families. They were brought up to cherish basic values, to appreciate their country, to abide by the law. To them, the money offers were attempts at bribery and they just didn't take bribes.

Louis Kurtz and Joseph Hartzell, for example, were summoned one July afternoon from their homes, which are next door to each other, by Karlavage and Rogers, who sat in a car outside, blowing the horn. The two men, both officers of the same local, climbed into the back seat, not knowing what the meeting was about. Karlavage and Rogers made them an offer. If they supported Boyle, Hartzell would receive $500 and Kurtz and the other officers of the local $200. The men refused. Recalled Hartzell later, "It was not a question of money. I didn't want money and I was not interested. I said I would give them an honest election and every vote would be recorded according to the man's wishes."

John Pacosky, the aging president of the same local, was also called from his home to a meeting in a parked car with Karlavage and Rogers. As Pacosky later recounted it: "Mr. Karlavage said, 'John, we don't want much from you but I want you *not* to run a nomination meeting and for this you get $100.' When I heard that I was so scared I run out of the car. That was the end of the conversation. . . . I was scared because it never happened to me in my whole life, you know. Was never offered nothing from anybody and would never accept anything for anything like that, you know. Not to run the meeting. It was impossible for me not to do that because we advertised the meeting in the local newspaper according to the constitution. As the President my duty was to go to the meeting and open up the nomination, and that is what was done. . . . I didn't ask nobody to vote for either Yablonski or Boyle because I thought myself the best thing for an old man over eighty years old was to be neutral, you know, because each and every man, each and every member can think for themselves. . . . My daughter is living with me and I didn't say nothing to her but she says, 'Pop, what's the matter with you, you are looking so different than any other time,' you know. So then I was thinking for a while and then I thought I ought to tell her, you know. And I did tell her what Mr. Karlavage said and what he offered. So she says, 'Pop, don't worry about it; you just go about according to the United Mine Workers Constitution and that is all.' So she did encourage me a little by saying that. I was very nervous. . . . According to the constitution, you have to give a fair deal to anybody. Anybody wants to run, let them run for office."

Elsewhere in the coal fields, men like Pacosky who could not be bought were resisting the overtures of free-spending district officials. In District 28 in Virginia, for example, two Yablonski supporters gave sworn testimony to this incident. The two men, Ray Hutchinson and Albert Matney, and other miners were taken by district officials to Pittsburgh on Tuesday, July 29. They met with District 5 officials, who urged them to support Boyle and gave them campaign literature. They were also told a variety of tales of Yablonski's alleged misdeeds. From Pittsburgh, they were taken to Washington, where they got a pro-Boyle pep talk from George Titler. They returned to Virginia on Friday, August 1. Their lost wages, lodging, travel, and meals were paid for by a check drawn on the District 28 treasury, and they were paid six days wages although they missed only four. Soon afterwards, Hutchinson was called into District 28 headquarters by Carson Hibbitts, the district president and a key Boyle lieutenant, and offered a job as a part-time campaigner for Boyle. Hutchinson turned it down.

In District 5, a number of the so-called "bogey" locals that had been allowed to exist for so long in the face of clear prohibition by the UMW

Constitution began to be de-chartered by the hierarchy. The purpose seemed obvious. This was Yablonski's home district and he was much more likely to have pensioner support here than in other districts. At other locals, men were offered up to $20 by district officials to vote for Boyle's nomination. Others were simply told they would be "taken care of" if they supported Boyle. The Boyle men seemed not to care who saw them in action. For example, Joe Daniels, a Yablonski supporter and candidate for International Auditor, tried to have Yablonski's name placed in nomination at one District 5 local at Cokeburgh, Pennsylvania, but was told by the president of the local that only nominations for the Boyle slate would be permitted. Daniels went to the nomination meeting anyway. The Boyle team was nominated, seconded, and voted through without any opportunity for mention of other candidates. The meeting was jammed with District 5 officials and pro-Boyle miners who did not belong to the local, but who voted nonetheless. At Fairview, in northern West Virginia, Yablonski was nominated by one local, forty-nine to forty-five. After some discussion, during which a number of members left, another vote was taken. Boyle was then declared the winner, thirty-six to thirty-five.

In Washington, reports of these and dozens of similar incidents poured into Yablonski headquarters and were passed along to Beverly Moore, the young law student assigned by Nader to assist Rauh. Moore checked out the reports as best he could by telephone and solicited affidavits from those willing to give them. A series of letters detailing the election violations was then sent over Rauh's signature to Secretary of Labor George Shultz, the bland former economics professor regarded as the chief liberal in the Nixon cabinet. Four such letters were sent Shultz in July. Each requested that he use his powers under the Landrum-Griffin Act to order an "immediate and continuing investigation . . . of the illegal activities of the officers of the union seeking to prevent the nomination of Mr. Yablonski and Mr. Brown. . . ." The letters cited section 601 of the act, which says, "The Secretary shall have power when he believes it necessary in order to determine whether any person has violated or is about to violate any provision of this Act . . . to make an investigation. . . ." Although the first two letters from Rauh detailed more than thirty violations, Shultz wrote back on July 23 that there would be no investigation. "Although the Secretary of Labor does have the power under Section 601 . . . to investigate election irregularities at any time," Shultz wrote, "it is the Department of Labor's long-established policy not to undertake investigations of this kind without having a valid complaint . . . after an election has been completed. In the absence of such a complaint the Secretary of Labor lacks the enforcement authority prescribed in Section 402." Section 402 empowers the Labor Department to investigate alleged violations after an election and then to ask the courts to invalidate the election and order a new one. Shultz's position was that, since he could do nothing to overturn the election until after it was over, it was pointless to investigate until then. While a pre-election investigation would have been unprecedented, to Rauh and the Yablonski camp, Shultz's position was incredible, especially in an administration elected on a promise to restore law and order to the land. Wouldn't evidence of election violations be more easily obtained shortly after they occurred rather than months later? Wouldn't the fact that the government had moved in to investigate tend to deter further violations? Couldn't evidence of election fraud, such as doctored tally sheets and records of misused money, be destroyed if the government didn't move quickly? Certainly the Yablonski camp thought so. But Shultz did not agree and made this clear in his letter. "Assuming that a Department of Labor investigation will establish that the unremedied violations which you allege have occurred," he said, "I fail to see what corrective effect such an investigation will have, absent any enforcement authority at this time." Nevertheless, two days after his letter was sent to Rauh, W. J. Usery, an assistant labor secretary, sent a warning to Boyle that unless fair election procedures were observed, the department might find it necessary to investigate before the general election on December 9. This gave Yablonski and his supporters some hope that Shultz's refusal was not final—that if the violations continued, the department might eventually move in. So they continued to bombard the Labor Department with letters detailing more violations and pleading for reconsideration of the decision against an investigation.

The day after the Shultz letter arrived, Rauh went to see the Secretary to ask him to reconsider. He pointed out to Shultz that there had already been violence against Yablonski and that there might be more. If this occurred, Rauh warned, the secretary would have it on his conscience forever. Shultz was unmoved. He was not a lawyer, and he was getting his advice from the department's ambitious, excitable general counsel, Laurence Silberman, whose opinion it was that Congress intended the Labor Department to avoid interfering in internal union affairs as much as possible. Therefore, despite the fact that the Landrum-Griffin Act empowered the Secretary to order an investigation "when he believes it necessary," Silberman felt that Shultz should avoid breaking precedent, and not order the department into the Mine Workers' election until after the vote, if at all. This line of reasoning, of course, made the warning to Boyle of a possible pre-election investigation hard to explain. Such inconsistencies didn't bother either Silberman or Shultz.

Shultz's refusal was not Rauh's first rebuff in his efforts to interest the government in the UMW election. On June 28, he had visited Henry Peterson, head of the Justice Department's labor rackets group, to ask him to see that a thorough investigation was made into the slugging of Yablonski in Illinois. More urgently, Rauh asked that protection be given Yablonski for the rest of the campaign. Rauh never got an answer from Peterson.

In contrast to the union-wide organization of paid employees that was the nucleus of Boyle's campaign team, Yablonski's forces were pathetic indeed. The "Miners for Yablonski" campaign headquarters was a tiny, barely furnished one-room office behind an unmarked door in an old Washington office building across Connecticut Avenue from Rauh's office. It was manned by Chip Yablonski, on leave from his job at the National Labor Relations Board, and John Bowers, the Nader "raider" loaned to the campaign. Bowers soon discovered, however, that he had little rapport with the candidate and was eventually assigned elsewhere by Nader. This left Chip to run the headquarters and act as press agent. Although intelligent and immensely likeable, the young Yablonski knew nothing of the news business and, although he did his best to crank out press releases and stimulate coverage for the campaign, his efforts were largely ineffective.

Despite the ragtag nature of his organization, Yablonski remained confident that he would win at least fifty nominations, although he knew the heavy duty efforts of the Boyle organization would keep his total from being impressive. So, in accordance with his plans, Yablonski did relatively little campaigning in the nomination period. There were a few rallies organized by his longtime supporters in Pennsylvania, and one in Matewan, West Virginia, set up by Elmer Brown. Much of Yablonski's time was spent in Washington, where his suit for reinstatement at Labor's Non-Partisan League at first made it necessary for him to pay close attention to his disputed job. Most of his weekends were spent at home in Clarksville in the company of a group of veteran union men who could accurately be described as his henchmen. Most of them had held elected positions in the UMW, either as local or district officers, and they represented a cross-section of the ethnic groups that made up the population of the coal regions of southwestern Pennsylvania and eastern Ohio. Among them were Mike Trobovich, Marion Pellegrini, Mike Encrapera, Peter Halvonik, Lou Antal, Nick DeVince and Karl Kafton. Several of them still worked in the mines and were the objects of periodic wooing by the union hierarchy. Antal, for example, was repeatedly approached with job offers, which he refused. Turning down a job offer from a union that one believes is corrupt and tyrannical is not as simple as it might seem. These men, for all their intelligence and anger, still had to go down in some coal mine every day to perform dangerous, difficult work. A job with the union offered more money, an expense account, relatively easy work, and, above all, got them out of the mines. If they were hired as so-called "organizers," it would not be hard for them to convince themselves that they would give it their best and work within the organization to bring the needed changes. Dozens of men on whom Yablonski had counted for support did take such jobs and turned against him. But many others, like Antal, refused. It says much about them that they did.

Yablonski knew his close friends and personal following among the miners in the three union districts in southwestern Pennsylvania would bring in a number of local endorsements, despite the efforts of the Boyle machine to undercut him. He would probably also do well in District 6, just across the river in Ohio, which was probably the most rebellious district in the UMW. Some locals in Elmer Brown's area of southern West Virginia might also support him, and he could count on endorsements in the anthracite region, although they might be limited by the extreme measures union officials were taking in that area.

Yablonski, outside of his old friends in Pennsylvania, had nothing that could be called an organization—no one to plan and organize rallies and meetings for him, no one to make it possible for him to go into a strange area and "campaign." Under court order, the union in late June had been forced to send out a mailing of Yablonski campaign literature, however, which was beginning to get results. Letters, many of them containing small contributions, began to come in to the "Miners for Yablonski" office in Washington. Early in July, Yablonski's wife, Margaret, an extremely pleasant, dark-haired woman of fifty-seven with a creative touch (she had written several plays, of which one about coal miners, entitled "Shorty," had been put on by a theater group in Pittsburgh) had put together with help from Mike Trobovich and others a four-page tabloid newspaper on Yablonski's campaign. It contained pictures of Yablonski and Brown and a point-by-point rebuttal of the charges in Boyle's "Election Bulletin." It summarized Yablonski's platform under what was to become the oft-repeated slogan, "A Bill of Rights for Coal Miners." The paper also carried an open letter from Yablonski. Although the publication was rather crude, it was easy to read and provided something that could be sent to those who wrote "Miners for Yablonski" requesting literature.

While Yablonski did not barnstorm the coal fields, he did make some important alliances in June and July. Bill Savitsky contacted him shortly after his announcement and offered his help. The two men spoke often by telephone and Savitsky's thin, slightly high-pitched voice and humble manner gave Yablonski the impression—until he and Savitsky finally met—that he was dealing with a much older and less energetic man. But Savitsky, in his unassuming way, had been a one-man movement in the anthracite region for years. A tall, greying man with blunt, plain features and a stoic expression, Savitsky was not especially well spoken. But he was intelligent and thoughtful and could express himself well in writing. And he had done a lot of writing. His files were stuffed with carbon copies of handwritten letters of protest on yellow legal sheets, which had gone to newspapers, UMW officials, and a variety of government agencies. Although the union and the government had been little help, Savitsky had established himself with the local press as an honest man with a legitimate cause. In addition, he was highly regarded by the dissident miners in the area, particularly the embittered pensioners who had formed a group called the Pensioned Miners Protest Committee. Savitsky would prove to be a fearless and tireless ally in a region where Yablonski's potential was great and the work of the union officials most intense.

In July, Yablonski met with a group of about twenty West Virginia miners at the home of Levi Daniel in Beckley. Daniel, a solidly built black man with a calm, reassuring manner, was one of the authentic rank-and-file leaders in his area. He was recording secretary of his local and was widely respected. Also at the meeting were Arnold Miller, Charles Shawkey, Woodrow Mullins, and others who had been active in the black lung drive. It was crucial to Yablonski to win over these men, for they were the nucleus of the rebel movement that had started around the black lung issue and was now in search of a new battle-ground. As Arnold Miller later remembered it, "We were kind of suspicious of him at first. But Jock sat down and asked us what we wanted to talk about. He took off his coat and loosened his tie and sat there with us for several hours. He gave straight answers to all our questions and he looked you in the eye when he spoke. We were really impressed."

Another miner who had received word of Yablonski's candidacy was Ed Yevincey, a redheaded six-footer in his early thirties with the build of a football player, who worked a steamshovel at a strip mine in the union's District 23 in west Kentucky. This was an area remote from the eastern coalfields and considered to be strong Boyle territory. Yablonski did not expect much support here. But Yevincey showed up at Yablonski's home in Clarksville while on a visit to see relatives in Pennsylvania and offered his help. "He was the kind of guy," Chip Yablonski later remembered, "that you just knew didn't take any shit." Like many of the other men who rallied to Yablonski's cause, Yevincey was president of his local and had the two ingredients essential for leadership among the working men: intelligence and personability.

Yablonski's support among the black lung crusaders was further aided when Drs. Rasmussen and Wells called a press conference late in July in Charleston to endorse him publicly. Their statements in support of Yablonski were well covered by the press, radio, and television. Throughout the meeting with reporters, held in a conference room of a downtown motel, Dr. Buff sat impassively at the end of the table where Wells and Rasmussen spoke. Rasmussen, whose idea the endorsement had been, had asked Buff to join him and Wells in backing Yablonski. But Buff liked to think of himself as the miners' saviour; he wanted to be the focus of attention in the coal controversy. So he refused, to the great annoyance of the other two. During the news conference, he did pipe up that his silence on Yablonski was not to be taken as an endorsement of Boyle. Earlier, on July 4, Buff had staged a well-publicized but sparsely attended rally for the health and safety legislation on the steps of the Jefferson Memorial. Yablonski appeared, but was not permitted by Buff to speak. Also mingling in the crowd were several UMW officials, including Suzanne Richards, the powerful, $40,000-a-year executive assistant to Boyle. Yablonski, still smarting from the karate blow he had received just a week earlier, strode up to Miss Richards and barked angrily, "You can't scare me off. You'll have to kill me to get me out of this."

Meanwhile, Yablonski's victories in court helped give his campaign an aura of momentum. His first and easiest triumph had come in mid-June, when the Federal Court in Washington ordered his campaign literature distributed to the membership. At about the same time, Rauh filed suit to have Yablonski reinstated at Labor's Non-Partisan League and had asked the court to award him damages for the firing. At first, Boyle claimed that Yablonski was dismissed for neglect of duty. But Yablonski countered this charge with his itemized statement of how his time had been spent since his assignment to Washington. When the matter went before the International Executive Board, a new rationale was used in the resolution approving the firing—namely that Yablonski had opposed the official policy of the organization. On July 15, therefore, District Judge Howard Corcoran ruled that the firing was a political reprisal and ordered Yablonski restored to his job. The issue of damages was put off, pending a thorough trial.

In August, another major suit was filed. Although it did not involve Yablonski directly, it added fuel to one of his key campaign issues—the management of the welfare and retirement fund. The suit charged the UMW, the welfare fund, the National Bank of Washington, and the Bituminous Coal Operators Association with "willfully defrauding" miners and their families out of at least $75 million in a conspiracy for private gain. The plaintiffs were seventy-eight active, retired, and disabled miners and widows of miners, joined by the leaders of the four-thousand-member West Virginia-based Disabled Miners and Widows, Incorporated. The Disabled Miners and Widows had been formed three years earlier in an attempt to obtain welfare fund benefits for thousands of miners and widows who had been unable to meet the fund's shifting criteria for them, or who had seen their benefits cut off. Representing the plaintiffs was Harry Huge, a young Washington lawyer on leave from the prestigious firm of Arnold & Porter, who was spending a year with a public-interest law firm called The Washington

Research Project. Huge had first become acquainted with the grievances of the miners and widows while in West Virginia six months earlier to work on a magazine article about black lung. He got to know the
officers of the widows and miners association and agreed to take their
case. He had spent most of his time thereafter gathering information
for the complaint. Specifically the suit charged what many already
knew: the fund had engaged in bizarre investment policies—such as
keeping up to $70 million in non-interest-bearing checking accounts—
which deprived the fund's beneficiaries of huge sums of money. Huge
told reporters at a Washington news conference at which the suit was
announced that the fund's assets had also been improperly used to
benefit certain coal companies, in addition to being used to fatten the
coffers of the UMW-controlled National Bank of Washington. The defendants, said the suit, "intended to and did use the welfare fund for
their own financial purposes." Asked to comment on the suit, Assistant
UMW *Journal* editor Rex Lauck said, "pure hogwash."

By late July, word of nominations was being heard from the union's
roughly 1,300 locals, and the Yablonski camp was keeping careful track
in anticipation of a possible flim-flam with the official count by Secretary-
Treasurer John Owens. Self-addressed postcards had been mailed to
the recording secretaries of most locals; the officers were asked to fill
out the cards and return them with the results of the nomination in
their local. By the first week in August, Yablonski had received good
news from well over fifty locals. He scheduled a news conference for
August 11 to claim nomination, hoping his announcement would discourage the Boyle administration from trying to pull a last-ditch fast
one. His count showed him with eighty-five nominations the morning of
his news conference. A surprising number—a dozen—had come from
west Kentucky, where Ed Yevincey had been passing the word. Yablonski also ran strong in Ohio, with at least fifteen nominations, and in
his home area, where he had expected to do well. He received at least
scattered support from every district. "I can report today a total victory
in the first round of . . . the struggle to oust Tony Boyle from the
leadership of the Mine Workers," Yablonski told the reporters who
gathered at the Mayflower. "Five years ago, in a desperate effort to
prevent future challenges to his presidency, Boyle had the Mine Workers Constitution amended to increase the number of local union nomi-

nations required for a place on the ballot from five to fifty. Boyle assumed that, with all the power at his command, no man could ever win the nomination of fifty local unions. But he was wrong; in the last thirty days, eighty-five local unions have voted to nominate me for president. We have verified each of these eighty-five nominations. And about an equal number have voted to nominate Elmer Brown for Vice-President on our ticket. This was accomplished by rank-and-file miners with no money and very little organization. . . ."

The next day, UMW headquarters, apparently chastened by the Labor Department's warning, made it official. Yablonski had gotten ninety-six local endorsements, Elmer Brown eighty-six. Both would be on the ballot. And Tony Boyle? He got 1,056.

10

In the atmosphere of magisterial privacy that had surrounded the Boyle administration until the Farmington disaster, the union's procedures for dispensing money had grown rather informal, to say the least. When a district asked the International for one of the so-called "loans" that all districts received to operate their offices, all that was required was a letter giving some general justification for the money, such as "organizing expenses" or "administration." Upon receipt of the request, Boyle would instruct Secretary-Treasurer Owens to send the money and a check would be forwarded immediately. The check would be either deposited in the district's bank account or, in some cases, cashed by a district official. No documentation beyond that contained in the letter of request was required and the districts kept no detailed records of how the money was spent. In 1967 and 1968, the International paid out $3.2 million in this fashion. In 1969, with the election upcoming, the "loans" grew larger, particularly in the districts close to Yablonski's home territory. By the end of the year, for example, the International had pumped $360,000 into District 5, compared to $180,000 the year before. In nearby District 2, the amount jumped from $315,000 to $480,000. In District 31, encompassing northern West Virginia, the figure zoomed from $81,000 to $252,000. The year's total for all districts exceeded $2 million.

The hierarchy was equally cavalier about salaries and expenses. Boyle regularly raised the salaries of various officials, including members of his family and relatives of other international officials, without consulting the International Executive Board, which has sole authority under the union constitution to fix salaries. Expense account vouchers were submitted without even a hint of documentation—no hotel bills, no credit card receipts, nothing—and paid without question. It was not unheard of for officials to claim expenses of as much as $20 a day while on vacation. Mileage estimates in expense vouchers were based upon the wildest guesses. Between 1967 and the end of 1969, the International paid its officers and employees $1.5 million to cover some 2,500 expense account vouchers submitted without documentation. Also paid without question were the medical bills of Boyle and his co-officers, as well as the tab for Boyle's foreign travel.

In the district offices, the pattern was the same. Officials submitted unsubstantiated vouchers for so-called "organizing expenses," which were paid without question. More than nine hundred of these were paid from 1967 through 1969 at a total cost of nearly $750,000. There were also seven thousand regular expense accounts—similarly undocumented—totaling $2.3 million paid by the district office in the 1967–69 period. District 12 Board Member Jesse M. Ballard, for example, was reimbursed for mileage and other expenses during a five-day period throughout which he was hospitalized. Two other District 12 officials made a practice of turning in grossly overestimated mileage vouchers which they justified to one inquisitor as referring to "short miles."

From 1967 through the 1969 election, the Boyle administration spent a total of more than $10 million for which it could not account in any way that came close to satisfying the Labor Department's interpretation of the bookkeeping requirements of the Landrum-Griffin Act. No one will ever know for sure what happened to all of this money, but there can be little doubt that much of it was used, in one way or another, to promote Boyle's re-election. During the campaign, nineteen local union presidents in District 5 were put on the payroll for six weeks for a so-called "organizing drive" in Butler and Mercer Counties, in Pennsylvania. There is no record that any mines were organized, but the men were paid approximately $1,650 apiece for their services. Later ten of them made another six-week trip into the same area and were paid at about the same rate. When Ray Hutchinson, Albert Matney, and the others made their trip to Pittsburgh and Washington, the bill for their travel and lost wages, which came to $3,180, was charged to

District 28 "organizing expenses." In the same District, the Boyle campaign organization operated out of the district office using union personnel. The same was true across the border in District 30 in eastern Kentucky.

In this free-spending atmosphere, it is not surprising that Yablonski's candidacy attracted no defectors from the ranks of the union's officials. He was the underdog, after all, and they were, almost to a man, accountable to Boyle for their comfortable jobs. So most worked feverishly to re-elect the incumbents. To augment this awesome political machine, Boyle sought outside professional help. He hired Oscar Jager, a veteran labor and political public relations man who had edited a variety of union publications. A portly, balding man who looked like a shorter, fatter Phil Silvers, Jager was paid close to $1,500-a-week for his services. Because Jager could not devote full time to the project, Boyle also hired Alex Bilanow, a Washington newspaperman, to operate the "Miners Committee for Boyle–Titler–Owens" headquarters, which opened in an office building across the street from the UMW shortly after Yablonski's nomination became official.

Joe Rauh was astonished when he heard that Boyle had hired Jager. He had known Jager for years and had once served with him on the board of an Americans for Democratic Action chapter. Although Jager was no militant, in his years as a labor and political publicist he had always been associated with liberal causes. One of his top accounts, for example, was that of Democrat Milton Shapp, the Pennsylvania millionaire, who had made a strong bid for the governorship in 1966 and was planning to make the race again in 1970. Rauh telephoned Jager, who maintained an office in Washington, to find out why he had taken the account. Jager hemmed and hawed about the matter, but insisted that he had not taken it on for the money. Snorted Rauh afterwards, "If he didn't do it for the money, then what in the hell did he do it for?"

Jager soon found himself on the defensive with newsmen. "I'm not saying these are the greatest union leaders," he cautioned one interviewer. Asked about the huge checking accounts maintained by the welfare fund in the union-owned National Bank of Washington, Jager replied, "They have been able to use the income from the bank to hold down their dues." It was an explanation that had not been heard before and has seldom been heard since. Why did Boyle refuse to allow the election of district officers? "Because of vested interests in the union and

the shadow of John L. Lewis," said Jager. Did this mean that Boyle
would like to establish district democracy? "I think he would love to,"
said Jager, adding, "I didn't take this thing until I conferred with them.
There are conditions that I have laid down. They have told me they
mean it."

The Boyle administration was clearly in a weak position on most of
the issues Yablonski had seized. The incumbents were destined to remain on the defensive unless some issues could be found—or fabricated
—to give Boyle something to campaign on. Here is where Jager's advice was important. He urged that Boyle come out for a vast program
of reform, and announce ambitious objectives for the next contract.
This tactic would give him a platform other than his record. To discredit Yablonski, Boyle should pound away at the fact that Yablonski
had gone along with the incumbents for years, publicly heaping lavish
praise upon them almost until the very day he announced his candidacy. Coupled with this clearly legitimate issue would be the claim that
Yablonski was the tool of "outside" forces seeking to take over the
UMW.

Both camps kept a low profile in August. But while there was not
much campaigning there were some important developments. Yablonski could not afford the services of a professional political publicist like
Jager, so he looked instead for a capable newspaperman who could act
as press secretary and hold down the Miners for Yablonski office in
Washington. Although it did not seem likely that a good reporter would
be willing, or even able, to get a four-month leave of absence to take
such a hectic job at relatively small pay, Yablonski was lucky. Fred
Barnes, a young reporter for the Washington *Evening Star*, heard about
the opportunity at a time when he was growing increasingly bored with
his job covering the city courts. Barnes had followed the UMW story
through the papers and the reporters' grapevine. He felt Yablonski had
all the issues on his side and that it was a worthy cause. He got the
required leave of absence and signed on with Yablonski in August at
$200 a week.

While Yablonski was making this alliance, another one was in the
process of dissolution. Ralph Nader had expected that Yablonski would
set out from the day he announced his candidacy to carry his message
to every coal town in the country. He envisioned an aggressive, barn-
storming drive in which Yablonski would emphasize not only union

issues but the broader issues that the candidate had spoken of in his May 29 statement. Instead, Yablonski seemed to be taking it easy. Before he won nomination, he spent relatively little time in the coal fields, and now that his place on the ballot was assured, he seemed to be no more aggressive. For the first three weeks in August, he did virtually no campaigning. The image of Jock Yablonski as the embodiment of a "new politics" in the labor movement was not being projected and Nader was growing disillusioned. Reporters who visited the Miners for Yablonski office and talked to Chip were impressed with how vague the campaign plans seemed and with how amateurish the publicity was. This situation was immediately improved by the addition of Barnes to the staff, but he, too, was disappointed at the lackadaisical quality of the crusade, which was enhanced by Yablonski's announcement to his staff that he would do no campaigning in eastern Kentucky or in Tennessee. "Why not?," he was asked. "What are you trying to do, get me killed?" he would growl, then lapse into moody silence. Word of all this reached Nader and seemed to confirm his fears. Yablonski seemed a reluctant warrior. Furthermore, Nader and Gary Sellers had both seen the "Election Bulletin" circulated by the Boyle team and reportedly were troubled by its allegations. Everyone associated with Yablonski insisted that they were scurrilous lies, but doubt apparently remained. If there were any skeletons in Yablonski's closet, this was the kind of campaign in which they would undoubtedly be revealed. Nader's name was linked to Yablonski's already; if he played the major role in the campaign that the Yablonski forces expected, the association might be reinforced. Should Yablonski come out of the campaign looking like a crook instead of a crusader, Nader's reputation would also be damaged. Since Nader's greatest resource was his credibility, he apparently decided not to run the risk of becoming too closely associated with the Yablonski campaign. He became increasingly hard to reach. The advice and other assistance—such as help in raising money—that Yablonski had expected from Nader did not materialize. "What's the matter with Nader? Why haven't we heard from him?" Yablonski was wondering aloud by the final weeks of August.

Joe Rauh, on the other hand, never flinched. He seemed more committed to the effort as time went on. Despite a busy schedule, he gave many hours to the campaign. Although a trial of Yablonski's suit for damages from his firing was a distant prospect, the case gave Rauh the opportunity to take Boyle's deposition, a bitter pill indeed for Boyle, considering the hatred which he and his associates had quickly developed for the aggressive Rauh. It was a tense session, held in Rauh's office on August 21, with Boyle attended by three lawyers. Rauh was alone except for Beverly Moore, who sat in more as spectator than participant. At one point, however, Boyle became extremely agitated at Moore, whose facial expressions apparently failed to hide his reaction to Boyle's testimony. Suddenly, Boyle said, "And you can snicker all you want to because I will yank you by the long hair if you fool around with me. . . . You fool around with me and I will grab him by the hair. Put that on the record." Later, gesturing toward Moore, he shouted at Rauh, "He won't make too many more faces at me when you don't see him. I will say that." Despite the outburst, Rauh was able to extract some revealing answers from Boyle. The UMW President asserted, for example, that Yablonski had plenty of notice that he might be fired from his job. "Mr. Yablonski was on notice," said Boyle. "Plenty of notice. He gave his own warning on May 29." By his actions on that date, said Boyle, "he was in violation of the constitution" and "wasn't carrying out the policies of the international organization or its convention." The statement Yablonski issued to reporters that day as he announced his candidacy "is in violation of the principles and policies enunciated by the organization down through the years since 1890," said Boyle.

At the same time, Rauh continued to pressure the Labor Department for an investigation. In mid-August, he sent another letter to Secretary Shultz detailing twenty further violations of the election procedures of the Landrum-Griffin Act. By now, Rauh had notified the department of more than fifty such alleged violations with most of the charges buttressed by affidavits or other evidence. Rauh even had canceled checks drawn on the District 28 treasury to back up his charge that union money was used to pay for Ray Hutchinson's propaganda tour to Washington and Pittsburgh.

In an effort to counter Yablonski's allegations, Boyle proposed that a five-member "Fair Elections Committee" be appointed to supervise the campaign and "make certain that the forthcoming election shall be carried out strictly in accordance with the UMWA constitution and the laws of the United States of America." The proposal sounded good, but Rauh immediately smelled mischief in it. He and Yablonski sent back a letter rejecting the idea and suggesting instead that either the American Arbitration Association or the Honest Ballot Association be hired to watch the election. "It is ludicrous," the letter said, "to propose a five-man panel to insure an honest election count at more than a thousand locals scattered across the United States and Canada and involving more than 150,000 active and retired miners. It is downright laughable to think that this small committee could cope with the gigantic task of tracking down the daily violations of the law you are committing in your campaign. And the stealing of votes, like your stealing of nomination elections, will occur in the precincts—not in Washington. . . . Running an honest election in December is not for a five-man panel in Washington, but for a nationwide organization in the business of honest elections." A copy of the letter was sent to the Labor Department with the request that Secretary Shultz use his "good offices" to convince the Boyle administration to accept the Yablonski proposal. Boyle, predictably, rejected the idea and repeated his original offer. The Labor Department soon afterward again turned down the appeal for an investigation and refused also to take part in the appointment of an outside organization. "I think it would not be appropriate for the Department of Labor to urge the adoption or rejection of either" plan, wrote Assistant Secretary W. J. Usery, Jr.

Rauh also went to court, on August 26, to ask for equal space for Yablonski in the UMW *Journal,* which had mentioned Boyle 166 times since Yablonski announced his candidacy while referring to the challenger only once outside the official roster of union officers published each month. The case was set for trial in mid-September.

As these developments unfolded in Washington, strikes broke out on two fronts in the coal fields. In southern West Virginia a wave of wildcats started over a contract dispute and closed thirty-six mines in three counties before dying out. At issue was a new graduated vacation clause which granted extra annual leave to men with ten years' experience. It is characteristic of the UMW contract that it failed to make clear whether this meant ten years' experience of any kind or ten years with the same company. Naturally, the companies favored the latter interpretation, the miners the former. When the inevitable conflict arose, the miners disdained the formal grievance procedures set forth in the contract and resorted to direct action. The result was a stalemate in which the companies demanded that the union get the men back to work and the union officials protested that the strike was unauthorized and out of their control. Gradually, the men trickled back to work with the issue still unsettled. It was a familiar pattern.

In northern West Virginia and southwestern Pennsylvania another contract dispute led to the firing of five men at Consolidation Coal's large Humphrey Number 7 mine at Morgantown, West Virginia. Roving pickets fanned out through the region, and within a week eight thousand men were out of work at about thirty large mines in West Virginia, Pennsylvania, and Ohio. Although the miners again chose direct action over the formal grievance machinery, the union's handling of the matter provides a good example of why the grievance procedure was held in such low esteem. After the strike had been on about ten days, Boyle dispatched two members of the International Executive Board to try to resolve it. The issue seemed clear: the company was required by the contract to post job vacancies so miners with the necessary seniority could exercise their claim to them. At Humphrey Number 7, the company had simply been ignoring this provision. The firings grew out of the resulting dispute and touched off the strike, which spread rapidly to other companies; coal miners are notoriously unselective in the targets of their wildcat strikes. After several days of negotiation between Boyle's agents and Consolidation, a settlement was announced—the five fired men would be reinstated with full seniority, but not until after a thirty-day suspension. The strike had been on for two weeks by this time and most of the miners were ready to go back to work, so the strike ended. But there was considerable grumbling over the agreement. After all, the men argued, the company had been flouting the contract and the five fired miners were right. Why should they be punished at all? Such settlements as these made many miners reluctant to put their contract problems in the hands of UMW officials through the formal grievance procedure.

As the union and company representatives met to settle the dispute, Yablonski went into the heart of the strikebound region for his major campaign rally of the month. It was held August 24, a sunny, sweltering Sunday, in the grimy Ohio industrial town of Bellaire, on the banks of the Ohio River. About 250 miners, most of them from the militant Ohio District 6, turned out to hear Yablonski. With him were two of his fel-

low insurgent candidates, Elmer Brown and Joe Daniels, who was running for International Auditor, and several of Yablonski's close friends
from Pennsylvania, including Mike Trobovich and Marion Pellegrini.
The chairman of the meeting was Karl Kafton, perhaps Yablonski's
ablest and most loyal supporter among the rank and file. In this friendly
atmosphere, Yablonski was at his best as a campaigner. Before the
meeting, he mingled with the incoming crowd at the gate of the high
school stadium that had been rented for the occasion. He already knew
many of these men, but those he did not know got an enthusiastic
handshake and a friendly, "How're you doing? Glad to see you," in
Yablonski's raspy, deep voice. Although he moved quickly from one
knot of men to another, he managed to do it without seeming imper-
sonal or distracted. The rostrum for the rally was set up on the edge of
the football field, across the cinder track from the covered grandstand
where the miners took their seats. A few benches were placed in the
bright sun behind the podium. Everyone spoke before Yablonski, and
some of the speakers were in no hurry. Joe Daniels, a man who looked
more like a card-sharp than a coal miner, in his shiny suit and snap-brim
hat, gave a good speech, and Elmer Brown, although no great orator,
made a favorable impression with his obvious sincerity. Finally, Yablonski rose to speak. He had taken his coat off and loosened his
tie in the oppressive heat. He looked good that way. His speech
was a rambling series of comments on various issues in the election. With each, Yablonski would start in normal tones, build as he
neared his point, and then open up to full volume as he hammered
home his message, often in blunt, off-color language. The response was
tremendous. The men chuckled when he ridiculed the two International Board Members whom Boyle had sent to settle the strike. He
called them "a couple of old gaffers, creaking at the joints." They
cheered and whistled when he denounced Boyle for his remarks at the
Farmington disaster. But what really sent the crowd was the way he
disposed of a rumor that had been making the rounds in the coal fields.
"Now some of you might have heard," he began quietly, "that if I'm
elected, I'm going to keep Boyle on as trustee of the welfare fund. That
this is part of a deal I made with him. Well, I'll tell you something. The
first thing I'm going to do when I take office [louder now, and faster] is
I'm going to go through the books and I'm going to investigate Boyle

for squandering your dues and the plunder of the welfare fund. And then I'm going to the Justice Department [now roaring, right hand raised, gesticulating] and I'm going to send Tony Boyle to the penitentiary." The men loved that. They jumped to their feet, laughing and cheering. They applauded for two minutes, while Yablonski, grinning, paused for a drink of water. "He's sure a good talker," said one man in the front row, shaking his head and smiling as the applause died down.

The Bellaire rally illustrated one of Yablonski's advantages—and one of his major problems. He came across well in person. He looked, acted, and sounded like a labor leader. He was forceful and persuasive, and he had a certain rugged charm that made men like him. Tony Boyle had none of these qualities. But for Yablonski to exploit this advantage, he would need to hold rallies like the one at Bellaire in every section of the coal fields. In Ohio, it was easy. The miners were longtime rebels and Yablonski had many friends among them. Elsewhere in the coal regions, however, he was a virtual stranger, with no friends and no organization. And the union officials were doing everything they could to undercut him. If his campaign were to have a chance, he would have to make contact with rank-and-file leaders in the vast sections of the coal fields where he was now unknown and win them over. With their support, he would have an organization of sorts to help him campaign, to hold rallies, and to meet the great number of miners he would need to know to overcome the recognition gap which was one of Boyle's great advantages. He received some encouragement in this respect the day of the Bellaire rally when he learned from Elmer Brown that the officers of the West Virginia Black Lung Association had voted the night before to support him. He would need their support and that of many more like them. He was aware of this; indeed, it was the principal reason he had not sought to barnstorm the mountains in the fashion some of his supporters had envisioned. He felt it would be fruitless to show up in areas where he was unknown and try to campaign. Not only did he consider it an unproductive way to campaign, but a potentially dangerous one as well. He had attempted this once, going to Illinois to meet a group of miners he did not know, and he had ended up with a karate chop for his pains. Besides, the election was still months away and he did not want to risk bringing his campaign to an early peak, only to watch it fade before the expensive onslaught he expected Boyle to mount in the final weeks of the race. So he decided to continue pacing himself until he had established the kind of rank-and-file contacts he would need to pave the way for the heavy campaigning he planned later.

The job of lining up miners to help Yablonski was assigned to Karl Kafton, who could not have been a better choice. Kafton was attractive and smart and held in high regard by his fellow miners. He had worked in coal mines in several states and knew men throughout the mining regions. Some of his friends were coal miners he had met in Carlsbad, New Mexico, where he had gone to work in the potash mines when times were hard in the coal industry. So Kafton took off from his home in Moundsville, West Virginia, to tour the coal fields in his pickup truck, which he drove at breakneck speed over the mountain roads. In the ensuing weeks, letters from Kafton arrived every day at Miners for Yablonski headquarters in Washington. They came from coal towns in West Virginia, Kentucky, Illinois, Indiana, and Alabama. Written in Kafton's hurried script, most were on letterhead stationery to which he had helped himself during a brief stay in the Aracoma Hotel in Logan, West Virginia ("Logan's Only Fireproof Hotel," the paper boasted). Each letter contained the names of miners Kafton had contacted, together with his assessment of their potential value to the campaign in terms of enthusiasm and willingness to work. He suggested ways Yablonski could increase their interest, such as telephoning or writing them, or simply sending them a shipment of campaign literature. Although Kafton was on the road just a few weeks, he covered most of the major mining regions where Yablonski was not well known. He succeeded in organizing an informal network of supporters and volunteer workers who could at least partially counteract the heavy campaigning for Boyle by the district and international officials. Later, these men would give Yablonski the contacts he needed to campaign effectively in unfamiliar territory.

Boyle officially kicked off his campaign with a Labor Day speech that was perhaps Oscar Jager's biggest single contribution to the campaign. Fifteen pages long, it covered every issue from wages to the environment. It was run off by the hundreds of copies by the *Journal* staff, who distributed it well in advance to the media with an attached press release declaring that Boyle was "in a fighting mood." Boyle delivered the speech twice that Monday, once in Logan and hours later at another rally in Elkhorn City, just across the line in Kentucky. At Logan, a crowd of about a thousand braved a rainstorm to hear him and to enjoy the free refreshments, country and western band, and full card of professional wrestling that were on the program. With District 17 President R. R. Humphreys holding an umbrella over his head, Boyle droned haltingly through the unfamiliar rhetoric, getting an even less enthusiastic reception from the milling crowd than he normally got for one of his extemporaneous tirades. Despite the indifferent reaction, the speech was a dramatic move for Boyle. It contained proposals that would have been inconceivable coming from him just months earlier. It promised, for example, to raise the miners' wages to $50 a day, $17 above the current maximum, by the final phase of the upcoming contract. Pensions would be increased to $200 a month and the welfare fund royalty would be doubled, if necessary, to make this possible.

Boyle promised an all-out lobbying effort for better health and safety conditions in the mines, and pledged to seek a guaranteed annual wage for coal miners. A new organizing drive would be undertaken to bring workers from coal-related plants into the union. Even the name of the union might be changed, he said, to the United Mine and Allied Workers. He would explore the possibility of investing in low-cost and moderate-cost housing for miners and would expand the union's education and manpower programs. "The UMWA, despite past gains, has tremendous catching up to do," he acknowledged. Later, he said, "Miners, both working and retired, should not be forced to live with smouldering culm heaps and polluted streams. We need to fill up and seal the abandoned mines. We need re-forestation and the restoration of clean waters." But on the key issue of democracy for the districts, Boyle hedged. He promised to name a "special commission of UMWA officers, together with rank-and-file members from each district" to study the matter.

The Labor Day promises gave Boyle a platform and got him partially off the defensive. Phase two of Jager's plan was an effort to discredit Yablonski, using legitimate issues—such as his earlier glorification of Boyle—when they could be found and fabricated issues when they couldn't. Out of the Miners Committee for Boyle–Titler–Owens headquarters came a stream of press releases, newsletters, and handbills aimed at cutting Yablonski down to size. The basic theme was that Yablonski was the agent of nameless "outsiders" bent on destroying the union. One September release, for example, quoted Boyle as accusing his opponent of "sleazy hypocracy" [sic] and "cheap opportunism" in his "transparent attempt to deliver the union to outside forces." The newsletters, entitled "Ammunition," featured glowing reports of Boyle's campaign activities and summaries of his press releases, most of which received little attention from the newspapers. A typical handbill was headlined "KEEP THE OUTSIDERS OUT!" It contained such innuendo-rich questions as "Who is paying Joe Yablonski's high-priced lawyers?" and "Who is manipulating Joe Yablonski like a puppet?" Another widely distributed handbill was called "The Two Faces of Joseph Yablonski." It contained quotations from Yablonski's speeches praising Boyle, juxtaposed with his more recent criticisms. It was illustrated with two crude drawings of Yablonski, one showing him with a halo above his head and his hands in prayer. In the other his mouth was wreathed in a malevolent laugh and his head had satanic horns. Later, thousands of recordings were made of Yablonski's adulatory speeches about Boyle and distributed throughout the coal regions.

Jager made an effort to be friendly and open to newsmen who sought him out with questions about the campaign and Boyle's new platform. He freely acknowledged, that he wrote Boyle's Labor Day speech. But when the questions got around to the unnamed "outsiders" who supposedly controlled Yablonski, Jager became uncooperative. He couldn't discuss the matter, he said, because to do so might "open a kettle of fish." What about Joe Rauh, he was asked, was there something sinister in his involvement in the campaign? "I just can't get into that," he said. "I think he's in this for reasons that go far beyond what meets the eye." Well, what reasons? "I just can't go into it." Jager found it increasingly difficult to justify Boyle's refusal to allow district autonomy even in the face of a government lawsuit to compel him to do so. "To come out for automony," Jager said, "would provoke internal squabbles in the union." While he usually tried to argue that he was actually on the side of union reform, he sometimes let down his guard. "Sure, I'm in this for the money," he admitted at one point, adding later, "I'm no longer so young that I can afford to be totally altruistic."

Although there was no matching Boyle's publicity operation for sheer volume, the Yablonski camp battled back gamely and with some success. In rebuttal to the Labor Day speech, Fred Barnes wrote and issued a statement in Yablonski's name which seized upon the acknowledgment that the union "has tremendous catching up to do." Boyle's speechwriters knew that "a progressive-sounding speech by Tony Boyle would be altogether preposterous if it did not contain some mention of how regressive Mr. Boyle has actually been," the statement said. It went on to accuse Boyle of "plagiarizing freely from my platform" and derided the incumbent for refusing to accept the invitation of a Charleston, West Virginia, television station to debate Yablonski on the air. The statement was released the day after Labor Day and benefited from the normal policy of newspapers and other media to publish replies to remarks made by opposing candidates. It received considerable play, even provoking a brief editorial in the *Charleston Gazette*. The editorial called Boyle "an insipid imitation of the indomitable titan who made his union to co-equal of management throughout the coal industry. Imagine John L. Lewis refusing to debate an opponent."

The Miners for Yablonski office also had printed thousands of copies of a so-called "Test for Coal Miners," which Margaret Yablonski had written. It had a series of questions with multiple choice answers. It asked, for example, "Why did Boyle appear only briefly at the Farmington disaster?" One of the possible answers was, "There was no Hilton Hotel in the area." Another question: "What great qualities of warm leadership do the big three have?" The answers: "Boyle, at sixty-five, keeps warm in bed with coal operators"; "Owens, at seventy-eight, even with a wig to keep his brain warm, is years behind getting his audits out"; "Titler, at seventy-three, is warmed by the fat around his belly and head." The tests had instructions to "Fill out and mail to Boyle," with his home address in Washington.

In mid-October, Yablonski scored a significant court victory in his suit to stop the Boyle-boosting in the UMW *Journal*. On October 12, Rauh interrogated Justin McCarthy before U. S. District Judge John Pratt on whether McCarthy had participated in the publication of the so-called "Election Bulletin." Rauh's only hope of winning the case lay in the Landrum-Griffin Act's strictures against the use of union member's funds and the official mailing list to promote a candidacy. Thus the court would have to find that the *Journal* was being used to boost

Boyle. Although this may seem obvious, the First Amendment makes courts extremely reluctant to judge editorial content. The "Election Bulletin" was important in this respect because it was labeled campaign material and, if it could be proved the *Journal* staff worked on it, would be a clear example of the use of the member's money for political purposes.

McCarthy testified that he helped with the editing of the publication, which was brought to him by Mike Budzanoski. He acknowledged that he had supplied pictures from the *Journal* files for the campaign bulletin. And, under close questioning by Rauh, he admitted that a temporary employee of the *Journal* had typed some of the copy. McCarthy insisted, however, that although this all happened in his office during the week, he was actually working on a day off which he had earned by working over the weekend. Would the union's records show that? asked Rauh. "I don't know that there are any such records," said McCarthy. Three days later, Judge Pratt ordered the union to stop using the *Journal* as a campaign instrument for Boyle. (Judge Pratt's injunction followed a temporary restraining order along the same lines issued by another judge after a preliminary hearing two weeks earlier. The restraining order had been upheld by the United States Court of Appeals.)

"This is a judgment decision which is made with full appreciation of the character of the *Journal* and similar publications of other national unions," Judge Pratt said in his memorandum. "We are aware that defendant Boyle, as the President of the union running for reelection, will in the nature of things be an important participant in many matters of interest to the membership and be more likely to have his participation in these matters the subject of inclusion in any report to the membership through the *Journal*. A line must be drawn between the use of the *Journal* to report the activities of defendant Boyle as President, which is permissible, and the use of the *Journal* in such a way in reporting such activities, as to promote the candidacy of said defendant. We find that this line has been breached and that the *Journal* in many respects has been used as a campaign instrument to promote defendant Boyle's candidacy."

Although Pratt ordered the electioneering in the *Journal* stopped, he declined to go along with Rauh's request that part of several ensuing issues be made available to Yablonski to help offset the effect of months

of Boyle-boosting. Nevertheless, Boyle was now stripped of one of his
most effective propaganda tools; the *Journal* for the rest of the campaign made scant mention of either Boyle or Yablonski.

In September and October, the Yablonski forces were strongly encouraged by the spontaneous opening of local Yablonski campaign
offices across the coal fields of Pennsylvania and West Virginia. In the
anthracite region, Bill Savitsky rented a storefront in downtown Shenandoah for $75 a month. It was used as a gathering place and as a
distribution center for Yablonski's campaign material. In District 5, a
second-story office was rented in Fredericktown, near Yablonski's home
in Clarksville, which Mike Trobovich and others from Yablonski's inner
circle used as a base for their campaign operations. Another District 5
office opened in a vacant storefront in New Kensington, near Lou
Antal's home.

In northern West Virginia, Elijah Wolford and his friends rented an
abandoned gas station on the outskirts of Morgantown for use as a
headquarters. Twenty miles to the south, the men who belonged to Bill
Fetty's local in historic Monongah proclaimed their local union hall
"Yablonski–Brown District 31 Headquarters," as a colorful sign on the
front of the building put it. The campaign attracted the interest of anti-
poverty workers in the mountains and one group, an organization
called Designs for Rural Action, made space available in their second-
story offices in downtown Charleston. The man most responsible for
this was Dave Biesmyer, a rangy DRA volunteer who had come to
know a number of the dissident miners in the area. He was particularly
friendly with Arnold Miller and Woodrow Mullins, who spent all the
time they could spare in the Charleston headquarters. In Logan, Elmer
Brown and his associates rented an office which instantly became a
popular gathering spot, partly, no doubt, because Brown spent $100 of
campaign funds on a television set for the place. In McDowell County,
a Yablonski storefront office was opened by a small, slender, inactive
miner named Posey Stewart who proved, as the campaign wore on, to
be one of Yablonski's most enthusiastic volunteers, although he was
somewhat slowed by chronic heart disease. He raised the $35 a month
to pay the rent on the headquarters and gave enormous amounts of
time to the campaign.

The local headquarters were not glamorous, but they gave the campaign an inestimable lift, particularly in West Virginia. Yablonski's strategy was to concentrate on Pennsylvania and West Virginia, the states with by far the most miners. In West Virginia, however, anything new is suspect and the campaign needed every sign of strength and legitimacy it could get. The local headquarters were helpful in this respect, as were the bumper and helmet stickers which Chip Yablonski began sending to the local headquarters for distribution. They were an instant hit. Within weeks, he had to order a second shipment and before the campaign was over, thousands of each had been given away. The bumper stickers said, "On December 9, Vote Yablonski and Brown." The helmet stickers read, "Your Safety First: Yablonski and Brown." Like the headquarters, the stickers were the kind of campaign trappings which made Yablonski look like a serious candidate to miners, in West Virginia and elsewhere, who might otherwise have regarded his campaign as hopeless.

The opening of the local headquarters apparently caused a stir in the Boyle camp, because in mid-October a press release was issued in Boyle's name citing the offices as proof of the big money that was flowing to Yablonski from the infamous "outsiders." "In West Virginia alone, Holy Joe has announced that offices are being opened in Monongah, Charleston, Beckley, Welch, and Williamson [sic]. These offices, the printing, and the other expenses associated with them come high. Somebody is footing the bill and it isn't miners," the release said. "Who pays for Joe? That is what miners want to know."

In fact, of course, it was miners who paid for the offices. Outside of Washington, Yablonski paid only three of his supporters: Bill Savitsky and Karl Kafton, who had taken leave from their jobs and were being paid by Yablonski to work for him full time the rest of the campaign, and Elmer Brown, who was occasionally sent money to cover expenses.

In Washington, Beverly Moore's place in the Yablonski organization was filled in October, after he returned to law school, by Clarice Feldman, an able young lawyer who had become a friend of Chip while both worked at the National Labor Relations Board. Across the street, the campaign staff grew in October when both Chip and Charlotte Yablonski left their jobs to work for their father's election. In the final months of the campaign, the Miners for Yablonski office became a noisy, crowded place. There was little furniture and no carpet in the one-room office and Fred Barnes's typewriter clattered loudly above the

voices of his co-workers as he hammered out press releases and struggled to keep up with the mail. Letters poured in from sympathetic miners, most of whom had a tale of woe to relate to the candidate. Many
who wrote were retired members who had failed to qualify for pensions
and wanted to tell their story. With help from his wife Barbara, who
spent hours at the office, Barnes answered as many of the letters as he
could. The two of them could be found at the office many evenings
working on the mail and press statements, fortified by a six-pack of
beer.

Chip and Charlotte were in the Washington office most of the time
also, manning the telephones, planning the candidate's travels, and
keeping in touch with his supporters in the coal fields. Later Chip and
his sister took on the awesome task of lining up volunteers to act as poll
watchers at each of the union's approximately 1,300 locals on election
day. The Landrum-Griffin Act entitles a candidate to have such observers and the Yablonski forces felt this was the only way of keeping
the balloting even reasonably honest. Chip knew the observers would
encounter resistance in locals where the officers were for Boyle, so he
had printed a highly authoritative-looking "Official Observer's Authori-
zation" to send to each Yablonski poll watcher. It was a smart idea, one
of many from Chip, who became an increasingly resourceful and valu-
able campaign worker as time went on. The "authorizations" were nothing but small sheets of paper, but they were printed with an elaborate
border similar to those on stock certificates. "This will certify that
—— has been designated by me as my election observer in Local Union
No. ——, District No. —— in the election of International Officers,
United Mine Workers of America, to be held the 9th day of December,
1969," the paper said. This bit of high-flown language was followed by
a space for Yablonski's signature which was put on by Chip with a
rubber stamp. In small print at the bottom, it said, "Anyone who inter-
feres with your duties is subject to Federal Prosecution." When the authorizations first came back from the printer, Chip thought they looked
sufficiently official to remark to his co-workers, "I hope the miners don't
try to go out and spend these things."

Late one October night, one of many long evenings Fred Barnes and
his wife spent at the Miners for Yablonski office, they were surprised by
two rough-looking strangers who suddenly walked in. The pair looked

so unsavory to Barnes that he immediately got up from his desk and walked toward them with the idea of getting them out of the office as quickly as possible. One of the men, his breath reeking of beer, said something about seeking directions to Little Rock, Arkansas, but Barnes barely let him finish. "Look, you can't come in here," he said. "You'll have to leave." The two men glanced around the room as if looking for something in particular. But they offered no resistance as Barnes ushered them out the door. He then locked it, something he had not normally done, and kept it locked thereafter. "I took one look at those guys," he later said, "and a bolt of terror shot through me. I had visions of every crime you could think of including rape and murder. I had never felt like that before. Barbara told me my face was absolutely white when I got up from the desk." Barnes mentioned the incident to a few friends, but since nothing came of it, he soon let it slip from his mind.

11

The struggle over a new Federal mine-safety law reached a critical point in October and the Boyle-Yablonski contest played an important part in the outcome. On October 2, the Senate passed a strong bill by a seventy-three to nothing vote. The bill not only completely revamped safety regulations but added new health standards, chiefly for dust control, to guard against miners' lung disease. Perhaps the boldest part of the bill was a section providing federal workmen's compensation of at least $1,600, and as much as $3,200, for miners with black lung who were unable to collect compensation from their states. This proposal had originally been in a separate bill which Senator Robert Byrd and several co-sponsors had introduced at the request of the UMW in the aftermath of the black lung uprising in West Virginia. But with important support of Senator Randolph, it had been incorporated into the mine-safety bill. Among the other important features of the bill was the elimination of the distinction between "gassy" and "non-gassy" mines under which mines in the "non-gassy" category had been allowed to use equipment considered unsafe for the "gassy" mines. This provision was fought hard by the lobbyists for the small, "non-gassy" mine operators, most of whose mines were in shallow seams where coal dust, rather than methane gas, was the chief explosion hazard. The small mine operators claimed the requirements for new equipment would impose an economic burden they could not bear.

The Senate bill vested broad rule-making power in the Secretary of the Interior, thus making it unnecessary for the department to seek Congressional legislation every time new safety regulations were needed to keep up with the changing technology of the industry. The bill established mandatory civil penalties of up to $25,000 for willful violations of the law. It also took the controversial step of abolishing The Coal Mine Safety Board of Review, which had been set up by the 1952 mining law to review, and possibly reverse, the Interior Department's decisions to close mines and take other action against offending companies. The review board normally consisted of two members "representing the viewpoint" of the miners and two "representing the viewpoint" of the industry. The chairman, however, was normally a noted industry official, so the companies had both control of the board and the power to overturn any disputed safety decision made by the Interior Department's mine inspectors. Such an appeals board was almost unheard of in industrial safety regulation, and its obvious imbalance on the side of industry caused even the mild-mannered Senator Harrison Williams to label it "bizarre."

The passage of a strong Senate bill, of course, was no assurance that such a measure would finally be enacted. The House had yet to vote on its version of the legislation, which had been voted out of its Labor Committee in mid-September. Thanks in large measure to the inside influence of Representative Burton, Gary Sellers, and Dave Finnegan, and to the external pressure from Ken Hechler, the bill was much like the one passed by the Senate. However, the board of review was retained in the House bill. The reason was that Boyle and his fellow officers had favored it—again putting themselves and the coal operators on the same side of a major safety issue.

As the Senate was about to take action on its bill, however, there was intense behind-the-scenes activity on the issue. Senator Winston Prouty, a conservative Vermont Republican, planned to introduce an amendment during the Senate floor action restoring the provision for the board of review to the legislation. Fearing that Prouty's move might succeed, Gary Sellers contacted Yablonski, who immediately put out a statement denouncing the board and blasting Boyle for supporting it. Sellers, never one to leave a stone unturned, then put through a call to Suzanne Richards. He warned her that Yablonski stood to make considerable political hay on the issue unless Boyle reversed himself and went against the board. A telegram was immediately sent to the members of the Senate Labor Committee informing them that Boyle had changed his mind and was now opposed to the review board. Although Prouty went ahead and offered his amendment, its chances of passage, never considered good, had been further diminished by Boyle's sudden switch, and it was beaten, fifty-three to twenty-four.

Shortly thereafter, Boyle wrote to all members of Congress that he was "entirely opposed to provisions vesting any board of review with the right to overrule the decisions of the Secretary of the Interior." While Boyle's turnabout made him no enemies among the chief Senate backers of the legislation, who had opposed the board all along, it had a different effect on the House. Over the objections of several committee members, including Burton, and under criticism from Hechler, Chairman John Dent of the Labor Subcommittee had insisted that a review board provision be part of the bill. He steered the controversial section not only through his own committee but through the full Labor Committee as well. So when Boyle changed his mind and began publicly denouncing the provision, Dent was furious. Boyle's insistence on the board was the only reason Dent had fought so hard for it, and he considered the UMW president's change of mind a brazen double-cross. Nevertheless, he went along and kept his anger to himself.

The incident illustrates one of the enduring realities of the entire UMW controversy: no matter what accusations and revelations came to light about Boyle and his associates, they were never without a small army of supporters in Congress who stood ready to defend their reputations, introduce their legislation, and fight for their viewpoint. It was perhaps because they were used to such treatment from politicians that they found Hechler's behavior so difficult to bear. They seemed as annoyed by Hechler's strong stance on mine safety—even though it frequently dovetailed with their own position—as they were with his criticism of them.

After the Senate action, when the debate was joined in the House over the review board, both Boyle and Hechler outspokenly denounced it. Boyle made known his feelings in his letter to all members of Congress and Hechler spoke against the board when the House bill came before the Rules Committee on October 16. He called the board "an unusual concept of administrative law—[a majority] of the members may retain their industry ties and overrule decisions of the Secretary of the Interior, a Cabinet officer."

A week later, the UMW transported five-hundred coal miners to Washington for a day of lobbying. They were briefed on the issues by the union safety director, Lewis Evans, and sent to Capitol Hill to call on their representatives. Shortly before noon, a group of about fifty miners walked into Hechler's office, surged past his receptionist, and swarmed into his personal office. He was standing in front of his chaotic desk getting ready to go to the House floor where he had reserved a minute to make a statement.

"Why aren't you supporting [Representative James] Kee's and Senator Byrd's bill? Why are you and Burton trying to weaken the mine safety bill?" one of the leaders demanded. Several others grumbled loudly. The mood of the group was ugly.

"I think my approach is stronger," Hechler began, but the miner cut him off. "You don't have the guts to support the Kee-Byrd bill," he sneered. Hechler, stepping forward, said, "I've explained . . . ," but the man shoved him back and said, "Don't talk to me like that."

Hechler began moving toward the door to leave, explaining, "I'm scheduled to give a one-minute speech on the floor and I have to leave."

"Yeah," shouted someone. "He's running out on us. He's chicken."

As Hechler made his way toward the door, he spotted a couple of miners he knew in the group. One of them came forward and said, "I believe you about your bill." As he hurried down the hall, he spotted Boyle and several of his associates. Hechler strode up to him and stuck out his hand. "Hello, Tony," he said, grinning good-naturedly. Boyle appeared not to recognize him, but one of his companions said, "That's Representative Hechler." Boyle turned to the Congressman and, in a low voice, said, "Why, I wouldn't shake hands with you." Then he turned his back and walked away.

Despite such discord among the proponents of new safety legislation for the miners, the way had been cleared for the removal of the board of review when the House bill came up for floor action on October 29, six days after Hechler's confrontation with the miners in his office. The amendment abolishing the board passed easily and the bill went through by a whopping margin of 389 to four. Even as the bill passed, Dent and its other managers were promising that a few other strengthening details would be attended to during the conference with the Senate. (It is a measure of the state of safety regulation in coal that the House bill included the first all-inclusive federal prohibition against the use of open-flame lamps underground. The bill also forbade the use of link-pin couplings on underground coal haulage trains, a prohibition that had been in effect in the railroad industry since the Safety Appliance Act of 1893.)

The House action, coming by so vast a margin, assured that a bill of historic proportions would soon become law. Although the Nixon Administration had expressed strong reservations about the federal black lung compensation provisions (workman's compensation had hitherto been the province of the states) there did not seem to be much likelihood that the President would veto a bill that passed both Houses with a total of four dissenting votes.

The passage of the House bill freed Yablonski from his lobbying duties, which he had performed diligently both because he was interested in the legislation and because he wanted to avoid giving Boyle any ammunition for his defense in Yablonski's damage suit over his earlier firing. Now Yablonski could devote himself full time to the campaign. During the next several weeks, he kept a heavy schedule of campaigning; his weekdays were devoted to visiting mines and to conferring with his supporters in each locality, and his weekends occupied primarily with rallies. Whenever he could, Yablonski also scheduled rallies on weeknights. In West Virginia, he was joined on the platform at virtually every rally by Hechler, who had no compunction about jumping into the UMW race with both feet, despite the obvious political risk. The rallies generally followed the same pattern as the one at Bellaire, Ohio. There would be several introductory speeches by local Yablonski supporters, usually those who organized the meeting, and by Elmer Brown and others from Yablonski's inner circle who accompanied him. After his experience in Springfield, Illinois, Yablonski insisted on having several of his closest allies accompany him on his travels and, since it was cheaper than buying several seats on commercial flights, Yablonski and his small entourage traveled the coal fields in a small private plane rented from a company near Yablonski's home. After the introductory speeches, Yablonski would take the floor and, with coat off, collar loosened, and sleeves rolled up, deliver one of his rambling, stem-winding harangues. The size of the crowd and the enthusiasm of the reaction depended largely on who had organized the rally. Yablonski normally had little or nothing to do with this phase of his campaign. Many of those who worked for Yablonski had been recruited by Karl Kafton, and Fred Barnes was chiefly responsible for coordinating rallies with them. Usually, Barnes would set a tentative date by telephone and later confirm it with the candidate. As the campaign moved into its final weeks, Barnes found that Yablonski's earlier reluctance disappeared and that he operated on a whirlwind schedule.

He made his first visit to the anthracite region of Pennsylvania, stumped southern West Virginia tirelessly, and made forays into Virginia, Illinois, and Indiana. He also campaigned in west Kentucky, where Ed Yevincey saw to it that he was well received. He even held one rally in eastern Kentucky despite his earlier vow that he would not go there. In addition, of course, he campaigned extensively in the more familiar territory of southwest Pennsylvania, northern West Virginia, and Ohio. Some of the rallies left Yablonski exhilarated. At Kincaid, Illinois, for example, the meeting had to be moved at the last minute because the school board abruptly withdrew permission to use a school auditorium. So the rally was held at another facility across the street. The school board's last minute action stirred considerable sympathy for Yablonski and hundreds turned out to hear him. They gave him a tumultuous response. Other rallies, however, were disappointing. At Montgomery, West Virginia, a weeknight rally organized by Arnold Miller drew only 150 people and, although the crowd was friendly, it did not give Yablonski the kind of cheering section he needed to be at his best.

Nevertheless, the campaign seemed to be gaining momentum and Yablonski was now showing great enthusiasm for it. But there was more to his enthusiasm than the mere scent of possible victory. Yablonski had been part of the union hierarchy for a long time and, although he had many friends among the miners in his home area, it had been many years since he had been in contact with rank and file leaders on anything but a casual basis. Many of the men that rallied to Yablonski's cause were miners who had been fighting the UMW hierarchy long before the idea of breaking ranks ever crossed Yablonski's mind. Some had stood up to threats and intimidation and rejected bribes. Although Yablonski had known Karl Kafton for years, he never realized fully how able, intelligent and courageous he was until Kafton went to work for his campaign. And before the campaign, he had never met such men as Ed Yevincey, Levi Daniel, Arnold Miller, and Bill Savitsky. The fact that these men took his side, undaunted by the allegations of Boyle's campaign literature, when they were offered nothing but a platform for change, deeply affected Yablonski.

One of those who became a staunch campaign ally was Ed Monborne, a squarely built, grey-haired miner of fifty-two who had worked in the coal mines of District 2 in southwestern Pennsylvania near Yablonski's home territory for forty years. Articulate, thoughtful, and deeply respected by his fellow miners, Monborne was one of those whose allegiance moved Yablonski most. He was a tireless campaign worker. During one November weekend, for example, he organized four successful rallies and also lined up a television interview. He had first heard of Yablonski when a news report of his candidacy came over the radio at Monborne's home in Ebensburg, Pennsylvania. "I just about flew three feet off my chair," he recalled. "I told my wife I'd like to talk to him; I wonder how I could contact him. She said why don't you call him up. So I called him in Clarksville in June and offered my services. I didn't know then, of course, what kind of man he was, but I knew we couldn't get any worse than what we had. Later, though, I got to know Jock just from riding around with him and listening to him talk. I realized then that he was really a humanitarian. I studied Jock as I talked to him and rode with him and as he told me of the suffering of the coal miner. Then I realized that this man was really something—that he was what the coal miners needed. I never worked so hard in my life as I worked for his campaign."

The candidate's newly inspired attitude and the optimistic reports from his supporters that followed his campaign stops gave Yablonski's staff in Washington the feeling that, if only the balloting were conducted fairly, Yablonski might win. Even Fred Barnes, by nature something of a pessimist, began to think that Yablonski now had a fighting chance. But establishing safeguards for the election was proving to be a formidable task.

On October 26, about forty miners, most of them from Ohio, chartered a bus and gave up a day's wages to come to Washington for a demonstration outside UMW headquarters. The men, all Yablonski supporters, set up a picket line outside the building and marched back and forth carrying signs with such messages as "We want an honest count, not a Boyle count," and "One miner, one vote." While bemused lunchtime passers-by stopped and watched, startled faces appeared at the windows of the grey union building. The miners chanted, "We want a fair election," again and again. Occasionally they would vary their chant by switching briefly to "Bye, bye, Tony, he's a phony." They plastered the first-floor windows of the building with Yablonski bumper and helmet stickers. It was an extraordinary sight. The labor union once feared as the most militant and mighty in the land was being picketed by an irreverent band of its own members, who sought, not exorbitant contract benefits, but merely an honest election. Ed Carey, union general counsel, arrived at the building, briefcase in hand, sporting a huge "Loyal to Boyle" button on his lapel. As he approached the front door, the crowd of miners swarmed around him shouting angrily. Carey raised his free hand in a V sign and shouted repeatedly, "Hurray for Boyle," then marched into the building. Not long thereafter, with the demonstration showing no signs of petering out, Secretary-Treasurer John Owens emerged from the building and stood on the steps to talk to the miners. He was greeted with a chorus of insults and shouts that the Boyle administration had been stealing the members' money. "Did your union steal it?" he asked, "your membership?" "No," came the answer, "you stole it." One miner shouted, "Did the sheep herder send you out?" This was a reference to a widely circulated rumor among UMW dissidents that Boyle had never actually been a coal miner, but had spent his salad days in Montana as a shepherd. Owens tried to convince the miners that he sincerely wanted to hear their comments, that he had come out, as he put it, "just to be with you." The men would not buy this, however, and his comments were greeted with another burst of insults. "You're too old for office," said one of them, "you shoulda retired years ago." The miner then turned to a newsman standing beside him and said, "He ought to have retired years ago. He's too old. He's got a toupee. He's bald as a cue ball."

The demonstration lasted well into the afternoon before the miners, tired and hungry, decided to break for lunch and resume their picketing at the Labor Department later. When the time came for them to head back to the coal fields, there was no sign that their uprising had brought about any action, but the miners, to a man, seemed to have enjoyed themselves immensely. They talked enthusiastically of coming back soon for another chance to raise an embarrassing ruckus at union headquarters.

That week, Rauh filed suit on Yablonski's behalf, asking that the Honest Ballot Association be ordered to supervise the election and that other election procedures spelled out in the Landrum-Griffin Act be followed, including permitting Yablonski observers at the polls. A few days later, the Yablonski camp got word that the UMW's printer, a suburban Washington firm, was preparing to run off the ballots. Fred Barnes called the printer and asked if he could be present to watch the printing. The plant manager agreed, but later changed his mind and called back to say that he needed formal permission from union officials. Rauh immediately prepared a motion asking that the ballot printing be held up until the full hearing on the election suit—by then just a few days away—could be held. In court the next morning, UMW General Counsel Carey said the ballots were already in the process of being printed and mailed. He told the court that the names of all candidates were on the ballots and that the correct number would be sent to each local union. Judge Matthew McGuire, therefore, denied Rauh's motion.

When the hearing on the election suit itself was held several days later, however, some new light was shed on the issue. Carey, put on the witness stand in a surprise move by Rauh, acknowledged that he had called the printing company after being informed of Rauh's motion to stop the printing. Carey acknowledged that he ordered the printer to "get the job out as quickly as possible." Thus when the hearing on Rauh's motion was held the next morning, Carey could truthfully say that the printing and mailing were under way. This was not all. Secretary-Treasurer Owens was questioned closely in connection with Yablonski's request that he be shown a membership list as provided by the Landrum-Griffin Act. Although Yablonski's first mailing of campaign literature had gone to 1,469 locals, Owens at first testified that there were only 1,338. He then called his office and told the court that there were 1,350. When the court was informed that a subsequent Yablonski mailing had gone to only 1,297 locals Owens again changed his testimony and said this was the correct number of locals. He was equally fuzzy about the number of members. At first, he used the figure 225,-000, then switched to two hundred thousand. Finally, after another check with his office, he announced that the true total was 193,500. All of this left Judge George Hart astonished. At one point during Owens's testimony, he remarked, "You're supposed to be the secretary-treasurer of this organization. If you were the secretary-treasurer of AT&T, I don't know what would happen." But Owens had not made his most startling revelation—namely, that although there were fewer than two hundred thousand members, the printer had run off 275,000 ballots. Owens explained that 10 percent more than the number of potential voters was always sent to each local. In addition, he testified, 51,000 extra ballots had been retained at headquarters. Why? Rauh asked. "Because sometimes the ballots don't reach the locals," he said. Were there any such incidents during the previous election in 1964? "I don't recall that we ever had any complaints," he said. His testimony still left an excess eleven thousand ballots which were never explained.

Owens's testimony also revealed that the union kept no up-to-date membership list despite the Landrum-Griffin Act's requirement that such a list be maintained. Further, he acknowledged that the union constitution's requirement that the membership be sent a detailed tabulation of election returns had been ignored in 1964. Why? "The candidates agreed it wasn't necessary," said Owens. Judge Hart interrupted here, "The candidates can't waive the constitutional rights of the membership. That's ridiculous." At another point, the judge observed that the UMW officers "pay attention to the constitution when they want to and don't when they don't."

The Landrum-Griffin Act, however, gives the courts limited jurisdiction over union elections, leaving most of the regulatory authority to the Labor Department which has never acted except after an election. As Judge Hart put it, "The Secretary of Labor can act ex post facto. If you want to say that's a funny way to do things, I couldn't agree with you more." Hart lacked authority to grant the kind of relief Yablonski was seeking. "If you are talking about a fair election, you are talking about something this court is powerless to do." Nevertheless, Judge Hart was able to get the union to agree to put away for good the extra ballots and to send a letter to the districts setting forth legally required election procedures such as secret balloting. Also in the letter was a stipulation that Yablonski could have an observer at each polling place.

The Yablonski forces considered Judge Hart's action a victory in view of the court's limited powers. But the UMW's general counsel, Ed Carey, did not agree. Carey said the judge's decision was a victory for the Boyle side, because Yablonski had been trying to disenfranchise the union's pensioned miners by his lawsuit and this attempt had failed. The charge that Yablonski was trying to keep the pensioners from voting became a mainstay of the incumbents' arsenal of accusations, a tactic which made obvious political sense because the pensioners were expected to favor Boyle heavily anyway, particularly after their recent increase in income. Anything Boyle could do to keep Yablonski from cutting into his support among the old-timers, and to make them feel it was important to vote, was a plus for him.

Translating the court-approved agreement on observers into reality was not easy. It was first necessary to know where and during what hours each local would vote. On October 30, Chip Yablonski had sent a letter over his father's signature to the officers of every local asking for this information and enclosing a self-addressed post-card. Out of the almost 1,300 sent, only 345 responses were received. In some cases where no post card was returned, the Yablonski camp was able to find out from a friendly member where and when the voting would be held. But as election day approached, the challenger still had no information on a vast majority of the locals in the union. So Chip, with help from his sister Charlotte and a friend who sometimes visited the office, began telephoning local union officers in areas where he knew he would have observers available. Posing as reporters, the three asked for information on the time and place of balloting, supposedly so a photographer could be sent to take pictures. In this manner, they were able to get polling information on about sixty more locals. Still, at least seven-hundred locals would vote with no Yablonski observer present.

Boyle's campaign, meanwhile, had moved into high gear. Boyle himself was touring the coal fields on a tight schedule organized by the UMW's safety director Lewis Evans, who was acting as campaign manager. Rex Lauck was at Boyle's side throughout most of his travels, although there was no coverage of the campaign in the *Journal*. Everywhere Boyle went, he was quickly shunted to and from his public appearances, never stopping to answer reporters' questions and never, of course, confronting Yablonski himself, who was eager for a debate. When a Charleston television station made available time in September for such a head-to-head debate, Yablonski accepted, but Boyle refused. So Yablonski was interviewed adjacent an empty chair, symbol of Boyle's absence. Later, when WOAY-TV in Oak Hill, West Virginia, invited Boyle to appear on a half-hour interview program, he accepted —but then reneged when the station refused to confine itself to a list of questions submitted by Rex Lauck. In the final weeks of the campaign, the Boyle organization staged a television and radio blitz that was awesome for a labor union election. It cost about $50,000 and reached every corner of the eastern coal fields with a barrage of pro-Boyle slogans and messages. Bathhouses across the coal regions were bombarded with records of Yablonski's adulatory introductory speeches for Boyle. The records cost about $18,000.

In Washington, campaign literature produced by the Boyle–Titler–Owens committee staff continued to pour off the presses. The most impressive piece of literature was a slick, four-page newspaper called the "UMW Campaign Express," which was mailed to the membership in the final weeks of the campaign. The newspaper sounded the same themes Boyle had used throughout the campaign—mainly, that the incumbents had made great progress for the membership and that Yablonski was one of Boyle's chief admirers "before certain outsiders last May decided that he would make a swell puppet-president."

The records of the Boyle–Titler–Owens committee showed that about $141,000 had been spent by the Washington office for salaries, literature, television and radio time, postage, stationery, newspaper advertising, and overhead. Significantly, despite the fact that this office was supposed to be the nerve center of the Boyle campaign, the telephone bill was only about $350, indicating that most of the planning and phoning had probably been done from headquarters across the street. All but a fraction of the Boyle campaign money was raised by contributions from his appointed underlings. The top international officers, for example, contributed $3,000, while most lesser officials contributed $1,000 or $500, depending on their salaries. All who gave later received pay raises commensurate with their contributions. Donations were received from less than one percent of the rank-and-file.

There can be little doubt, however, that the Boyle campaign cost considerably more than $141,000. One authoritative official estimate later placed the cost at closer to $250,000, with the money raised and spent at the district level included. This figure, however, did not take into account what it cost the membership to have salaried union employees out campaigning full time for Boyle and union facilities used in the campaign.

Yablonski, of course, could muster nothing like this kind of money. Chip once estimated that his father spent about $60,000 in all, most of it from his own money or money put up by his brother Edward, a well-to-do Pennsylvania businessman who controlled the water works around Clarksville. At one point in the campaign, the Boyle organization began accusing Yablonski himself of being a "water tycoon" who came by his holdings dishonestly. Fred Barnes obtained a letter from the Pennsylvania Public Utility Commission certifying that neither the candidate nor anyone in his immediate family owned any interest in water companies. This ended the "water tycoon" issue.

Although Yablonski spent less than Boyle, in some ways his campaign was more effective. Instead of the news releases written in story fashion which the Boyle camp was sending out, Barnes prepared statements on issues in the campaign for release in conjunction with Yablonski's appearances at rallies. The full text of the statements, together with a brief note explaining where and when the statements would be released, was sent to the regional bureaus of both wire services throughout the coal regions. Although Yablonski's speeches at the rallies often had nothing to do with the statements Barnes sent out in advance, this was no problem because it is perfectly common for political candidates to issue written statements along the campaign trail which do not reflect what they are saying in their speeches. Since most rallies were held on weekends when news is scarce, especially in a wire service bureau which must come up with fresh news for its broadcast wires every hour, the Yablonski statements were normally given the full treatment by both AP and UPI. These stories got only limited space in newspapers, but it was enough to keep the candidate's name before the public. And Yablonski's supporters in the fields reported that stories about his statements were constantly being heard on radio. Although Boyle's press releases were widely distributed, they apparently failed to reach the strategic regional wire service bureaus and were not given the same play Yablonski's received.

Boyle's publicity organization had other difficulties. Throughout the campaign, Oscar Jager repeatedly told newsmen that a major revelation of corruption on Yablonski's part was forthcoming. Finally, in November, the long-promised allegation appeared. Jager took Margaret Kilgore, a UPI Washington reporter who had covered much of the action concerning the UMW, and Neil Gilbride, the AP's veteran labor reporter, to lunch at Duke Zeibert's, a posh downtown Washington restaurant. There he told them the Boyle organization had uncovered documents which proved that Yablonski had been paid $10,000 for "mining rights" to his property in Pennsylvania by the Republic Steel Company. At the same time, said Jager, Yablonski, as District 5 president, was supposed to be enforcing contracts with the company. Jager called it "a serious conflict of interest." That afternoon, both reporters called Fred Barnes to get Yablonski's side of the story. Barnes, having no idea whether the story was true, put them off while he tried to reach the candidate. When he finally contacted him, Yablonski explained that he had never owned the mining rights to his property—they had been owned by Republic Steel for years. What had occurred was that the company was mining beneath Yablonski's land and needed space to drill a bore hole so that electrical wires could be lowered underground. For $1,000, Yablonski leased them a tiny piece of his property for ten years. Apparently, one of Boyle's researchers, digging through the Washington County, Pennsylvania, courthouse had come across the record of the transaction, and passed along a confused version of it to Jager. Barnes, feeling no obligation to straighten the matter out for Jager, simply told Gilbride and Miss Kilgore that Yablonski had never owned the mining rights to his property. In the face of such a flat denial, neither reporter used the story. The next day, Jager, with copies of the documents in hand, again tried to peddle the conflict of interest story, this time to Donald Finley, the UPI labor reporter in Washington. Finley, however, read the documents carefully, concluded that they did not support Jager's allegation, and also refused to use the story. It ended up being sent out in one of Boyle's press releases.

Although Yablonski came out ahead in this episode, the over-all press coverage of the campaign was one of his biggest disappointments. Yablonski felt he could overcome Boyle's money and manpower advantage only with exhaustive coverage by the media in the coal fields and the newspapers and magazines with impact in Washington. He did not expect biased or favorable reporting, only thorough reporting. If the press looked behind the charges he was making against Boyle, Yablonski felt, they would find that they were true. And if they did the same with Boyle's allegations about the takeover plot by unnamed "outsiders," they would report that the charge was unfounded. Unfortunately for Yablonski, almost no one paid this much attention. The *Washington Post,* an ambitious newspaper of national reputation and influence, covered the black lung drive in West Virginia thoroughly and with an eye for the picturesque quality of the movement. At the time, the reporter on the story, Hank Burchard, wrote a perceptive news analysis piece on the UMW leadership's indifference to the rank and

file. But after Yablonski announced his candidacy the *Post* lost interest
in the story, although it had given all-out coverage to Ralph Nader's
allegations against the union only weeks earlier. The job of covering the
union campaign thereafter was shuttled about from one reporter to another, and the result was that the *Post* did a shallow job. It tried to
catch up with a front-page summary in the final days of the campaign,
but the story was done by a reporter who had no background in the
material; he did a perfunctory piece, talking about the charges and
counter-charges made by the candidates, never attempting to find out
which side was telling the truth. Joe Rauh felt throughout the campaign
that the *Post*'s non-coverage of the story was a major reason the Labor
Department could not be prodded into action. He may have had a
point. The *Post* is without question the most influential paper in Washington and anything it covers in depth is bound to get attention—and
very likely, action—from the resident bureaucrats and politicians.

In the coal fields, neither Pittsburgh paper paid much attention to the
campaign. But the most disappointing performance was that of the
Charleston *Gazette*. As the state's most influential—and most liberal—
paper, it had shown courage and energy in battling the special interests
and the corrupt Democratic machine that had ruled the state for so
long. The *Gazette* had also taken a tough stand on mine safety after
Farmington—it had devoted a whole issue of its Sunday magazine to
articles on the subject, some of which were highly critical of the state's
coal companies—and it seemed likely to the Yablonski forces that the
Gazette would fully appreciate the potential of a reformed UMW.
After all, the union hierarchy had always been closely allied with the
worst elements of the old Democratic machine. "Wally Barron never
broke a promise to us," Rex Lauck would say. Moreover, Yablonski and
his supporters set much store by the *Gazette*'s coverage because they
felt that this paper's interest would influence the state's television sta-
tions and smaller newspapers to take a similar interest. But, like the
Post, the *Gazette* wasn't interested. It assigned no reporter to cover the
story and relied mainly on wire copy for what stories it carried. As
the election approached, the *Gazette* published a deeply pessimistic
editorial which asserted that neither candidate represented the working man and wishing that these "parasites" would go away.

Neither major wire service did an in-depth job on the campaign, but
this was not expected because the wire services have so much ground to

cover and so few personnel. Nevertheless, both AP and UPI did a work-manlike job of covering Yablonski's court actions in Washington, and the regional bureaus made full use of any campaign story that was available to them.

The *Wall Street Journal,* despite detailed coverage of the 1964 upris-ing in the UMW, did only a superficial job on the Yablonski campaign. Often its stories were contrived to work in the question of whether developments in the union controversy might lead to a strike. Although unauthorized strikes were a way of life in the UMW, the Yablonski campaign did not occasion any, and the stories written from this angle were both irrelevant and misleading. The best example of this was the *Journal's* story on Yablonski's candidacy announcement. "The nation's coal producers are worried about the prospects of a bitter fight for con-trol of the United Mine Workers Union," the story began. It quoted "one coal industry official" as expressing "fear that strikes might spread across the coal fields as supporters of each man attempt to demonstrate how much backing he has. Ultimately the whole industry could be closed down. . . ."

Although all three major television networks did a good job on the black lung movement, they also seemed to lose interest in the union election. On September 23, CBS broadcast a half-hour news special en-titled "Challenge in the Coal Mines: Men Against their Union," which gave an accurate, if not especially probing, version of the internal strife in the union. (CBS sought to interview each of the international officers but they all refused. Carey acted as their spokesman, and announced that the Boyle administration was in favor of "total democracy" in the union.) After the September broadcast, CBS's coverage was spotty. NBC devoted half of one weekend evening newscast to a report on the campaign but did little more than spot coverage outside of that. ABC was invisible.

There were, however, exceptions to this rule of press indifference. Ben Franklin, *The New York Times's* regional correspondent for Ap-palachia, became deeply interested in the whole coal story after Farm-ington and provided exceptional coverage of all aspects of it, including the UMW controversy. It was Franklin, for example, who first reported the details of the Boyle family's controversial dealings in Montana. Be-fore Franklin's story, Boyle's background had never been explored ex-cept in a series of articles by a newspaper in Billings, Montana. Although Franklin's editors sometimes were skeptical about the reader interest in his stories on coal, they ran them without exception.

Even better than *The Times*'s coverage was that of the *Louisville Courier-Journal,* whose Washington bureau chief, Ward Sinclair, clearly understood the relationship between the Farmington mine disaster, the black lung uprising, and the Yablonski candidacy—a related chain of developments, each growing out of the one before it. His coverage, not limited by the space problems Franklin encountered, included all the important day-to-day developments, plus a series of investigative stories. An example of the enterprise of the *Courier-Journal* came after Yablonski charged in his reply to Boyle's Labor Day speech that Boyle continued to tolerate "sweetheart" contracts in West Virginia and eastern Kentucky that made a mockery of his promise of a $50-a-day wage for miners. Yablonski's comments were published in the *Courier-Journal* and promptly and hotly denied by Carson Hibbitts, president of District 30 in eastern Kentucky. Not content to leave the matter hanging, Sinclair got in touch with Yablonski and obtained the names of mines where Yablonski backers had reported "sweethearts" in effect. The matter then was investigated by the newspaper's east Kentucky correspondent, Kyle Vance. The result was a story conclusively showing that the "sweetheart contract remains a recognized instrument in eastern Kentucky coal production." The story cited the "ten or twenty" mines Yablonski had mentioned in one Kentucky area, but said that, instead of the ten or twenty Yablonski listed, "The Courier-Journal . . . has found the number of such operators to more closely approach sixty or seventy truck mines paying as little as $20 a day." The story quoted Carson Hibbitts as saying that he was unaware of any mines paying less than the union scale wage and would investigate if a grievance was filed. But it also quoted a "sweetheart" operator as saying the UMW "told us . . . that if a man was satisfied with his job and didn't come to them with a grievance, they would do nothing."

This of course was precisely the kind of investigation Yablonski had hoped would be made into many of his campaign allegations. But outside of Franklin's and Sinclair's stories, such digging was rarely done. There were, however, two other newsmen who took an interest in the issue and did some investigating on their own. One was Norman Davis, the editorial director of WTOP Radio and TV, a Washington station owned by the Washington Post Company. Davis followed the UMW controversy closely and broadcast a number of hard-hitting editorials. It was he, for example, who first revealed that the union officers had lifted $850,000 out of the union treasury to set up a private pension fund for themselves—a fund that by 1969 had grown to $1.5 million. Another editor whose work deserves comment is Bill O'Brien of the tiny *Evening Herald,* which serves the anthracite towns of Shenandoah, Ashland, and Mahanoy City, Pennsylvania. Although he was desk-bound much of the time and not able to get out and dig for stories, he saw to it that the campaign received full play in the papers and augmented this coverage with a series of trenchant columns. He personally covered the June rally in Shenandoah that was broken up by the Boyle men and made this the lead story in the paper the next day. In an accompanying editorial, he labeled the incident "A Disgraceful Performance": "We couldn't believe that this was a scene in America which we witnessed Sunday afternoon in Shenandoah Valley High School auditorium, when a group of union goons refused to allow the speakers to present their message in behalf of the UMWA candidacy of Joseph Yablonski." The editorial went on to name the names of the leaders and to report that the "goons" were paid $20 for their work. "It's obvious," the editorial added, "that the Yablonski forces are going to have to ask for federal government supervision of the forthcoming election to prevent the goons from intimidating men who cast ballots at local union elections." O'Brien concluded, "The goons may be able to stifle free speech, but they won't gag the free press."

As election day drew near, Joe Rauh made a final appeal to the Labor Department to begin an investigation. His letter to Labor Secretary Schultz cited the fact that Yablonski had found it necessary to go to court to obtain basic rights conferred by the Landrum-Griffin Act, and it also pointed to the revelations by John Owens in the most recent trial. "This, Mr. Secretary," the letter said, "is the sorry record of illegal conduct of the incumbent officers of the UMWA. That they intend to steal the election a week from tomorrow has been shown over and over again in these pages. We ask you to start an investigation at once so that evidence of these illegal actions will be obtained before the trail is cold and so that those local officials of the UMWA who want to resist Boyle's orders and who want to comply with the law will be strengthened by the presence of the Department.

"So, Mr. Secretary, these are your choices: You can allow the Boyle team to steal the election and start a long four-year process toward a new election with cold evidence which will cost the government millions of dollars and the union its democracy for another four years; or, Mr. Secretary, you can stand up, investigate, have an agent at every poll and make the LMRDA [the Landrum-Griffin Act] a reality." Five days later, Rauh got his answer. There would be no investigation, no poll watchers, no government intervention.

But although the department refused to investigate the election, it did, late in November, make public a report summarizing the findings of an audit it had begun of the union's books the previous March after Ralph Nader's allegations of nepotism. Although the summary did not contain much that was new to those who had been following the matter, it did officially confirm many of the allegations that Nader, Yablonski, and Hechler had been making. It listed the various relatives of top officials on the payroll, described the establishment of the special pension fund for the top officers, and detailed the way expense accounts were submitted and paid "improperly" without documentation. "Some officials," the summary said, "have claimed reimbursement for hotel expenses during periods when they were at their places of residence, some have claimed expenses for hotels and travel practically every day of the year, and some have claimed identical amounts for hotel and automobile travel for every day spent in travel." The report was released with the announcement that the information on which it was based had been turned over to the Internal Revenue Service and the Justice Department for further investigation. Although there was not much that was new in it, the fact that it was official made it front-page news in Washington and across the coal fields.

The Boyle camp was furious. Campaigning in west Kentucky, Boyle issued a statement calling the report "a smear job and open union-busting." "Nothing was spelled out," said Boyle. "It was all allegations. . . . There were only the same allegations hashed over by Yablonski. It is an attempt to panic UMW members into voting on December 9 for the man now fronting for the federal bureaucrats and other outsiders trying to take over the union. It is an effort to force union members to elect only officers who have a rubber stamp of approval from the federal establishment."

The spirits of Yablonski's staff, which had been high earlier in November, had sagged considerably in the face of Boyle's juggernaut campaign in the final stretch. They had been receiving gloomy reports from many locals where Yablonski had earlier seemed to have a strong lead. "They've just moved in with all the money and all the union officials, using television and radio, and they're just crushing us now," Fred Barnes said. But the release of the Labor Department's report—which came on November 26—and the furor it created buoyed their spirits. Who could gauge the impact of such a thing? After all, this was the government accusing the Boyle administration of illegal conduct two weeks before the election. To those like Charlotte and Chip Yablonski, who still wanted to believe that their father could do it after all, the Labor Department's report provided room for hope. The two of them worked feverishly in the final days of the campaign trying to line up election observers, always believing that their father would win anywhere the voting was honest. Charlotte, a short, sturdy-looking woman with jet-black hair and her father's fiery spirit, never seemed to lose the conviction that victory was possible. "Oh, he'll win all right, if we can just keep it honest. There's never been any doubt about that," she said.

By election night, however, no realistic observer could take Charlotte Yablonski's optimism seriously. For one thing, despite the fact that hundreds of college students and scores of pro-Yablonski miners had agreed to be poll-watchers, most locals had no observers. The Yablonski camp had not even known where hundreds of locals would hold their balloting. Besides, the Boyle organization's final blitz had been effective. Scores of locals earlier thought to be safely in Yablonski's column had reportedly shifted to Boyle.

At the UMW *Journal* office a block and a half from the main union headquarters, Justin McCarthy stood by a large blackboard posting returns for the benefit of the dozen or so reporters who shuttled back and forth between the *Journal* office and Yablonski headquarters a few blocks away. The returns were being phoned in from the district offices to the main headquarters. Those the administration wanted posted would then be relayed to McCarthy. On the *Journal* board, Boyle quickly built a sizable lead which appeared insurmountable by midevening, although there were still no reports from regions such as the anthracite where Yablonski was expected to do well. The first total to appear was from District 19, home of the hardhats from Tennessee and

Kentucky who had made a name for themselves at the 1964 convention. The count was 3,723 for Boyle to 87 for Yablonski. Although this figure was said to be a preliminary total and was posted only a short time after the polls were supposed to have closed, it never changed all evening.

At the Miners for Yablonski office, the early returns made it an even race, but Boyle soon began to pull away. In his home District 5 for example, Yablonski fell behind after losing at Republic Steel's Clyde Mine, which was the operation which tunneled under his property, and a local he felt sure he would win. In general, Yablonski did well where he had observers. He carried the anthracite in the final total by 6,365 to 4,225 and won District 6 in Ohio, 4,577 to 2,747. Although Yablonski lost District 5, 4,983 to 4,251, he won in Elmer Brown's home District 17, 6,310 to 5,574.

In the districts where Yablonski had few or no observers (which, of course, were also the districts where he had the least organized support), Boyle rolled up tremendous majorities. In District 20 in Alabama, Boyle won by 4,651 to 391. In tiny District 14 in Kansas, where Yablonski had no observers and had made no visits, Boyle won by 816 to 62. The totals in all districts were roughly the same for the presidential and vice-presidential candidates. (Incumbent Secretary-Treasurer John Owens, of course, was unopposed.) Shortly after midnight, Boyle, with Carey in tow, appeared at *Journal* headquarters to claim victory. By then, the blackboard showed him ahead by 75,680 to 43,307. Yablonski, who had awaited the returns at home in Clarksville, refused to concede, calling the balloting "the most dishonest election in the history of the American labor movement." Yablonski vowed that he would "see Boyle in court."

Indeed, Yablonski had plenty of reason to believe he could have Boyle's election overturned. Within days of the balloting, reports of dozens of election violations by the Boyle organization had been reported by Yablonski's observers and supporters. By the end of the week following the voting, Chip Yablonski had assembled an affidavit, based upon reports from the field, which enumerated eighty-six examples of alleged fraud, intimidation and vote-stealing. Here are a few samples:

"The polling places in Logan and Chatteroy [West Virginia] were the local headquarters of the Miners Committee for Boyle, Titler, and Owens. Those who appeared at the polls were not afforded the right to vote in secret. They had to cast their ballots on the table right in front of the tellers. Frequently, the tellers interfered with the voters. Moreover, Yablonski-Brown observers were denied the right to inspect the voter eligibility list or to watch the voting. When the polls were closed, District official R. Runyon picked up the ballots in Logan and Chatteroy and put them in his car. The votes were not counted at the Chatteroy site.

"At Local 7692 in the Gilbert-Matewan area [West Virginia], no notices of election were mailed to members, but an observer did appear and saw, among other things, coal operators voting in the union election.

"At Local 975 [Pennsylvania anthracite], the President of the local marked twenty-five ballots himself.

"In District 29 [southern West Virginia], wholesale voting of pensioners under the premise that they 'needed help' occurred. In the District's two huge locals composed mostly of pensioners, assistance by district staff people occurred with great frequency. A cab company and dozens of men were hired in Beckley to seek out pensioned miners with aid of membership lists and bring them to the polls. These elderly people were intimidated into accepting 'help' in voting without protest. The lopsided totals in these locals, Local 5997 in Welch and Local 7086 in Beckley, further demonstrate the counterfeit nature of the 'election.' Yablonski was defeated by identical eight and a half to one ratios in both locals (364 to forty-three in Local 5997 and 842 to ninety-six in Local 7086).

"In Quinwood, West Virginia, at Local 6200, the vice president, Ronald Sayre, was designated a Yablonski observer. He was physically ejected from the polling place after he complained of numerous instances of improper interference with voters. Local President Kyle Brewster, a Boyle backer, openly and brazenly told union members to vote for Boyle while dozens of Boyle supporters loitered and electioneered in the polling area."

In addition, the union hierarchy's own records would later show that no election return sheets were received from about two dozen locals. At least three others turned in more votes than the local had members.

Chip Yablonski's affidavit formed the basis for yet another appeal by Rauh to Secretary Shultz, asking him to begin an immediate investigation. On December 13, Rauh wired Shultz requesting that the Labor

Department impound the ballots. The telegram, sent in Yablonski's name, warned, "The next days will be immediately used by Boyle to juggle figures at headquarters and in the field to bring them in line with his previously announced totals." When Chip's affidavit was ready a few days later, it was sent to the Labor Department to buttress the request for immediate action. Simultaneously, a letter with the affidavit attached was sent to the union's international tellers asking them to begin an investigation. While nobody on Yablonski's side thought this move had any chance of producing action, it was a necessary formality because the Landrum-Griffin Act requires that aggrieved union members exhaust all their so-called "internal remedies" before turning to the Labor Department or the courts for action. An exception can be made where there are extraordinary circumstances and, of course, Rauh and Yablonski felt the UMW election had been extraordinary, at the very least. But the Labor Department's past behavior gave them little hope that Shultz would agree, so the letter to the international tellers was sent.

Rauh got his reply from Shultz on December 23, and it was true to form. This time, Shultz did not reply in person, but had one of his assistant secretaries write the letter. "The impounding of ballots would be an extraordinary action and justified only in the event of convincing evidence that the integrity of the ballots or records were directly threatened," the letter said. "The information made available to us does not satisfy the criteria."

Although Yablonski had been defeated by a large margin and his final appeal for immediate action by the government failed, he was far from discouraged. An examination of the vote totals, local by local, convinced him that he had run Boyle an even race among the working miners and had been defeated by the massive pensioner turnout for Boyle. Since it was Yablonski's position that countless pensioners were improperly apportioned in the "bogey locals" and that they had been ruthlessly manipulated and intimidated into supporting Boyle, he thought his disadvantage with them might be overcome if they were all reassigned to active locals, and if a rematch election with Boyle were conducted under federal supervision.

Moreover, the nearly forty-six thousand votes which the final official tally gave him was more than any insurgent UMW candidate in memory had gotten. "I have a constituency now," Yablonski said with satisfaction, "and I intend to represent it." The weekend after the election, his supporters in West Virginia organized a rally at Sophia, near Beckley, which was designated "Irregularity Day." Dissident miners by the hundreds turned out for the gathering and many took the platform to relate their tales of election day shenanigans by the Boyle organization. The entrance road to the parking lot of the Sophia High School, where the rally was held, was lined with cars filled with men. The cars were plastered with "Loyal to Boyle" bumper stickers. The men came into the meeting and watched in silence, scanning the crowd, but their presence did not noticeably affect the rally. Yablonski gave one of his patented stemwinding speeches, full of defiance and hyperbole. The miners especially enjoyed this comparison of his race with Boyle to a Presidential election: "You can imagine it right now if in 1971, the beginning of the year, President Nixon issues orders to the three million federal employees to begin campaigning full time for him, adds another half million employees to pick up whatever slack they leave, throws open the doors of the U. S. Treasury to buy votes, people, or anything else, and then has the audacity and the gall to say to his opponent, 'I am not even going to tell you where one half of the polling places are going to be.' That is how fair this election was."

Aside from his conviction that the election had been, from beginning to end, so corrupt as to make certain its eventual invalidation, Yablonski had other reasons to hope that his reform effort would ultimately succeed. On December 4, Rauh had filed a suit on behalf of Yablonski and about a dozen of his rank-and-file supporters, seeking to force Boyle and his associates to make restitution to the union treasury for millions of dollars used for questionable purposes, ranging from packing the conventions to padding the payrolls. Although the suit received little public attention in the last hours of the campaign, Yablonski and Rauh both felt it had an excellent chance of succeeding. And even if the suit failed to force the Boyle administration to reimburse the treasury, it provided a legal wedge with which Rauh could force the hierarchy to reveal a vast amount of embarrassing information, thereby keeping Boyle and his allies surrounded with the aura of scandal.

In addition, a federal grand jury had been convened in Washington to investigate "circumstances surrounding the dispersion of certain union funds during the first six months of the year." Justice Department officials said privately that they planned to look no further than the

indoctrination trip to Pittsburgh and Washington made by Ray Hutchinson and the other miners from Virginia, and the withdrawal of money
from the union treasury by District 5 President Budzanoski and Secretary-Treasurer, John Seddon. Although this seemed to Yablonski a
needlessly narrow scope for such a probe, he thought nevertheless that
another avenue to reform had been opened.

Optimistic though he was in the weeks following the election, Yablonski was still bothered by a nagging premonition that his defection from
the Boyle camp might still provoke some extreme reprisal, particularly
now that the election was over and Yablonski showed no signs of giving
up. "Ed," he had said to Ed Monborn after the campaign, "I think
they're after me." Mrs. Yablonski had reported seeing a strange car
bearing Tennessee license plates parked near the entrance road to the
Yablonski home a number of times during the final weeks of the campaign. The car so troubled Yablonski's brother Edward that he insisted
that Jock borrow one of his shotguns to keep in the house. Then one
night, not long after the election was over, when Yablonski and a
number of his close friends, including Karl Kafton, were gathered at his
home, two rough-looking young strangers knocked at the door. Yablonski answered. The two men identified themselves as coal miners from
Beckley, West Virginia. They said they were out of work and had
come to Pennsylvania seeking employment. They asked if Yablonski
could help them, but he told them there was nothing he could do and
quickly closed the door. Everyone in the house was suspicious. A short
time later, Yablonski, his older son Ken, and Karl Kafton drove into
Clarksville to see if the men were still in the area. They spotted their
car parked along a street in the center of the tiny town. It bore
Ohio plates. Now Yablonski was convinced that something was wrong.
He took down the license number and called the state police as soon as
he got back to the house. He gave the police the license number and
asked that the two men be questioned. He was promised that the police
would follow up. He heard nothing thereafter; he assumed that the
matter had been looked into and that nothing out of the ordinary had
been uncovered. In fact, however, the police never bothered to go to
Clarksville that night to look up the two strangers.

Joseph and Margaret Yablonski were sound asleep in their bedroom
on the second floor of the old fieldstone farmhouse shortly after one

o'clock the morning of December 31. Charlotte slept in an adjacent bedroom, her black hair in pincurls. A car containing three men drove slowly onto the property, turned around and stopped. The men got out and moved quietly and certainly through the darkness. It was familiar territory; they had been there several times before and had once entered and explored the house while no one was home. They had even become friendly with the Yablonskis' grey terrier puppy, Rascal. The men let the air out of the tires of the two Yablonski cars, removed the distributor cap from one of them, then cut the telephone lines. One of the men carried a .38 caliber pistol, another a .30 caliber M-1 rifle. They carefully removed the frame from a screen door at the side of the house, then reached in and opened the main door, which was unlocked. Once inside, they took off their shoes and climbed the circular stairs to the second floor. Rascal watched them without making a sound. One of the men walked into Charlotte's bedroom and stood beside her bed. He held the .38 pistol next to her head and pulled the trigger twice. She was killed instantly. Mrs. Yablonski awoke screaming. Yablonski jumped up and groped for the box of shells he kept under the bed to load the rifle his brother had loaned him. It was too late. The men were in the room now and they opened fire. Mrs. Yablonski was struck in the arm and chest, killed before she could get out of bed. Seven shots were aimed at her husband, all but one finding their mark. He slumped to the floor beside his bed, the box of shells under his body. The men hurried out of the house and sped off into the darkness.

EPILOGUE

The bodies of Joseph, Margaret and Charlotte Yablonski were found five days later when Ken Yablonski stopped at his parents' house to find out why no one had been answering the phone. The murders shocked the nation. Yablonski and his insurgent campaign suddenly became a matter of great national consequence. Reporters swarmed into the tiny town of Clarksville to cover the aftermath of the killings. Their stories were splashed across the front pages and given top priority on the evening news broadcasts for days.

The government officials who had spurned Yablonski's calls for help displayed a similar reaction. Attorney General John Mitchell, whose department had earlier refused Yablonski protection, ordered the FBI into the murder investigation. Labor Secretary Shultz, after a brief hesitation, ordered a full investigation of the election.

Among Yablonski's supporters there was little doubt as to the reason for his murder. As Chip was about to board a plane to fly home the day the bodies were discovered, he was asked if he thought the union was involved. "I am sure of it without even knowing," he snapped. Later, he and his brother issued a formal statement blaming the killing on "professional assassins" and charging that it was "an outgrowth" of the challenge to Boyle.

Meanwhile, Tony Boyle laid low at UMW headquarters. Except for one interview with a television crew which caught him on his way into the building, his talking was done by Ed Carey, who called a news conference on January 8 to announce the union was posting a $50,000 reward for the killers. "My theory," said Carey, "is that it had nothing to do with the Union whatsoever. . . . I'll bet my life that it is not connected with union activity."

The FBI, exploiting the lead furnished by Yablonski's effort to check out the two mysterious visitors to his home in December, made quick progress in its investigation. On January 21, sixteen days after the bodies were discovered, the FBI announced it had arrested three men in Cleveland in connection with the slayings. The suspects were a motley, disreputable trio: Paul Eugene Gilly, thirty-seven, a house painter; Claude Edward Vealey, twenty-six, a man with a drink problem and a long criminal record; and Aubran Wayne Martin, twenty-three, another small-time crook who was serving fifty-five days in the county work house at the time of his arrest for punching a policeman. All three lived in a section of East Cleveland heavily populated by emigrants from Appalachia. Gilly was originally from a tiny Kentucky mountain town called Defiance, Vealey from Ronda, West Virginia, and Martin from Madison, West Virginia.

The arrests were immediately cited at UMW headquarters as evidence that the murders had nothing to do with the union. But the supposed vindication was to be short-lived. Robert Krupansky, the capable, ambitious Federal District Attorney for Cleveland, announced that a grand jury was being convened to go further into what he somewhat cryptically termed the "broadening aspects" of the Yablonski case.

Although Krupansky did not say so publicly, the "broadening aspects" grew out of a full confession extracted from Claude Vealey the day of his arrest. According to Vealey, the murders were the climax of months of unsuccessful stalking of Yablonski to execute a murder contract for the total sum of $5,200. He said he was first contacted about the matter sometime prior to July 4, 1969 by Gilly, who "said that he knew this guy that wanted a person killed and asked me if I would help him with it. . . . Gilly told me that the guy was willing to pay $4,200."

In October, Vealey said, he and one Charles James Phillips were charged with housebreaking in Youngstown, Ohio, and jailed, unable to make bond. Gilly came to Youngstown and offered to bail him out if he would take part in the planned murder. Vealey agreed and he and Phillips were bailed out. The three of them drove to Washington the next day to hunt for Yablonski. They failed to locate him at the Miners for Yablonski office and telephoned his office at UMW headquarters and were told he was staying with Chip. They went to Chip's home in suburban Bethesda. Chip told them his father was in Scranton, Pennsylvania. So the three drove to Scranton. While there "Gilly said he called his wife and told her to call Tony. . . . Tony was supposed to know everything about Yablonski. Someone called Gilly while we were in Scranton and we learned of the whereabouts of Clarksville, Pa. and the Yablonski farm." Yablonski was not home, so the three returned to Cleveland. The next day they tried again. "Phillips and I proceeded to the Yablonski residence, found it unlocked and entered. Gilly stayed in the car and drove around. After casing the house we rejoined Gilly in the car since there was no one home."

After one more unsuccessful trip to Clarksville, Vealey said, Phillips began to have second thoughts and decided to back out. "Sometime in November, 1969, Paul Gilly made a trip to Tennessee. I do not know the purpose of the trip. Upon his return, he informed me that Tony had called and that Tony was in a hurry and wanted the job done." They kept pursuing Yablonski.

At one point in December, Vealey said, "we were parked in Gilly's Chevrolet next to a telephone booth in Clarksville and a green Pontiac pulled up behind us and then left. . . . It was on this date that Gilly had gone to the Yablonski home, knocked on the door and Mr. Joseph Yablonski came to the door. We talked with him about employment. Yablonski stayed inside all the time and we remained outside the house. I was armed with a chrome-plated six-inch Smith and Wesson .38 caliber revolver with white grips. Paul Gilly was armed with a .25 caliber automatic. We had planned to kill Joseph Yablonski at this time but chickened out.

After still another failure in Clarksville—on Christmas day—another man joined the murder team, Vealey said, "an individual I am acquainted with and know as Buddy Martin." The trio met in the Family Tavern, a favorite gathering place for transplanted Appalachians living in East Cleveland. "Paul informed me that the price had been upped by a thousand dollars and was now a total of $5,200 being offered by

Tony for the killing of Yablonski. We set a time of noon on December 30, 1969 that we would leave for Clarksville, Pennsylvania, to kill Yablonski."

On their way, Vealey said, they bought some Stroh's beer and a pint of 7-Crown whisky to take with them. "We then proceeded to Clarksville, drove by the Yablonski residence, and then drove up to a vantage point located on a hill behind the Yablonski residence where we drank the six-pack of beer and a good portion of the 7-Crown. We threw the Stroh's beer cans out the car window while parked at the vantage point."

Later, he said, "we drove back down past Yablonski's and on the main street we stopped at the first bar on the left. . . . In there I bought six throwaway bottles of Iron City Beer. This occurred about ten-thirty or eleven P.M. We then drove back to the vantage point, drank the beer and threw the bottles out the window of the car. While sitting up there in the car watching Yablonski's, Paul came up with all kinds of ideas on how to get in the house and shoot Yablonski. He said that it would be best to go ahead and kill Yablonski and anybody else in the house and get it over with. Buddy Martin agreed to this and so did I so we could get it over with." At about one A.M., Vealey said, they drove to Yablonski's home, parked the car and let themselves into the house, slipped quietly up the stairs and shot the Yablonskis to death. Then they went back to Cleveland, stopping along the way to throw their weapons into the Monongahela River.

Using Vealey's confession and information obtained from a cooperative Phillips, Krupansky quickly obtained indictments against two other persons. The first came as no surprise. It was against Annette Lucy Gilly, the hard-looking, twenty-eight-year-old blonde wife of Paul Gilly. After Mrs. Gilly's indictment, the grand jury heard testimony from a series of witnesses, including several top UMW officials. The investigation focused on the source of the money paid the three alleged killers, and in that connection James Kmetz, a member of one of the most entrenched UMW dynasties and Yablonski's successor as director of Labor's Non-Partisan League, was called. It was not known what he said, but he told reporters afterward that the authorities were on the wrong track. "They should be investigating the Communists," he asserted. Also called were Albert Pass, the secretary-treasurer of District 19—home of the hardhats of 1964 convention fame and one of the most violence-prone regions of the union—and William Prater, a field representative from the same Tennessee-Kentucky district. After his testimony, Prater said, "If I have to stay here six months, I'll be convinced the union has nothing to do with this thing. Throughout our entire history, people are always trying to pin things on the union, and this is no exception."

The key witness, however, proved to be Silous Huddleston, Annette Gilly's white-haired sixty-one-year-old father, the president of UMW local 3228 at LaFollette, Tennessee, an all-pensioner "bogey local." When first called on February 6, Huddleston took the Fifth Amendment. He was kept in Cleveland by a subpoena until February 25, when he was briefly recalled. He emerged from the grand jury room, triumphant. "I'm going home to Tennessee," he said. "I'm very happy to be going home. . . . The people who work for the Federal government are among the nicest people I've ever met."

No sooner had Huddleston left the courthouse, however, than he was seized by FBI agents, charged by the grand jury with being the man who organized the murder plot and obtained the money to pay the killers.

The government had moved quickly in rounding up those who allegedly organized and executed Yablonski's murder. But finding out the original source of the money used for the job proved far more difficult. Vealey's mention of a man named "Tony" was legally meaningless, although the authorities were known to believe that Huddleston was a close ally of Boyle's. Furthermore, Huddleston was unshakable in his refusal to cooperate with the government investigation. This brought the investigation to a virtual standstill because Huddleston was considered the only one of the suspects who actually knew where the money had come from. Richard Sprague, the crack Assistant District Attorney from Philadelphia who was made special prosecutor for the case, then decided to seek the death penalty for all five suspects. This was apparently an attempt to break down the uncooperative Huddleston. Meanwhile, however, the Ohio courts took months processing the defendants' appeals of court orders extraditing them to Pennsylvania for trial. For almost a year and a half, progress in the case came to a near halt.

Although the Justice Department was stymied in its efforts to locate the source of the murder money, its suspicion that top union officials, including Boyle, were involved led to a decision to move against the union on other fronts. Two lawyers in the Department's criminal division, Thomas Henderson and Charles Ruff, began to delve into any potentially fruitful allegations of illegal activity by the union hierarchy. These included several charges which Yablonski had first raised during his campaign, but which the Department had passed over as trivial.

Senator Harrison Williams's Labor Subcommittee also got into the act. Early in February it began hearings as part of an investigation of irregularities in the UMW pension fund and in the conduct of the election. Chip Yablonski was its first witness. He appeared on February 5, the one-month anniversary of the discovery of his father's body. Speaking clearly, but in a voice barely able to conceal his emotion, the young Yablonski made his statement extemporaneously. The hearing room was crowded but absolutely silent as he spoke.

"I would implore this subcommittee to get to the heart of this matter," he said. "I don't know how you go about doing that. All I know is this: when I went home for the last time I was shocked to walk into my parents' bedroom and see three guns lined up on the walls and on the window sills; to know the way my father abhorred guns, wouldn't have them in the house; to see our home an armed camp; to know the reign of terror under which he was living at that time, after the election.

"I couldn't comprehend the full scope of it then; I can now, because I was raised by a good man who told me, 'Keep guns out of your house. Your children won't be hurt. You can protect yourself.'

"But yet he had to bring guns into his home, he was so terrified. And now in the wake of his death and the murder of my mother and sister, I, who would never have a gun in my home, go to sleep each night, a loaded pistol under my pillow, and my wife tosses and turns.

"I know the thousands of people who supported my father living under that same reign of terror. They feel, as I feel, that unless the Government of the United States, whether it be the Secretary of Labor, the Department of Justice, the U.S. Senate, or the combined will of them all, gets to the roots of the corruption and tyranny in the United Mine Workers Union, they won't sleep well.

"I feel that way personally. I make that appeal to this committee. I hope you will heed it. I hope that my father didn't die in vain, that the coal miners will some day be given an opportunity to vote in a democratic election. I know they were denied that right in this past election by the most violent and coercive intimidation that I have ever know."

Exactly one month later, the Labor Department made known what the two hundred investigators it had assigned to probe the union election had come up with. The Boyle administration, said Secretary Shultz, had failed to provide adequate safeguards for a fair election, denied Yablonski the right to post observers, failed to obey its own constitution, failed to provide for secret balloting, and, in some cases, denied members the right to vote at all by not holding elections at some locals. Moreover, Shultz charged, some miners were made "subject to penalty, discipline, or improper interference or reprisal" in attempting to vote for the candidate of their choice. And, he added, the incumbents used the members' money to "promote the candidacy of its international officers." The Department was filing suit in Federal Court to ask that the election be set aside and a new one ordered, Shultz said. The Department was also suing the union to force it to begin keeping the required financial records.

The flow of unfavorable publicity which the Boyle adminstration had been getting since the Farmington disaster had now become a tidal wave, and Boyle's usual spokesmen, such as Ed Carey, were not doing much to stem it with their unconvincing rebuttals to each new attack. Carey, for example, told a news conference that the government's suit to overturn the election that was the work of low-level bureaucrats in the Labor Department who "may be trying to embarrass President Nixon by making him seem anti-labor." Although the allegations made by Shultz could hardly have been more sweeping, Carey insisted that they were "minuscule."

To offset the evident public suspicion that Boyle and company were behind the murders, Boyle announced that the union was setting up its own investigative commission to look into the murders and into Yablonski's "questionable associations." The press, Boyle told a Pittsburgh news conference—which he left without answering questions—was conducting a "journalistic lynching bee." A few days later, Boyle hired Thomas Deegan Associates, the famed New York public relations outfit that handles Pepsi-Cola and other major accounts, to help polish the union's tarnished image. The first advice he got was to try to rid himself of the aura of a man with something to hide. Hold a big news con-

ference and throw it open to questions, he was told. Boyle agreed and
a veteran Washington publicist named Reg Mitchell organized the affair
in the National Press Club ballroom on March 14. The place was
jammed. Boyle read a fifteen-page statement in which he denied every
charge in sight and some that were not. He was especially vehement in
claiming that he did not even know Silous Huddleston. Afterwards, the
reporters stood in line at a microphone to question him. Seldom has a
public figure taken such a beating. The Washington press corps, which
had previously been indifferent as a whole to the UMW scandal, had
caught up by now. Their questions were trenchant and they persisted
when Boyle failed to answer responsively. As John Herling, the literate
labor columnist, put it, Boyle "started off the proceedings by swearing
to high heaven that he was now prepared to tell the truth, the whole
truth, and nothing but the truth. But in the question period which followed his fifty-minute recital of his position, the most reporters could
get were snippets of answers, frequent evasions, sly innuendoes and
elaborate non-sequiturs." This was to be Tony Boyle's last press conference and the end of his brief fling with the Deegan firm. The investigative commission Boyle named faded out of sight after a couple of
farcical meetings.

The suit to overturn the election did not get the Labor Department
completely off the hook in the UMW controversy. The Labor Subcommittee wanted to know why the Department had failed to move before
the murders. After at first refusing to appear, Shultz finally trundled up
to Capitol Hill on May 4 to explain. His testimony could hardly have
been more surprising to those who had followed the controversy closely.
"The Department should not, as a matter of policy, and I believe may
not, as a matter of sound statutory construction, investigate and publi-
cize the activities of one faction in an election in order to assist the
campaign of the other," Shultz said. "I think it is fair to say that the
basic thrust of the appeals that were made to the Department of Labor
by and on behalf of Mr. Yablonski were that we give him assistance in
his campaign." Further, Shultz made the bold assertion that, "We have
no evidence that the murders were connected with the election."

Shultz further asserted that the government had not been negligent
in following up the Yablonski side's allegations of violence during the
campaign. He pointed to an FBI report on the June 28 incident in
Springfield, Illinois, where Yablonski charged that he was karate-

chopped from behind during a meeting with miners. The assailant had finally come forward, *after the murders,* Shultz said, and claimed that he had slugged Yablonski on the jaw in a moment's rush of anger at something Yablonski had said. Shultz thus made it plain that he accepted the version advanced by the assailant rather than that of the victim.

The subcommittee also took several days of testimony on the pension increase which Boyle had engineered during the campaign. The whole story came out—how the operators' trustee, George Judy, had been misled into thinking Boyle had Josephine Roche's proxy in his pocket and had voted for the increase because he thought it was fruitless to do otherwise. Boyle denied it and his testimony was backed up by Carey and by Suzanne Richards. But Senator Williams was not inclined to believe any of them. He concluded that there was "political motivation" behind the increase.

A few months later a General Accounting Office study of the fund, made for William's subcommittee, concluded that the pension increase would drive the fund to insolvency by mid-1975.

By August, the subcommittee had before it another issue affecting the miners: the failure of the Bureau of Mines to enforce the new mine safety law. The Nixon Administration had fired John O'Leary and then had left the bureau director's office vacant for a time before naming Dr. J. Richard Lucas of Virginia Polytechnic Institute to the job. The appointment was arranged by Linwood Holton, the Republican Governor of Virginia, on behalf of a group of small mine operators in his state who were dead set against the new law. Several of these operators had gone to court to prevent the enforcement of the law. They felt that Lucas, a gentle, pliant man with an almost childlike emotional attachment to the coal industry, would see them through once the law finally took effect. Lucas's qualifications were dimmed by the fact that he had previously been considered for the post during the Johnson Administration but had been rejected because the FBI unearthed allegations that he had plagiarized a professional paper—a charge that Lucas denied and one which was never proved. Lucas also had considerable mineral holdings. Revelation of these facts in the press and noisy opposition from Ken Hechler succeeded in delaying confirmation. The Administration then accepted Lucas's request that his nomination be withdrawn. So the Bureau drifted rudderless into the summer months with the death rate from mine accidents running higher than the previous year's. The Bureau rationalized that it was having a hard time finding enough qualified men to fill the many new inspector's posts needed to enforce the law. Williams concluded that the Bureau's performance, inspectors or no inspectors, was "outrageous."

Thousands of miners agreed with him. In June, a wildcat strike protesting the non-enforcement of the law shut down 150 mines and idled as many as twenty thousand men across the eastern coal region. The strike leaders were the so-called Miners for Democracy, a loose organization made up of dissidents who had supported Yablonski. The combined legal weight of the union and the companies finally got the men back to work on June 25, after a court issued an antistrike order against Miners for Democracy. The labor peace was brief, however. On July 13, a group of disabled miners and widows began setting up picket lines in West Virginia, Virginia, and Kentucky in protest of Boyle's failure to carry out his campaign pledge to shape up the Welfare and Retirement Fund, where business had been going on as usual. The coal companies quickly got about two dozen restraining orders against those they identified as leaders of the walkout, but the strike went on for weeks before finally dying out.

On August 5, the Justice Department's efforts to dig up prosecutable offenses by members of the Boyle organization bore fruit. Mike Budzanoski and John Seddon were indicted by a federal grand jury in Pittsburgh on charges of filing false expense accounts and financial reports. The key witnesses were Yablonski's supporters on the District 5 executive board, Marion Pellegrini and Peter Halvonik, who had been told to fill out fake vouchers themselves as a means of diverting union money into Boyle's campaign. This charge had surfaced during the election, of course, but the Justice Department thought it too small a matter then because Budzanoski and Seddon had put the money in a safety deposit box and had not yet turned it over to the campaign.

The allegation was particularly painful to Budzanoski, who was standing for re-election in December against Lou Antal, the peppery Yablonski supporter who was a stalwart in Miners for Democracy. To help Budzanoski, a district constitutional amendment permitting absentee voting was rammed through the district convention prior to the balloting. The incumbent obviously hoped the out-of-state pensioners could be importuned for the extra margin of support he might need.

He needed it, all right. When all the other ballots had been counted after the December polling, Antal led by a slim margin—slim enough to be overcome by a strong absentee showing for the incumbent. Before the absentee ballots had been officially processed, a group of Miners for Democracy members barged into a back room at District 5 headquarters and found Seddon and several of Budzanoski's loyal supporters closeted with the absentee ballots. The ballot box was unlocked and there were razor blades, glue, and extra blank ballots on the table. This irregularity was reported to the Labor Department, which seized the ballots on December 14 and turned them over to the FBI. The Labor Department later reported that a number had been tampered with. Again pointing to its alleged impotence under the law, however, the Department returned the ballots to the Budzanoski administration and announced that their disposition was up to him. Shortly thereafter, he was declared the winner. Antal, with Chip Yablonski representing him, then had to begin the long process of exhausting his "internal remedies" before again approaching the Labor Department for action.

On December 30, the first anniversary of President Nixon's signing of the mine safety bill, the worst fears of those who felt the new law was being scandalously under-enforced were confirmed. An explosion touched off by illegal blasting procedures ripped through a so-called "non-gassy" mine near Hyden, Kentucky. Thirty-eight men were killed. The Bureau of Mines had made an inspection only days before the blast and a check-up visit was planned but never made because the inspector went on leave. At the hearing held after the explosion one miner asserted that his section foreman had ordered the illegal detonating device known as "Prima-Cord" used in the mine. Another said the foreman at least knew that the cord was being used. The foreman denied it. Soon thereafter, he was hired by the Bureau as an inspector. When Ward Sinclair of the Louisville *Courier-Journal* got wind of this, the ex-foreman was confined to desk duty on orders of Henry Wheeler, the Bureau deputy director for health and safety. "I don't want a man like that inspecting mines for me," said Wheeler, who called the hiring "incredible."

In December, acting on information provided by the Internal Revenue Service, the Justice Department's Thomas Henderson took up with a grand jury in Washington the legality of contributions made by Labor's Non-Partisan League to various candidates between 1967 and

1969. The grand jury, meeting once weekly, heard testimony from fund officials, including director James Kmetz, and also from other union figures such as John Owens and Suzanne Richards. Simultaneously, it began looking into the union-funded trip made to Pittsburgh and Washington by Albert Matney and the others from District 28 during the campaign. The latter charge, of course, had been raised during the campaign but had been deemed minor by the Justice Department. On February 2, Ray Thornbury, a District 28 official, was indicted in connection with the incident on charges of embezzling a total of $1,784. A month later, the grand jury came out with the most serious official accusation yet made against Boyle and his fellow officers. It alleged that $49,250 had been illegally channeled from the union treasury into the campaign coffers of a number of politicians including Hubert Humphrey, who got $30,000 for his 1968 presidential race. Boyle was charged with making the illegal donations and with embezzling $5,000 of the money to do it. Also charged were Kmetz and John Owens. Boyle appeared at District Court for arraignment the next day in a white trenchcoat with his hat pulled over his eyes. He pleaded not guilty, as did Kmetz and Owens.

Boyle's indictment was the most devastating blow he had yet suffered, but it was soon followed by another of equal force. The multimillion dollar damage suit filed in August, 1969, by the group of seventy-eight miners and widows challenging the management of the welfare fund, was tried in February, 1971, before U.S. District Judge Gerhard Gesell in Washington. Harry Huge, the young Washington lawyer representing the plaintiffs, did an exceptionally thorough and meticulous job of preparing the case and moving it expeditiously to trial. Moreover, Gesell was one of the nation's best judges. Dedicated and orderly, he had an extremely penetrating mind capable of easily sorting out the complexities of an issue such as the welfare fund management. And some of the testimony in this case made his job easier. Josephine Roche, John L. Lewis's longtime confidant and ally, acknowledged that the fund had kept too much money in the checking account at the National Bank of Washington. This practice, of course, was the heart of the plaintiffs' case. "There's no excuse, perhaps, for it at all," the eighty-four-year-old fund director said. "I know how terrible it looks to have so much money sitting there." She was also asked about the fact that Thomas Ryan, the fund's comptroller, was also a director of the bank. "I, being old-fashioned, said, 'My goodness, I hope this isn't conflict of interest,'" Miss Roche remembered saying to Lewis. "But then I thought it couldn't happen to Tom Ryan." What was Lewis's response? she was asked. "He just smiled," she said. "It was very insignificant. It was only my personal experience. Against his wisdom."

After two weeks of testimony, including a full examination of the circumstances of the pension fund increase during the campaign, Gesell took the case under advisement. On April 28, Gesell issued his findings. They were as close to an all-out triumph for the plaintiffs as could be imagined. The judge found that the union, under Lewis, had conspired with Josephine Roche and Barney Colton, the former president of the National Bank of Washington, to enrich the bank by keeping the fund's money on deposit in non-interest-bearing checking accounts up until the time of Lewis's death. While postponing the determination of damages, the judge ordered all of the fund's money withdrawn from the bank by June 30. By that same date, he also ordered Boyle to get off the board of the fund, although he found that Boyle had not taken part in the conspiracy. "Boyle, however, violated his duty as trustee in several particulars. His actions in forcing through the pension increase, partly by misrepresentation, in haste and without consulting the neutral trustee, reflect an insensitivity to fiduciary standards," Judge Gesell said. Boyle appointed Carey to be the new trustee, but Carey remained on the bank board, so Gesell promptly ordered Carey off the bank board.

On May 6, the hierarchy got more bad news when Budzanoski and Seddon were convicted in Pittsburgh on all counts of conspiracy and falsifying the union's records. In June, Thornbury was also convicted in Washington, although on only one of the six counts of embezzlement with which he was charged. Sentencing was postponed in both cases.

By the middle of 1971, Tony Boyle and his fellow officers were under siege as never before. Even the long-delayed suit to establish democratic rule in the districts was finally set for trial and it appeared there would be no more delays this time. The Labor Department had won its case to force the union to keep the required financial records. Three high-ranking union officers stood convicted of federal crimes and Boyle himself, along with Owens and Kmetz, was under federal indictment. Moreover, the Justice Department showed no signs of letting up. Indeed, it had just received a fresh batch of leads when the Williams subcommittee completed its field investigation into the use of union funds in Boyle's campaign and passed the top-secret findings along to the Department. Richard Sprague, the determined prosecutor heading the murder investigation, was pulling no punches in his effort to crack the mystery of who financed the killings. In late June, he brought Vealey into court to plead guilty and to make public, for the first time, his eighteen-month-old confession. This story made headlines across the nation, with prominent reference to the man named "Tony" who was alleged to be the source of the money. Carey immediately called a press conference to deny vehemently that the "Tony" cited in Vealey's confession was Tony Boyle.

At about the same time, the Labor Department decided there was sufficient evidence of fraud to try to set aside Budzanoski's re-election, although it elected to postpone filing suit on the say-so of Carey that the hierarchy itself might overturn the election. The government's suit to set aside Boyle's re-election was set for trial later in the year. Further adding to the hierarchy's woes was the Landrum-Griffith case filed by the Yablonski faction near the end of the campaign to force the union leaders to make restitution to the union treasury for money spent on a vast variety of allegedly wasteful projects. This suit was far from going to trial, but Clarice Feldman and Chip had set up shop in Washington, supported by a foundation grant, to devote themselves full-time to pressing the rebel miners' cause. High among their priorities was this suit. There could be no doubt that they intended to see it through.

Certainly it must have seemed at times to Boyle and those around him that the end of their dominion was near. Each day seemed to bring a new dose of unfavorable publicity and they lived in the knowledge that the government, as well as the rebel faction of the membership, was bent on toppling them. Yet there was no sign that they were weakening under the stress. The UMW *Journal* was again crammed with propaganda for the regime and Carey, now virtually Boyle's sole spokesman, was missing no opportunity to trumpet the administration line and to shout defiance at Boyle's detractors. Embattled though he was, Boyle still had a firm grip on the reins of power. Even if he were convicted on the campaign funds charge, there would be appeals which would take years. He was still collecting his $50,000-a-year salary, still exercising his power of appointment over nearly every official in the organization. And if the government won its cases to democratize the districts and to hold a new presidential election, he and his men would still be the incumbents. Besides, who would the insurgents put up against him? Yablonski might have been a grave threat the second time around. But Boyle didn't have to worry about him.

November 20, 1968: Smoke pours from the Llewellyn portal of Consol. No. 9, Farmington, West Virginia. (*Wide World Photos*)

Tony Boyle. (*Wide World Photos*)

John L. Lewis. (*Wide World Photos*)

Ken Hechler tells a rally in Charleston what he thinks of the UMW's work for the miners' health and safety. (*Ferrell Friend, Charleston Gazette*)

Dr. I. E. Buff.
(*Jeanne M. Rasmussen*)

Dr. Don Rasmussen.
(*Jeanne M. Rasmussen*)

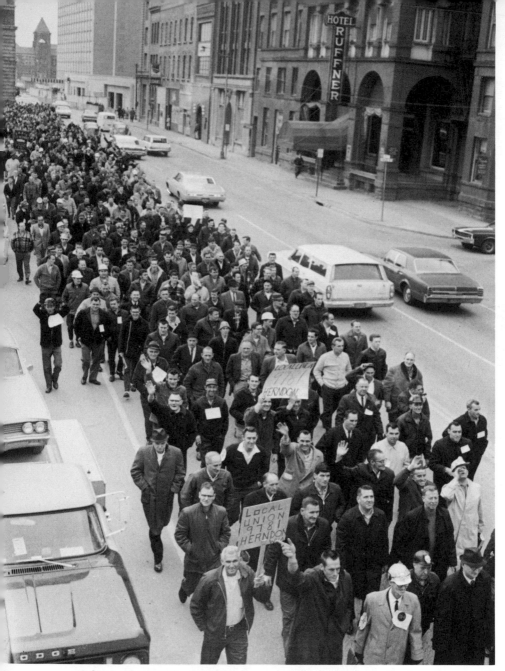

February 26, 1969: the Black Lung march up Kanawha Boulevard. (*Ferrell Friend, Charleston Gazette*)

May 29, 1969: Joseph A. Yablonski announces his candidacy for the UMW presidency. (*Wide World Photos*)

Yablonski campaigning. (*Jeanne M. Rasmussen*)

Yablonski's house in Clarksville. (*Wide World Photos*)

Murder suspects Buddy Martin, Claude Vealy, and Paul Gilly. (*Wide World Photos*)

Murder suspect Annette Gilly. (*Wide World Photos*)

Silous Huddleston talks to reporters minutes before his arrest. (*Wide World Photos*)

March 3, 1971: Boyle leaves U.S. District Court in Washington after arraignment on charges of embezzling UMW funds. (*Wide World Photos*)

INDEX